Sociality and Responsibility

Sociality and Responsibility

New Essays in Plural Subject Theory

Margaret Gilbert

ROWMAN & LITTLEFIELD PUBLISHERS, INC.
Lanham • Boulder • New York • Oxford

ROWMAN & LITTLEFIELD PUBLISHERS, INC.

Published in the United States of America
by Rowman & Littlefield Publishers, Inc.
4720 Boston Way, Lanham, Maryland 20706
http://www.rowmanlittlefield.com

12 Hid's Copse Road
Cumnor Hill, Oxford OX2 9JJ, England

British Library Cataloguing in Publication Information Available

Library of Congress Cataloging-in-Publication Data

Gilbert, Margaret.
    Sociality and responsibility : new essays in plural subject theory / Margaret Gilbert.
      p.   cm.
    Includes bibliographical references and index.
    ISBN 0-8476-9762-2 (cloth : alk. paper) — ISBN 0-8476-9763-0 (paper : alk. paper)
    1. Social groups.   2. Social action.   3. Collective behavior.   4. Political obligation.
I. Title.
HM716.G55 1999
305—dc21   99-046263

Printed in the United States of America

∞™ The paper used in this publication meets the minimum requirements of American National
Standard for Information Sciences—Permanence of Paper for Printed Library Materials,
ANSI/NISO Z39.48–1992.

Contents

Preface

In my book *On Social Facts* I argued that social groups, group languages, and other central social phenomena are *plural subject* phenomena. That is, a special type of commitment—what I call a *joint* commitment—underlies them. When people are jointly committed to doing something as a body, they form a plural subject in my sense.

In subsequent work I have explored further the nature of plural subjects and their relevance to a variety of issues from the nature of everyday agreements to the nature of love. In other words, I have continued to develop the theory of plural subjects. My book *Living Together: Rationality, Sociality, and Obligation* includes a number of relevant studies. The refinement and extended application of this theory is a continuing project.

As the title indicates, the essays in the present work, *Sociality and Responsibility: New Essays in Plural Subject Theory,* continue the development and extend the application of plural subject theory. The book addresses central topics in ethics, political philosophy, the philosophy of law, the philosophy of science, and the philosophy of action and emotion.

The chapters have been drawn from a variety of sources, including specialist journals and collections of essays for specialists in a particular area. In collecting them together I have aimed in part to make the individual essays more accessible, in part to advance my argument for the importance of an understanding of plural subjects to an understanding of human life as a whole. Each essay on its own helps to make this point; it becomes clearer when they are brought together.

Each essay is intended to be relatively self-contained. At the same time, some amplify points that are only sketched in others. I have generally kept previously published articles intact. Any changes are editorial rather than substantive. The introduction provides an overview, noting the major themes of the book. An abstract precedes each of the chapters.

There are references throughout this book to *On Social Facts* and *Living*

Together. The reader is encouraged to look at these earlier books, which probe a number of related topics and provide a variety of supporting arguments.

Acknowledgments

Many people have contributed to this book in one way or another. Each chapter includes a note of gratitude to the particular people whose comments or suggestions were most helpful to its development. Special thanks to James Phelps and Dan Blair for helping to put the manuscript together. The index was prepared with the help of Adam Potthast.

Two institutions deserve particular thanks in connection with this book. One is King's College London where I was visiting professor in the humanities from January 1996 through December 1998. While in London I had helpful conversations on topics related to these essays with many King's faculty including Keith Hossack, David Lloyd-Thomas, David Papineau, Thomas Pink, and Mark Sainsbury. The other institution is the University of Connecticut, Storrs, my academic home base for many years. The views expressed in several of the chapters have been subjected, at some stage of their development, to the lively critical scrutiny of my Philosophy Department colleagues at one of our regular brown-bag lunchtime discussions.

The interest in and expressions of support for my work on sociality from many colleagues at a variety of places have meant much to me. I shall not attempt an exhaustive list, but such a list would include Michael Bacharach, Annette Baier, Michael Bratman, Angelo Corlett, Justin Gosling, John Greenwood, Gilbert Harman, Virginia Held, John Horton, Christine Korsgaard, David Lewis, Robert Nozick, Gianguido Piazza, Joseph Raz, Frederick Schmitt, John Searle, Amartya Sen, Gabriele Taylor, and Raimo Tuomela.

I should like to make special mention in this connection of the late Martin Hollis. Martin's supportive interest in *On Social Facts* and related work was deeply encouraging. His continuing contribution to the field in which we both work was cut short tragically and far too soon.

SOURCES

Chapter 2 is reprinted with minor revisions from *Contemporary Action Theory,* ed. G. Holmstrom-Hintikka and R. Tuomela, vol. 2, *The Philosophy and Logic of Social Action* (Dordrecht: Kluwer Academic Publishers, 1997), 65–85, with kind permission from Kluwer Academic Publishers.

Chapter 3 is reprinted with minor revisions from the Italian translation, "Credenze collective e mutamento scientifico" (trans. G. Piazza), in *Fenomenologia e societa,* n. 1 (1998), anno XXI, 32–45. It is published here with permission of *Fenomenologia e societa.*

Chapter 4 is reprinted with minor revisions from *Utilitas,* 11, (1999), 143–163. It is reprinted with permission of the Editor and Edinburgh University Press.

Chapter 5 is reprinted with minor revisions from *Law and Philosophy,* 18, (1999), 141–171, with kind permission from Kluwer Academic Publishers.

Chapter 6 is reprinted with minor revisions from *Ethics,* 109 (1999), 236–260. It is reprinted with permission of *Ethics* and the University of Chicago Press. © by the University of Chicago. All rights reserved.

Chapter 9 is reprinted with minor revisions from *Philosophical Explorations,* 1 (1) (1998), 233–241, and appears with the permission of the Editors of *Philosophical Explorations.*

Sociality and Responsibility

1

Introduction: Sociality and Plural Subject Theory

1. INVESTIGATING SOCIALITY

Philosophers through the ages have included in their reflections many fundamental aspects of the world. They have pondered, among other things, the nature of time, space, causation, and mentality. What of sociality, or the social realm?

The most prominent discussions of sociality were written by philosophically minded sociologists at the turn of the nineteenth century. Seeking foundations for their discipline, Max Weber, Emile Durkheim, and Georg Simmel all attempted in deep and subtle discussions to provide a general account of the social realm.[1] They focused on the sociality of human beings, as does this book.[2]

Durkheim and Simmel, each in his own way, insist that social phenomena involve a connection between individuals so close that it justifies one in saying that the relevant people constitute a *unit*. Weber, in contrast, sees human sociality as solely a matter of individuals acting with other people in mind. The field was thus left open for further debate.[3]

Contemporary analytic philosophers have not tended to investigate the nature of sociality.[4] Some have proposed accounts of particular paradigmatic social phenomena such as social conventions.[5] These accounts commonly express a Weberian stance, insofar as they are couched in terms of the acts, expectations, and so on, of individuals.

One reason for the prevalence of this approach may be that those like Durkheim and Simmel who have proposed something different tend to couch their views in relatively obscure terms. What they say is suggestive but not overly precise.

My pursuit of a satisfying account of sociality has led me to what I call *plural subject theory*. According to this theory paradigmatic social phenomena are, in a specified technical sense, *plural subject* phenomena.

1

People form a plural subject, in my sense, when they are jointly committed to doing something as a body, in a broad sense of "do." In the next section I amplify this description. In particular I say something about the important notion of *joint commitment*.

As will emerge, a joint commitment unifies the participants in a significant fashion, providing an intelligible basis for talk of *our* acts, expectations, and so on. To that extent my theory accords with the perspective on sociality of Durkheim and Simmel, and diverges from the prevalent Weberian stance.

I first argued for plural subject theory at length in *On Social Facts*. That book discusses a variety of central social phenomena, incorporating extended examinations of related historical and contemporary material from Weber, Durkheim, Simmel, David Lewis, Peter Winch, and Saul Kripke (the last two for their interpretations of Wittgenstein on the social nature of language and thought). The phenomena most fully considered are social groups, collective beliefs, social conventions, and group languages. Each of these, I argue, is best understood as a plural subject phenomenon.[6]

A second book, *Living Together: Rationality, Sociality, and Obligation*, continued the discussion of plural subject theory. There is some reworking, in briefer compass, of material in *On Social Facts* and much new material. Topics covered in depth for the first time include the nature of everyday agreements, coerced agreements and the sense, if any, in which they obligate the parties, the sense of union that commonly arises within a long marriage, group membership and political obligation, and the intelligibility of guilt feelings over what one's group has done. The introduction explains some developments in my characterization of plural subjects since the publication of *On Social Facts*.

Living Together also includes studies that focus on the difficulty of coordinating one's actions with those of others within the pared-down framework envisaged by game theory. This argues for the practical utility of plural subject formation even for those whose primary intent is meeting personal goals.

The present work, *Sociality and Responsibility: New Essays in Plural Subject Theory*, is a collection of essays that continue the investigation of the nature of plural subjects and their prevalence and central role in human life. A range of issues that tend to be discussed by practitioners of different branches of philosophy—ethics, political philosophy, philosophy of law, philosophy of science, philosophy of mind and action—are all discussed from the unifying perspective of plural subject theory.

Some of the issues are classic and long-standing: What are obligations and rights? Are there political obligations that can be explained by something akin to a contract? Some have begun to attract sustained attention more recently: What is science, and how do the tenets of science change? What is it for a group—as opposed to an individual—to endorse a rule? What is it for *us* to intend? Is there such a thing as collective moral responsibility? Others have so far failed to receive the attention they deserve: How are we to understand everyday talk of group emotions, such as collective remorse? Is the only proper object of remorse one's own action?

In the next three sections I informally review some central aspects of plural subjects. This overview may be particularly useful for readers unfamiliar with plural subject theory. The individual essays discuss these matters to a greater or lesser extent in the context of their specific concerns, sometimes in considerably greater detail than is given here.

2. PLURAL SUBJECT THEORY: BEYOND INDIVIDUALISM

Suppose that—in accordance with standard practice—we call the standard, Weberian approach to sociality I have outlined a form of "individualism" and its opposite "holism." One who is wedded to this form of individualism is unlikely to arrive at plural subject theory because, at the base of any plural subject in my sense, lies what I call a "joint commitment."[7] The relevant concept of a joint commitment is a holistic one in the following sense: it cannot be analyzed in terms of a sum or aggregate of personal commitments.

A paradigmatic context for the genesis of what I am calling a *personal* commitment is the making of a personal decision. If Jane decides to go fishing, for instance, she is now personally committed to going fishing, as long as she does not change her mind. A joint commitment is the commitment *of two or more people*. The joint commitment of Jane and Joe is the commitment of Jane and Joe, as opposed to the conjunction of Jane's personal commitment and Joe's personal commitment. A joint commitment, by its nature, may be said to tie or bind its participants together into a unit or whole.

Insofar as the core concept of plural subject theory is this holistic concept of joint commitment, and insofar as, according to plural subject theory, there are joint commitments, the theory may reasonably be characterized as both conceptually and ontologically a holist theory. In other words, it goes beyond individualism both with respect to the concepts it uses and in its understanding of what there is.[8]

It is worth emphasizing that this does not mean that plural subject theory goes beyond the plane of *humanity* in characterizing human sociality. It does not invoke any ontologically suspect kind of "social spirit" or "group mind." Human beings create joint commitments together and thereby constitute plural subjects. I say something about how they do this later. When they do so it is consequential in many ways, as much of the discussion in this book makes clear, but it does not move them beyond the human plane.

3. JOINT COMMITMENT AS THE CORE OF PLURAL SUBJECTS

According to plural subject theory, joint commitments—foundational for plural subjects—play a fundamental role in the life of human beings. They may be regarded as the core of human sociality.[9]

This contention is grounded in the fact that satisfying accounts of a wide variety of everyday social phenomena can be given in terms of some kind of joint commitment. For example, as I argued in *On Social Facts,* what goes on in ordinary conversations is the continuous production of different joint commitments of a specific sort.

Suppose Pat and Joe are walking together and Pat says to Joe "It's hot!" Joe demurs, replying "I wouldn't say so, I'd say it's warm." Pat may then reply "I guess that's right." Regardless of whether Pat personally thinks it is warm rather than hot, she will understand, as will Joe, that at this point something has been established between them. I argued that this can be understood in terms of the *joint* acceptance of the proposition that it's warm or, in other words, a joint commitment to accept as a body the proposition that it's warm.[10]

I argued further that when people speak of what "we believe" or (in that sense) "accept," they typically refer to a situation involving a joint commitment to accept a certain proposition as a body. What is it for us to accept some proposition *p as a body*? I take it that, roughly, this is for us, by virtue of the acts, including utterances, of each to constitute as far as possible a single body that believes that *p*.

People can jointly commit to instantiate as a body not only cognitive concepts but psychological concepts in general. Thus they can jointly commit so to intend, for instance. The idea of people who are jointly committed to instantiating a psychological concept as a body is what I refer to as the idea of a plural subject.

Why do I use the phrase "plural subject" in this context? If Pat doubts that Tim will phone her tomorrow, she can appropriately say "I doubt that Tim will phone me tomorrow." In other words, she constitutes what one might call a singular subject of doubt. Now if Pat says, of herself and Joe, "We doubt that Tim will phone me tomorrow," she may mean to refer only to a conjunction or aggregate of personal doubts. Then it would be equally, if not more, appropriate for her to say "We both doubt that Tim will phone me tomorrow." But sometimes this would not be appropriate, for this is not what she means. She may intend to imply that there is something other than two singular subjects of doubt, something that can appropriately be seen as, on the contrary, a plural subject of doubt.

My use of the phrase "plural subject" in the sense I have given it corresponds to a contention argued for in a variety of ways in *On Social Facts.*

When people refer to "our" doubts, and so on, and mean to imply that there is something other than two singular subjects of doubt, they suppose—however inexplicitly—that the people referred to constitute a plural subject of doubt in my sense.[11]

This conclusion has some intuitive plausibility. As one might put it, the joint commitment involved in a plural subject in my sense serves as a single "command center" that is apt to lead the several participants to constitute—as far as is in their power—a single doubter. That is, it unifies a plurality of persons into a plural subject of doubt.

4. FORMING JOINT COMMITMENTS: A SPECTRUM OF CASES

How are joint commitments formed? The obvious answer is that the contribution of each party is required. More specifically, each party must express to every other party his or her personal readiness to be jointly committed in the relevant way. The mechanism by which joint commitments were formed would then parallel the mechanism by which personal commitments were formed. That is, just as I form or bring into being my commitment, you *and* I form or bring into being our commitment. In other words, without a special background I can't jointly commit you by my own efforts, and vice versa.

I take this obvious answer to be essentially correct for the basic case of joint commitment, although it can be clarified further.[12] I take there to be non-basic cases in which people are jointly committed by means of an open-ended basic joint commitment, such as a commitment to accept as a body that a certain individual is to form certain plans for us.[13] If we focus on the basic case of joint commitment, we must still take care to distinguish between different types of joint commitment formation.

In *The Republic* Plato proposed that when enquiring into the nature of justice one should start with the city as opposed to the individual citizen. He argued that since the city is larger than the citizen, the character of justice will be more clearly discernible in the city. It is not clear how serious Plato was in this passage. In any case, one might argue for the opposite position when what is being investigated is joint commitment. Small-scale examples—such as that of Jane expressing to Joe her readiness to be jointly committed with him in some way and his responding in kind—are plausibly claimed to be those through which we can most easily arrive at an understanding of the way joint commitments are formed. For this reason I often focus on small-scale cases, as do the following remarks.

Many cases of joint commitment formation involve what are properly characterized as agreements. Thus, Jane may ask Joe "Shall we go fishing this afternoon?" and Joe may reply "Fine!" Now they are jointly committed to uphold as a body the decision to go fishing that afternoon. We can properly say, also, that Jane and Joe agreed to go fishing that afternoon.

We should be careful not to conclude from this that all joint commitments involve agreements. This is not so.

Suppose that, as she leaves the house, Claire informs Paul that she is going out for a walk. Paul responds, "Wait a moment, I'll join you!" Claire waits by the door, Paul comes up to her, saying "I'm ready!" and they proceed out of the house together. I doubt that one can properly say that Claire and Paul agreed to go for a walk, yet what transpired between them appears sufficient to ground a joint commitment to accept as a body the current goal of going for a walk together.

It may be tempting in such cases to invoke something one refers to as an *implicit* agreement. If, at the same time, one judges that Claire and Paul did not agree to go for a walk, one must admit that a so-called implicit agreement is not an agreement proper. It may, of course, be something deeply akin to an agreement. This is what I would argue: both agreements and so-called implicit agreements are processes with the same important result—they set up a joint commitment.[14]

Further, joint commitments are not always saliently brought into being at a particular point in time, as typical agreements are.[15] There may be several encounters or a relatively long continuous period during which one person's understandings about the other are clarified to the point that a joint commitment arises. Even if a particular interaction clinches the matter, the participants may not be aware that it has this status. That is, they may not consciously register what has happened in spite of their ensuing confidence that a joint commitment is in place.

A related point is that joint commitments are not necessarily brought into being with any clear conscious intent to do so. Putting these points together, people may relatively unconsciously take up one another's relatively unconscious hints to the point that they become confident that there is a joint commitment, without being able to point to the time it came into being. This confidence itself may be quite inexplicit, although if it is there it will probably manifest itself in a variety of ways.

The following example illustrates these points. John and Peter make an impromptu decision to have dinner together after work one Monday night. The following Monday Peter proposes to John that they again have dinner together after work, and John agrees. This happens again once or twice, and each surmises that, in effect, each is ready to be jointly committed with the other to accept as a body the plan of having dinner together after work on Mondays. Perhaps, without prior reflection, John will subsequently say something like "Where shall we eat this Monday?" and without any sense of surprise Peter may reply with a suggested venue. By this interchange each makes it clear to the other that his supposition about what each is ready to do is correct. Although on reflection either or both may see things in this light, it is likely that neither is ever consciously aware of the "clinching" nature of the interchange. They will probably see themselves as having just "fallen into" a joint commitment that they are—with good reason—confident they have.

5. SPECIAL FEATURES OF JOINT COMMITMENT: STABILITY, OBLIGATIONS, AND RIGHTS

Both personal and joint commitments have considerable practical signifi- cance. More specifically, both types of commitment are generally judged to trump mere inclinations from the point of view of practical reasoning. If I de- cided at lunchtime not to have dessert tonight, then the fact that now, after dinner, I am inclined to have some ice cream is "trumped" by my standing de- cision not to eat dessert. Thus I may well say to myself "It's true that I feel like some ice cream, but I decided not to eat dessert tonight."

In spite of this, a given personal commitment is not as useful as it might be in such contexts, insofar as I can always change my mind. In other words, I have the power both to give in to my inclination and to avoid having to act against a standing commitment. Thus, in a continuation of the previous story, I might say "It's true that I decided not to eat dessert tonight, but I really feel like having some ice cream. I guess I'll have some dessert tonight after all." The last statement functions, in effect, as the rescinding of the prior decision, replacing it with a contrary one.

Joint commitments in my sense have an important advantage over personal commitments in this respect, for no party to a standing joint commitment can unilaterally rescind it. This is so at least in the absence of the prior violation of the commitment by the other party or parties.[16] Thus joint commitments have the advantage of a special kind of stability over personal commitments.[17]

Another highly significant aspect of joint commitments is that—as I argue—they are a central context for our talk of obligations and rights. Thus the investigation of the nature of sociality leads to a deeper understanding of a central topic of moral philosophy: the nature of obligation. There are so- called obligations of importantly different kinds, with importantly different sources. Without a clear understanding of the distinctiveness of one of these sources—joint commitment—much confusion and misunderstanding can arise.

If one thinks about what a joint commitment is, focusing on its jointness, it may immediately seem reasonable to say that by virtue of one's participa- tion in a joint commitment with another person *one gains a special standing with respect to the actions of that other person.* Indeed, without prior analy- sis of the notion of an obligation or a right, it may immediately seem reason- able to say that each party to the joint commitment has a right to conforming actions from the other, and each is under a corresponding obligation to that other.

Thus it may not even seem we need to argue that a joint commitment in and of itself involves obligations and rights. That was my own initial reaction.[18] What, though, if this idea does not immediately convince? In "Obligation and Joint Commitment," (Chapter 4, this volume), I present a series of considerations in support of it. I previously argued for the same conclusion most fully in my article "Agreements, Coercion, and Obligation," reprinted in *Living Together*. Here I approach it afresh from a different perspective.[19] I shall not attempt to detail the arguments here.

This conclusion lends some credence to the claim by some moral theorists (who have received the label "intuitionists") that we know a priori—without appeal to the course of experience—that agreements and promises obligate. As I argue in a number of places, agreements are plural subject phenomena and thus have joint commitments—and hence obligations and rights—at their core.[20]

The idea that joint commitments involve obligations and rights is pertinent to a range of issues in addition to the question of the obligations and rights associated with agreements. Several of the chapters in this volume attest to this.

6. BRIEF OVERVIEW OF THE BOOK: CONNECTING THEMES

i. Introduction

Taken together, the essays collected here help to emphasize two major strengths of plural subject theory. The first is the theory's ability to explain what we are talking about when we talk about collective psychological states, such as our doubts or our beliefs. The second is its ability to shed light on a number of long-debated questions about obligations and rights. The theory provides a related explanation for a range of everyday responses people have to one another, including what I have elsewhere called "offended rebukes" and other forms of punitive pressure.[21]

ii. Collective Psychological States

People often speak of what we intend when they mean to refer to something other than what we both or all intend. They seem to imply that there is what we might call a "collective" or "shared" intention. But what might reasonably be so-called? More to the point, what is it we mean to refer to when we say that we intend in this collective sense?

Theorists who have specialized in the nature of intention have only recently attempted to characterize shared intention. A well-known, individualistic approach is that of Michael Bratman: on his view "our" intention is a complex of personal intentions. John Searle suggests something different. Instead of a collection of concordant personal intentions or "I intends," he suggests that, in effect, the participants in a shared intention must all think—or intend—in terms of what "we intend." Searle says little more than this, however.[22]

A problem for both views is how to explain a certain complex of attitudes that appear justified by the existence of a shared intention. For instance, if we intend to go shopping this afternoon and I announce that I have decided to go to the beach, you seem entitled to complain that I have no business making such a decision, at least without consulting you. In Chapter 2 I argue that a plural subject account of shared intention provides a satisfying explanation of the way people think, talk, act, and react in the context of what *we* intend. I compare and contrast my account of shared intention with those of a number of other philosophers, including Bratman and Searle, in Chapter 9.

Another common psychological statement concerns what we—as opposed to you and I both—believe. I have discussed such statements and the collective beliefs to which they refer in several places, including *On Social Facts* and *Living Together,* arguing for a plural subject account of collective belief. Collective belief in the sense of plural subject theory plays an important role in Chapter 3, "Collective Belief and Scientific Change."

Just as people speak of what "we" intend and believe, they often say that "we" are sorry or, more seriously, that "we" feel remorse when they mean something other than that each of us personally feels remorse. They seem to imply that there is a collective emotion, specifically that there is collective remorse.

In Chapter 7, after considering a number of alternatives, I offer a plural subject account of collective remorse. I argue that it is preferable to the alternatives.

I take the phenomenon I describe—a plural subject of remorse—to be a phenomenon of considerable practical importance, whatever its name. Among other things, collective remorse in the plural subject sense is likely to be an important agent of intergroup reconciliation and of stable peace, both on a small scale—such as the scale of families—and on a large scale, such as the scale of nations.

People can find themselves feeling remorse over what their group has done, even when they have no personal moral guilt in the matter. They may, indeed, have made their opposition to the group's act clear at the time it was carried out. It has been questioned whether such feelings make sense. Are they rational? In Chapter 7 I argue that plural subject theory can allow for the intelligibility of such feelings. Given their special nature, we need a helpful way of referring to them. I refer to remorse of the kind in question as "membership remorse."

Both collective remorse and what I call membership remorse appear to presuppose that a group can not only act but can act culpably. In other words, they apparently presuppose that a group can be morally responsible for its actions and, in the case of a bad action, can bear moral guilt.

In the wake of the World War II and again today, the idea that there is such a thing as collective guilt has been debated not only by philosophers but among thoughtful people in general. Concern has centered on the relationship of collective guilt to personal moral responsibility. If there is such a thing as collective guilt, does it mean that everyone in the relevant group is morally guilty, or does it mean that no one in that group is? Many have—reasonably enough—found both implications repugnant, which has led them to reject the very idea of collective guilt.

Discussions of collective guilt have not generally been accompanied by careful consideration of what it is or might be for a group to act, let alone to act culpably. As I argue in Chapter 8, a plural subject account of group action can help to show that there is an intelligible concept of collective guilt, a concept whose ramifications for personal moral responsibility are in no way outrageous.

The question debated in Chapter 5, the nature of social rules, can also be construed as, at base, a question about collective psychological properties. One can think of a social rule as the rule of a group, and construe the latter as a rule a group accepts. Without explicitly following this particular route in this chapter, I argue for a plural subject account of social rules.

Durkheim said that collective ways of acting, thinking, and feeling had their "substrate" in society as opposed to a set of detached individuals. I say something similar: such "ways" have at their foundation not a set of detached individuals but individuals associated or unified through a joint commitment.[23]

iii. Obligations, Rights, and Rebukes:
The Explanatory Power of Joint Commitment

Chapter 4 argues from a variety of angles for the idea that a central context in which we talk of obligations and rights is the context of an existing joint commitment. The chapter also compares the obligations of joint commitment with obligations in the relatively narrow sense recommended by H. L. A. Hart in his famous essay, "Are There Any Natural Rights?"

Chapter 4 does not purport to cover all contexts in which we talk of rights and obligations. If there are obligations individuals are "born into" or otherwise have *irrespective of any thoughts or actions of their own,* these are not obligations of joint commitment.

Nonetheless, as indicated earlier in this chapter, obligations of joint commitment can arise in a variety of circumstances, not only in the context of the agreements and promises that are the focus of Chapter 4. That this is so is important to the arguments of several chapters, including in particular Chapter 1.

This argues both that actual contract theory has more to be said for it than might be thought and that a plural subject theory of political obligation has more to be said for it than has actual contract theory. Although it can resist the common criticism that it assumes an unrealistic freedom of action on the part of the contractors, actual contract theory falls to the criticism that few have actually agreed to support and uphold the institutions of their country. Plural subject theory is not susceptible to this objection.

The obligations and rights of joint commitment and associated rebukes and other forms of pressure play a significant role in several of the other essays. Thus in Chapter 3 I argue that the assumption that scientific communities are plural subjects of belief suggests important constraints on the development of science. In Chapter 4 I argue that the responses of punitive pressure that, as H. L. A. Hart emphasizes, are associated with social rules, can best be explained by an underlying joint commitment with its associated rights and obligations. A related argument is used in arguing for a plural subject account of *our* intention in Chapter 2. Chapter 4 provides important background material for all of these essays which themselves include only relatively sketchy explanations of the link between joint commitment and obligation.

iv. Summary

Taken together, these essays help to suggest the fertility and scope of plural subject theory. None is intended to close the relevant discussion. On the contrary, it is my hope that these essays stimulate further exploration of both the important topics they address and the plural subject approach to these topics.

The concluding coda (Chapter 9) compares and contrasts plural subject theory with some of the major competing theories in the contemporary literature, with special reference to the topics of shared intention and action and social convention. The chapter explores the way in which plural subject theory is holistic as opposed to individualistic and emphasizes its ability to explain the important normative aspect of social phenomena. This helps to make clear both the power and the distinctiveness of plural subject theory.

NOTES

Thanks to John Troyer and Donald Baxter for comments on a late draft of this introduction.

1. See, for instance, Emile Durkheim, *The Rules of Sociological Method,* trans. W. D. Halls (New York: Free Press, 1982), from the 1895 French original; Georg Simmel, "How Is Society Possible?" in *Georg Simmel: On Individuality and Social Forms,* D. N. Levine,

ed. (Chicago: University of Chicago Press, 1971), from the 1908 German original; Max Weber, *Economy and Society*, 1, G. Roth and C. Wittich, eds. (Berkeley: University of California Press, 1978), from the 1922 posthumous German original.

2. For some reflections on "the question of [nonhuman] animals" in relation to the plural subject theory discussed in this book, see Margaret Gilbert, *On Social Facts* (London: Routledge, 1989), 442–444.

3. For discussion of core claims by these authors, see Gilbert, *On Social Facts*, chapter 2 (an extended critical discussion of Weber's technical concept of "social action"), chapter 4 (on a central claim of Simmel's in "How Is Society Possible?"), and chapter 5 (on Durkheim's discussion of social facts in *Rules*).

4. "Analytic philosopher" is a somewhat vague category that I shall not try to define here. There is an implied contrast with philosophers who work in the post-Kantian "continental" tradition from Hegel onward. My own work on sociality was developed from within the analytic tradition and uses the style of discourse and various techniques of that tradition. (See Gilbert, *On Social Facts*, chapter 1, for relevant discussion.) My positive views developed in the context of reflecting on relevant work within that tradition, particularly that of David Lewis (see the next note). Charles Taylor (who has a foot in both camps) was also an influence (see Gilbert, *On Social Facts*, preface and elsewhere).

5. For the most influential (and most debated) account of social conventions, see David Lewis, *Convention: A Philosophical Study* (Cambridge, Mass.: Harvard University Press, 1969). I offer an extended critique of Lewis's account of convention in Gilbert, *On Social Facts*, chapter 6. See also several of the essays in Margaret Gilbert, *Living Together: Rationality, Sociality, and Obligation* (Lanham, Md.: Rowman and Littlefield, 1996), and Chapter 9, this volume.

6. On social groups see Gilbert, *On Social Facts*, chapter 4; on collective belief, chapter 5; on social convention, chapter 6; on group languages, chapter 3, section 6. Chapter 4 also includes a sustained discussion of acting together.

7. The phrase "joint commitment" has been used by other authors. Sometimes it is clearly used in a different sense from my own; sometimes it is left undefined. I use "joint commitment" as a technical term of my own in a sense I define for my own purposes.

8. On the question of the objectivity of joint commitments, see Margaret Gilbert, "Sociality, Unity, Objectivity," in the *Proceedings of the 1998 World Congress of Philosophy* (forthcoming).

9. See Gilbert, *On Social Facts*, especially 441–442. See also the more extended discussion in "Concerning Sociality: The Plural Subject as Paradigm" in Greenwood, ed., *The Mark of the Social*.

10. See the introduction to Gilbert, *Living Together*, 7–8 for a note on my developing preference for explicit mention of joint commitment in accounts of particular social concepts. The discussion of conversation in Gilbert, *On Social Facts*, is at 294–298.

11. See Gilbert, *On Social Facts*, 154–203.

12. One aspect of such clarification is in terms of a condition of "common knowledge" in roughly the sense of Lewis, *Convention*. There has been much debate as to the best account of common knowledge since Lewis in 1969 and Steven Schiffer in 1972 independently published discussions of what looks like the same idea. Game theorist Robert Aumann published another independent discussion in 1987 (which shows that philosophical news does not travel fast). The most striking and, in a sense, the simplest way to define common knowledge is as follows: it is common knowledge between persons A and B

that *p* if and only if (i) *A* knows that *p*, (ii) *B* knows that *p*, (iii) *A* knows that *B* knows that *p*, (iv) *B* knows that *A* knows that *p*, and so on, ad infinitum. Many have objected to the "ad infinitum" on grounds of a lack of realism, and both Lewis and Schiffer propose alternative accounts. I offer an account of common knowledge and its relationship to the formation of joint commitments in Gilbert, *On Social Facts,* chapter 4.

13. On basic versus derived cases of joint commitment, see Chapter 2, section 4.ii (which refers to "simple" versus "complex" cases as opposed to the more informative "basic" versus "derived" cases) and elsewhere in this volume.

14. The idea of appealing to "implicit agreements" is discussed further in several of the essays in this volume, in particular Chapters 2 and 6.

15. I take it that a typical agreement consists of a proposal or an offer and a consequent acceptance of the proposal. In the standard case of two people in face-to-face contact, the agreement would saliently conclude at the moment of acceptance. I assume that what I have, following convention, referred to as the "conclusion" of the agreement is the moment at which the agreement comes into being. See Gilbert, "Is an Agreement an Exchange of Promises?" *Journal of Philosophy,* 90, no. 12 (1993), 627–649, and Chapter 5, this volume, for more on agreements and the consequences of this assumption, among other things.

16. See Gilbert, *Living Together,* 10–11, for further discussion of this *joint abrogation constraint* on joint commitments.

17. See Chapter 2 for reference to one relevant context, that of the coordination problem. I argue for the superiority of promises to personal intentions, decisions, and plans in the context of temptation in "Resisting Temptation: Plans Versus Promises," my comment on Michael Bratman's "Planning and Temptation" presented at the Conference on Methods, New York, 1994.

18. See Gilbert, *On Social Facts,* p. 198, for instance: "These people will be jointly committed to do A together when the time comes. . . . Each party to the joint commitment will have certain ensuing entitlements and obligations."

19. For a summary of the approach taken in "Agreements, Coercion, and Obligation," see Chapter 5, note 15.

20. For more on the relevance of my views to intuitionist moral theory see Chapter 5.

21. I focus on "offended rebukes" in "Remarks on Collective Belief," in *Socializing Epistemology: The Social Dimensions of Knowledge,* F. Schmitt, ed. (Lanham, Md.: Rowman and Littlefield 1994); reprinted, with amendments, in Gilbert, *Living Together,* as "More on Collective Belief."

22. Bratman's main papers on the topic have recently been collected (with amendments) in *Faces of Intention* (Cambridge: Cambridge University Press, 1999). The central reference for Searle's account is his "Collective Intentions and Actions," in *Intentions in Communication,* P. R. Cohen, J. Morgan, and M. E. Pollack, eds. (Cambridge, Mass.: MIT Press, 1990).

23. For a discussion of Durkheim's "social facts" in relation to plural subject theory, see Gilbert, *On Social Facts,* chapter 5, and Gilbert, "Durkheim and Social Facts," in *Debating Durkheim,* W. S. F. Pickering and H. Martin, eds. (London: Routledge, 1994).

2

What Is It for *Us* to Intend?

When people say things of the form "We intend to do *A*" they standardly mean something other than "We all intend to do *A*." In Michael Bratman's phrase, they are speaking of a *shared intention*. I propose three criteria of adequacy for an account of shared intention: the "obligation" criterion, the "permission" criterion, and the "compatibility with lack of the corresponding personal intentions" criterion. I then present an account of a shared intention as the intention of a *plural subject*: people form the plural subject of an intention to do such-and-such when they are jointly committed to intend as a body to do such-and-such. I argue that the plural subject account of shared intention satisfies the three proposed criteria of adequacy. I explain how shared intention on this account has practical value as a stable framework for bargaining and as an aid to the solution of coordination problems. It contrasts favorably in this respect with other phenomena that philosophers have identified with shared intention.

1. INTRODUCTION: "WE INTEND TO DO *A*"

Philosophers have long discussed what it is for an individual human being to intend to do something. People do not only speak of what you or I intend to do, however. They also quite commonly speak of what *we* intend to do. This mode of speech suggests, on the face of it, that something in some sense plural is unified in such a way as to count as the subject of a single intention—the intention that is *ours*.[1]

It may be that sometimes, when someone says "We intend to do *A*" he (or she) means "We both intend to do *A*" or "We all intend to do *A*."[2] But one who says "We intend to do *A*" does not always mean "We both intend to do *A*" or "We all intend to do *A*."

Consider the following example. Scott asks John what he plans to do this afternoon. Gesturing toward Alice, John says "We intend to go shopping." Intending a friendly echo, Scott responds, "I see, you both intend to go shopping." John replies, with some irritation, "No, no, that's not what I meant." We can all understand that John's reply may be perfectly appropriate. He didn't mean "*We both* intend. . . ." On the contrary, he meant "*We* intend. . . ."

We can imagine John continuing "*We* intend to go shopping," with an emphasis on the first person plural pronoun. Alternatively, he might add a significant word: "We intend to go shopping *together.*" Both answers would apparently provide the same information. For it seems that the intention appropriate to our *doing something together* is an intention of ours (in the relevant sense), and, moreover, *an intention of ours* (in the relevant sense) is an intention to do something together.[3]

The above considerations suggest that there is a standard sense of the English sentence form "We intend to do *A*" such that it is not equivalent to "Each of us intends to do *A*." In what follows I shall suppose this to be so. Indeed, I shall suppose (as is plausible) that there is a single standard sense of "We intend to do *A*" of this kind.

From now on I shall borrow Michael Bratman's phrase and write of a "shared intention" instead of "an intention that is 'ours' in the sense at issue." This phrase may not be entirely felicitous.[4] As long as its intended meaning is clear, however, it will serve. I believe that in Bratman's writings the intended meaning of the phrase "shared intention" is, at the outset at least, the same as mine is here.[5]

What is it for us to share an intention? In this essay I propose an answer to this question. I take the question to call for an analysis of the everyday concept of a shared intention. This is what I attempt to provide.[6]

My account of shared intention is along the lines of proposals I have made elsewhere regarding the attribution of other psychological states to "us." In a technical sense to be specified later, I argue that we must form a *plural subject* of intention. As noted above, that we must form a plural subject *in some sense* is suggested by the apparent structure of (shared intention) sentences of the form "We intend to do *A*." Plural subjects in my technical sense conform to this idea; they do so in a particular manner that I specify.

My main positive claims in this paper are, in fact, of two sorts. On the one hand, I propose some criteria of adequacy for an account of shared intention (in section 2). On the other, I propose an account of shared intention (section 3).

My discussion will be relatively compressed, and the reader will be referred to a number of discussions in other places for further relevant material. I shall largely eschew discussion of competing views of shared intention, but I hope that what I say here will provide material for comparison with other views.[7]

2. ANALYZING ASCRIPTIONS OF SHARED INTENTION: THREE CRITERIA OF ADEQUACY

In this section I consider some examples in which there is, by hypothesis, a shared intention. My examples will involve just two people in an informal setting. That they have a particular shared intention will be assumed to be "common knowledge" between them. For present purposes we can construe this as the assumption that, minimally, both parties know they share the intention in question and both know this is so.[8] It allows us to consider how people may reasonably react in the light of knowledge of their shared intention.[9]

I shall distinguish three features of shared intention situations of the sort I am focusing on and suggest that an adequate analysis of the everyday concept of a shared intention will explain at least these three features. They are all features of shared intention situations from an intuitive, or pretheoretical, point of view.

The following observations parallel observations I have made elsewhere concerning a number of related cases. These cases include what may be called "shared belief" and "sharing in an action."[10] The fact that similar observations can be made in quite a few cases strongly suggests that the everyday concepts in question have a common core. More generally, it suggests that there is a family of everyday concepts in relation to which such observations can be made by virtue of some common factor. I say more about this later.

i. The Obligation Criterion

Let us suppose that Tina and Lena have a certain shared intention. They have started out on a walk, sharing an intention to turn back in about half an hour.

Now imagine that after fifteen minutes Lena suddenly stops in her tracks and, without a word, turns around and starts walking back. Tina will presumably be surprised, but this is not the only reaction we can expect. She is likely to *object* in some such way as this: "What are you doing? We planned to go on for half an hour!" She is critical of Lena's deviation from the shared intention and rebukes her for it. We would expect both Tina and Lena to understand that Tina is entitled to rebuke Lena in this way. Indeed, she clearly has some special standing in the matter, by virtue of the shared intention.

These and similar considerations suggest three related features of shared intention. First, each participant has an obligation not to act contrary to the shared intention. More positively, each has an obligation to promote the fulfillment of the shared intention as well as possible. Second, corresponding to these obligations are rights or entitlements of the other parties to the appropriate performances. Third, if one participant does something contrary to the shared intention, the others have a special entitlement to rebuke that person.

I shall say that an analysis of shared intention fulfills the *obligation criterion* if it explains these interrelated features of shared intention. I see this as a criterion of adequacy for an analysis of shared intention, for in my view whenever we understand a shared intention to be present we understand the noted obligations and entitlements to be present: the connection is conceptual.[11]

ii. The Permission Criterion

Now suppose that Lena responds to Tina's rebuke as follows: "I've decided to go back. I'm just too tired." Though she may choose not to, Tina is surely now in a position to object somewhat as follows: "But you can't just decide to go back, just like that, even if you have a good reason to do so! *You can't just split off without my concurrence or permission.*" We would, in fact, expect both participants in the shared intention to understand that Tina would be right to say such things, by virtue of the shared intention.

Suppose that before turning back Lena had announced "I'm going back!" I believe this would not be acceptable. She *"can't just tell"* Tina that she's going back, as Tina might well observe. In other words, the problem does not lie in the fact that Lena did not tell Tina of her decision to turn back before she carried it out. The problem is, rather, that she "can't just decide," *whether or not she announces her decision to Tina.*

This discussion introduces what I shall call the *permission criterion*. Participants in a shared intention understand that they are not in a position to remove its constraints unilaterally by a simple change of mind, announced or unannounced. The concurrence of the other participants must first be obtained. I take this to be another conceptual truth about shared intention.

iii. The Compatibility with Lack of the Corresponding Personal Intentions Criterion

I shall call an account of shared intention "personal intention–based" if, according to that account, in order for us to share an intention to do *A,* each of us must have a corresponding *personal* intention. By this I mean that (at a minimum) each of us must personally intend to behave appropriately to our doing *A*. It appears that any such account is at least problematic with respect to our everyday notion of shared intention.[12]

Let us return to Tina and Lena. Out on their walk, they have a shared intention to turn back in half an hour. After they have walked for ten minutes, Lena begins to feel tired. She decides that she will turn back within the next five minutes. Soon after this she blurts out "I'm turning back!"

At this point Tina might object with an allusion to their shared intention: "What do you mean? We're supposed to be going on for half an hour!" Though she may not take this line, Lena might now say, firmly, "Well, *I don't intend to go on*." Rather than being understood as denying that "We intend to go on for half an hour," this may well be understood as an expression of defiance: Lena does not intend to act in conformity with the shared intention; indeed, she intends to act contrary to the shared intention.

Evidently, if a shared intention is or comes to be accompanied by one or more *contrary* personal intentions, there is more likelihood that the shared intention will in some way come to grief. In the example given, the parties might renegotiate their shared intention. Tina might respond to Lena's "I don't intend to go on" with a concessive "Well, if that's so, we'd better turn back now." If Lena concurs, a new shared intention has now been formed.[13]

Perhaps, though Tina "speaks up for" the shared intention in her initial response to Lena, she is secretly relieved at the opportunity to change it. She might confess to Lena "I didn't intend to go on that long either!" Thus *it seems that there could be a shared intention to do such-and-such though none of the participants personally intend to conform their behavior to the shared intention.*

I do not claim that it is common for one or more of the participants in a shared intention to lack the corresponding personal intentions. Nor do I claim that shared intentions are typically accompanied by one or more personal intentions that conflict with them. My central claim is that *it is apparently possible in principle that the corresponding personal intentions are lacking when a shared intention is present.*[14] Part of the task of an account of our everyday concept of shared intention is, I take it, to account for this.

Does it mean that a shared intention is not a function of the mental states of the participants? No, only that the relevant mental states are not personal intentions of the participants in favor of the corresponding behavior. Does it mean that shared intentions cannot motivate? No, only that insofar as they do motivate, their motivational force does not derive from the motivational force of corresponding personal intentions. Does it mean that a sensitive understanding of the nature of *intention* is not relevant to an understanding of shared intention? Not necessarily. In order to see whether such an understanding is or is not relevant and to go further on the other issues just raised, we could do with a positive account of shared intention. I now turn to my own proposal.

3. A GENERAL SCHEME OF ANALYSIS FOR COLLECTIVE PSYCHOLOGICAL PROPERTIES

i. Schema *S*

According to the account I shall propose, the everyday concept of shared intention is a member of the family of concepts I labeled the "plural subject" concepts in *On Social Facts* (Gilbert, 1989). The technical sense in which I use the term "plural subject" will be explained shortly.

The argument of *On Social Facts* as a whole suggests that, quite standardly, vernacular first person plural psychological statements are susceptible of a particular type of analysis along the following lines. (The schema and notes that follow continue this paper's focus on the two person case.)[15]

Schema *S*

For the relevant psychological predicate "*X*" and persons *P1* and *P2, P1* or *P2* may truly say "We *X*" with respect to *P1* and *P2* if and only if *P1* and *P2* are *jointly committed* to *X*-ing *as a body.*[16]

I explain what I mean by "joint commitment" in section ii. There follow here some further observations relating to Schema *S*.

a. Plural subjects

When persons *P1* and *P2* are jointly committed to *X*-ing as a body, they then constitute what I call a *plural subject.* In particular, they form a plural subject of *X*-ing. Joint commitment is an essential component of plural subjecthood in my technical sense.

b. "X-ing as a body"

I am not deeply committed to the formulation "*X*-ing *as a body,*" though this is what I tend to prefer. One possible alternative is "*X*-ing as a unit." Some further formulation might be even more perspicuous, but both of these, I think, give the general idea.[17]

c. The role of psychological concepts

Schema *S* incorporates the following idea about psychological properties that are "shared" in the sense at issue here, properties we may also call *collective* psychological properties. The individuals in question know what it is to possess the psychological property in question.

Note that I do not say they know what it is for there to be an *individual human being* who *X*s. There is no need here to preempt an answer to the question whether our conceptions of collective psychological properties are in some way parasitic upon or secondary to our conceptions of the psychological properties of an individual human being. There could be differences among the broad range of psychological properties in this connection.

This feature of the schema entails that our understanding of the concept of *intention* will be relevant to our understanding of shared intention.

d. Corresponding analyses

In *On Social Facts* I argued, in independent discussions, for a number of corresponding analyses. I proposed, for instance, that a standard interpretation of "We believe that such-and-such" runs along these lines.[18] I argued similarly with respect to several other broadly speaking psychological attributions to "us," including "We are doing this together," "This is our language," "We have this convention (governing action)."[19] I have also proposed that this form of analysis applies to some ascriptions of emotion such as anger and fear.[20]

These arguments, which will not be repeated here, support the proposal that Schema *S* captures a standard interpretation of first person psychological statements in general. My argument for a corresponding account of shared intention does not *assume* that Schema *S* holds for shared intention also. It gains support, however, from the plausibility of the proposal that there is a family of apparently related concepts susceptible of analysis in terms of that schema.

ii. "Joint Commitment"

In order that Schema *S* be fully understood, I must explain how I construe the technical term "joint commitment." The following discussion is intended to give the general idea.[21]

a. "Commitments"

Let me first say something briefly and informally about the sense in which I am using the term "commitment" here. I do not use it in a "socialized" sense such that my commitments are all in some sense commitments to others. Rather I see a personal decision, for instance, as involving a commitment.

Inclinations and enthusiasms do not yet involve commitments. If I have decided to do *A,* I am subject to a commitment to do *A.* In contrast, I can be inclined to do *A* but not yet subject to a commitment to do *A.* I shall not try further to specify the relevant sense of "commitment" in this paper.[22]

b. "Personal commitments"

In explaining what a joint commitment is, it will be useful first to introduce the notion of what I shall call a "personal commitment." Consider the case of a personal decision. When John decides to do *A,* he is the sole author of his decision. If he wishes to rid himself of it once it is made, he is in a position to do so. He need only change his mind. One might say that he has the authority unilaterally to rescind his decision.

A *personal commitment* may for present purposes be characterized as follows. John is subject to a personal commitment if and only if he is the sole author of a commitment and has the authority unilaterally to rescind it. Personal decisions, plans, and goals all involve personal commitments in this sense.

c. "Joint commitments"

I now turn to joint commitment, as I understand it. Ruth and Lil's joint commitment is, precisely, the commitment *of Ruth and Lil.*[23] Some brief remarks may help to clarify that general description.

A typical context for the formation of a joint commitment of two people involves the parties in face-to-face contact, mutually expressing their readiness to be jointly committed, in conditions of common knowledge. As the parties understand, the joint commitment is in place when and only when each of the relevant expressions has been made.

From what has just been said about the genesis of joint commitments, a joint commitment could be an aggregate of personal commitments, but it is not. The creation of Lil and Ruth's commitment is not a matter of Lil's creating (and expressing) a personal commitment of her own and Ruth's then creating (and expressing) a corresponding personal commitment of her own. Nor is it a matter of their somehow creating corresponding personal commitments simultaneously.

Ruth and Lil's commitment is not an aggregate of personal commitments, and in expressing her readiness to be jointly committed each one understands this. In so expressing herself she understands that no "part" of the joint commitment will be in place before the joint commitment is. More to the point, she understands that a joint commitment does not properly speaking have *parts.*

So it is not the case that each is the sole author of part of the joint commitment, let alone of the joint commitment as a whole. Rather, they comprise the author of the joint commitment together.

Neither one is in a position to be rid of the joint commitment simply by changing her mind. In other words, neither one has the authority to rescind the joint commitment unilaterally. They must rescind it together.

A joint commitment, then, is very different from a personal commitment as characterized above. Once their joint commitment is in place, Ruth is subject to a commitment such that she is not the sole author of the commitment, and she does not have the authority unilaterally to rescind it. The same goes, of course, for Lil.

Each of the parties to a joint commitment is indeed committed in the sense that each one is subject to a commitment. It is tempting, then, to refer to the parties' "individual commitments." If one does so, one must bear in mind that these commitments have important special features arising from their dependence on the joint commitment: these "individual commitments" cannot exist independently of the joint commitment, and the person who has a given "individual commitment" of this sort is not in a position unilaterally to rescind it. These individual commitments clearly are not *personal* commitments in the sense adumbrated earlier.

It is true that one party can deliberately violate or break a joint commitment. But as long as the joint commitment survives, what is done amounts precisely to a violation, as each party will understand.[24]

I shall return to the concept of joint commitment shortly, in connection with the obligation criterion. For now I hope somewhat to have clarified its content.

4. THE PLURAL SUBJECT ACCOUNT OF SHARED INTENTION

An initial account of shared intention can now be formulated. It follows Schema *S* with appropriate substitutions:

Persons *P1* and *P2* have a shared intention to do *A* if and only if they are jointly committed to intending as a body to do *A*.

Alternatively (now that we have introduced the notion of a plural subject):

Persons *P1* and *P2* have a shared intention to do *A* if and only if they constitute the plural subject of an intention to do *A*.

If we want a label, then, we may call this *the plural subject account* of shared intention. The key phrase "joint commitment" must, of course, be interpreted as indicated in the previous section. Some further notes on this proposal follow.

i. Extending the Account

This account can easily be extended to cover not only "intentions to" but also "intentions that." "Intentions that" are referred to in such statements as "We intend that the perpetrators be brought to justice." Saying this rather than "We intend to bring the perpetrators to justice" suggests that though we may not bring the perpetrators to justice ourselves, we are in a position to ensure that they are brought to justice one way or another.

The account can also be extended to cover an important type of case of "intentions to." Members of large populations—such as the many inhabitants of a large island—are unlikely to know or even know of one another personally. To allow that the members of such a population may share an intention, we will need an appropriate extension or version of the proposed account in which the people in question are picked out by reference to some common feature such as "living on the island."[25]

ii. Complex Cases

The proposed account is already tailored to cover a class of cases other than those I have focused on here. In those cases it was, by hypothesis, common knowledge between the parties to the shared intention that they had this particular shared intention. There appear to be cases of shared intention where the specifics of a certain shared intention are *not* known to all the parties.

Asked about his vacation plans, George might turn, in ignorance, to his wife, Rosa, and ask "What are our plans, love?"[26] In cases like this, one or more of the parties to our intention evidently has special authority to form intentions for *us*—intentions not all of us need to be aware of even after they are formed. Such authority is likely to be restricted to some particular class of intentions, though in principle it need not be.

Such cases may conform to the above account in the following way. To take our example, George and Rosa may be *jointly committed to accept as a body that Rosa is the one who decides on behalf of the two of them where they will take their annual vacation.* By some such mechanism, George and Rosa may become jointly committed to intending to go to Greece this summer, though George does not yet know of the commitment.

I call this a "complex case" because it sets up a shared intention in a relatively complex way. It is simpler mutually to express willingness to be jointly committed to intend as a body to do *A* in conditions of common knowledge. The more complex way is first to authorize someone (or some body) to set up shared intentions for the people in question and then to have that person (or body) go through the relevant mechanism. It is a two-stage process.

The account proposed covers both simple and complex cases of the kind noted, in part by avoiding any stipulation as to how the relevant joint commitment is formed. In particular, it does not stipulate that the parties must mutually express willingness to be jointly committed to intend to do *A* as a body. They must simply *be* jointly committed; and the available mechanisms for this allow that they need not, in fact, mutually express willingness to be jointly committed to intend to do *A* as a body in order to be so committed.

An alternative way of dealing with complex cases would be to include a mutual expressions of willingness clause in what was argued to be the core or basic definition of shared intention and to go on to explain how complex cases can arise. This has been my procedure in some related discussions.

iii. An Analogy with Personal Intentions

A personal intention is directly relevant to the practical reasoning of the person in question. Among other things, the existence of a particular personal intention to do *A* is apt to structure a person's further planning, as Michael Bratman has emphasized.[27] Broadly speaking, I take it that if one has a personal intention to do *A,* one then has reason to promote the satisfaction of the intention.[28] If shared intentions are anything like personal intentions, one would expect them to have this in common with personal intentions.

I take it that any *commitment* one is subject to gives one reason to act accordingly.[29] Therefore if Ruth and Lil are *jointly committed* to intend as a body to paint the kitchen today, each then has reason to act, make plans, and so on, in conformity to the joint commitment. Ruth has reason not to accept her friend Joe's suggestion that they go to the beach. Each has reason to discuss with the other whether any relevant materials need to be bought. And so on.

Given the plural subject account of shared intention, then, shared intentions are directly relevant to the parties' practical reasoning. Those with a shared intention have reason to promote the satisfaction of the intention in question by virtue of the underlying joint commitment.

Insofar as personal intentions have independent motivational force, of themselves giving reasons for acting, shared intentions have this in common with personal intentions. This makes for a significant analogy between shared intentions and personal intentions. It also accords with some by now well-known observations about inferences from premises about what "we intend."

iv. Relation to Standard Inferences from Premises about What "We intend"

A participant in a shared intention on the plural subject account can reason as follows: "We intend to clean the house today, my staying home is required for that, therefore I have reason to stay home." There is no need for anything further, in particular no need for any reference to a personal intention or desire. The premise stating that "We intend . . ." together with the statement of what is needed to satisfy the intention leads to a conclusion about what I have reason to do. In the absence of countervailing reasons, this is what I should do, from the point of view of practical reasoning.

The acceptability of the inference in question seems clear pretheoretically without any analysis of "We intend. . . ." The same goes for related premises such as "Our goal is. . . ." This was remarked upon (in more or less the same terms) by Wilfrid Sellars.[30] As I first argued in *On Social Facts*, an interpretation of such premises in terms of joint commitment would explain the intuitive propriety of such inferences.[31]

That the inference is justified by an account does not, in and of itself, clinch the argument in favor of that account.[32] However, given that mine is not a personal intention–based account, it is important to show that this inference can be accommodated.

It is an implication of the obligation and permission criteria of adequacy proposed earlier that a variety of other inferences involving the premise "We intend . . ." are acceptable as well.[33] My discussion of these criteria in the next section shows that these inferences, too, can be justified by the plural subject account of shared intention.

5. SHARED INTENTION AND MUTUAL OBLIGATION

I shall now argue that the plural subject account of shared intention satisfies the three criteria of adequacy I put forward earlier. I start with the criterion I stated first, which also merits the most discussion.

i. The Obligation Criterion

The obligation criterion appears to raise a large question: What are *obligations*? The term "obligation" has come to be used very broadly, and there is reason to suppose that—given this breadth of usage—there are obligations of very different types. For present purposes the general question about obligation need not concern us. Of specific concern is shared intention and the obligations associated with it.

Correlated with the obligations associated with shared intention are entitlements to an obligated person's performance and corresponding entitlements to rebuke that person for violating his or her obligation. My proposal about the obligations of shared intention is this: *the pretheoretical judgment that shared intentions involve obligations with corresponding entitlements responds to the presence, given a shared intention, of a joint commitment.*

Behind this proposal is another: *obligations with corresponding entitlements inhere in any joint commitment.* I have argued for this general claim about joint commitment in other places.[34] Given its importance here, some relevant observations follow.

Suppose Lena has made a certain decision. She could rescind it unilaterally, but she has not done so. Nonetheless, she finds herself acting against it. She might then reflect that she has in a sense *betrayed herself.* She has acted contrary to a personal commitment. The same may go, evidently, for other forms of personal commitment such as plans and goals.

Suppose now that Lena is party to a joint commitment with Tina. Lena is not in a position to rescind it unilaterally. She and Tina must rescind it together, and they have not done so.[35] Lena's violation of the joint commitment can surely be argued to constitute not so much a self-betrayal as *a betrayal of herself and Tina.* It appears, in other words, that *by virtue of her involvement in a joint commitment with Lena, and that alone, Tina gains a special standing in relation to Lena's actions, and vice versa.*

How might we describe this special standing? It seems very natural to describe it thus: *Tina is entitled to Lena's conforming action.* Correspondingly, *Lena is under an obligation to Tina,* an obligation to conform to the joint commitment. Tina thus has the standing to rebuke Lena should she not conform. In other words, *Tina is entitled to rebuke Lena for nonconformity.*

Pursuing this mode of description, these obligations and entitlements derive from the joint commitment alone. They *inhere in* the joint commitment in the sense that once the joint commitment exists, they exist also. Nothing further is needed.[36]

Someone might object that the obligations and entitlements we are talking about now are obligations and entitlements like no others. This may be so—it need not be decided here. I am happy to refer to "the obligations and entitlements of joint commitment" if this will help to keep their particular nature in focus.

Note that all that the participants need to understand in order to recognize that they have these obligations and entitlements is the nature of joint commitment, and this they will inevitably understand if they are parties to such a commitment. Given the observations made earlier about the tight connection between joint commitment and obligations, this is a desirable result, conformable to pretheoretical judgments.

I conclude that the obligation criterion is satisfied by the plural subject account of shared intention. Arguing this has required some explanation of the way in which, on this account, the parties are (of logical necessity) obligated to one another.

ii. The Permission Criterion

The permission criterion can be dealt with more quickly. Suppose that Tina and Lena have a shared intention—according to the plural subject account—to turn back in half an hour. This is common knowledge between them. They will then understand that neither has the option of unilaterally calling things off. The underlying joint commitment can only be rescinded by the two of them together. The concurrence of both parties is therefore a requirement of calling things off. Thus the permission criterion is satisfied.

iii. The Compatibility with Lack of the Corresponding Personal Intentions Criterion

Recall that by "corresponding personal intentions" I refer to personal intentions to conform one's behavior to the shared intention. For example, if we intend to turn back in half an hour then my corresponding personal intention would be the intention to go on walking for half an hour and then turn back.

Given the plural subject account, it is possible from a logical point of view for a shared intention to exist without the corresponding personal intentions. An intention that two people share is the intention of two people united by a joint commitment to intend, as a body, in the relevant way. They are indeed committed through their joint commitment, but they do not thereby accrue *personal* commitments as these were characterized earlier.

Given the rough and general idea of a commitment specified above, a personal intention may be counted a commitment.[37] If it is a commitment, it is a personal one. That is, it is a commitment over which the person whose intention it is holds sway: that person can dissolve the commitment he or she is subject to unilaterally, by a change of mind. Hence those who are committed through a joint commitment do not thereby accrue personal intentions in favor of the shared intention. Personal intentions are simply not part of the plural subject account of shared intention.

It is worth stressing that, on that account, *given a shared intention the corresponding personal intentions are redundant from a motivational point of view*. Once we have that intention, *we are already motivated to act according to the corresponding personal intentions*. (In the absence of the corresponding personal intentions we could not, of course, act *in light of* them.)

Of course, given a particular shared intention, many and various personal intentions are likely to be framed with an eye on conforming to the shared intention. Suppose that Tina has promised to phone her brother Max at 4 P.M., and she and Lena intend not to finish their walk until 4.30 P.M. Tina may decide to look for a call box on their route, intending to call Max from there. She can then both keep her promise and accord with the intention she shares with Lena.

6. CREATING SHARED INTENTIONS: EXPLICIT AGREEMENTS AND OTHER CONTEXTS

Shared intentions of the simple, informal sort I have focused on here often arise in a face-to-face interaction where an explicit agreement is made. For instance, Ben says "Shall we plan on cleaning the house today?" and Bill responds "Yes, sure." Here there is an explicit agreement to the effect that the parties will do something together.

Not all of the contexts in which shared intentions arise are of this sort. For instance, Bill is putting books from a large pile back on the bookshelves. Ben walks over to him and appears to be waiting for instructions. Bill says, "Put the travel books on this shelf." Here the parties have not explicitly agreed to refill the bookshelves together. Yet by the end of the story they may be deemed to share that intention.

Turning from shared intentions to joint commitments, all that these require are mutual expressions of willingness to be jointly committed in the relevant way, mutual expressions made in conditions of common knowledge. We can take Bill and Ben to have fulfilled this condition in the book-shelving case. They also fulfill it when they make an explicit agreement, as in the house-cleaning case.

One may be inclined to say that what has transpired in the book-shelving case is a "tacit" or perhaps an "implicit" agreement. This can only be regarded as a first start in explaining the matter. What precisely is a "tacit" or an "implicit" agreement? What, indeed, is an explicit agreement? What does it amount to?

I have argued elsewhere for a plural subject account of explicit agreements. An agreement is, in effect, a "shared decision," this being analyzable as a plural subject concept. At the base of an agreement, then, is a joint commitment.[38] This could explain why it is tempting to use the language of agreements (albeit "tacit" or "implicit" agreements) in connection with other phenomena—such as shared intention—susceptible of a plural subject analysis.[39]

Suffice it to say here that attention to the contexts in which we deem a shared intention to have been formed support the plural subject account of shared intention. These contexts include both the house-cleaning case (that involves an explicit agreement) and the book-shelving case (that does not).

7. SHARED INTENTION, BARGAINING, AND COORDINATION PROBLEMS

i. The Plural Subject Account of Shared Intention As a "Dual Control" Account

The plural subject account of shared intention might be referred to as a "dual control" account (in relation to a two person case). This has implications for its desirability as a framework for bargaining and as a mechanism for the solution of coordination problems. It contrasts favorably in this way with an account of shared intention that solely requires meshing personal intentions.

According to the plural subject account of shared intention, it is notable that one and the same thing—the joint commitment—constrains each of the parties' practical reasoning. In the case of meshing personal intentions, what constrains the parties' practical reasoning is different for each one—each party's reasoning is constrained by his or her own personal intention.

In the case of joint commitment, the single thing that constrains the practical reasoning of both parties is something over which neither party has absolute control. The joint commitment is under the control of both parties together: as both understand, no one party can unilaterally rescind the commitment. As a result, no one party can dissolve the shared intention by a unilateral change of mind.

In contrast, given a personal intention–based account of shared intention—with no further factor such as a joint commitment added—all that is required to, in effect, dissolve the shared intention is a change of mind by one party, something each party is in a position to bring about. For each party is in a position to rescind or change his or her personal intention, insofar as that intention is under his or her personal control.

There may, of course, be other operative constraints. If Fred knows that Rosie would prefer that the shared intention were not dissolved or that much hangs upon its continued existence as far as she is concerned, he may find this reason enough not to change his own mind. My point is that it is in his power to change his mind and (thus) to dissolve the shared intention should he wish to, and both he and Rosie will know this.

ii. Shared Intention and Bargaining

As Bratman notes, those with a particular shared intention may need to bargain or negotiate within the framework of that intention. For instance, people who intend to go for a walk together may have different preferences as to where to go and need somehow to resolve this conflict.

Regarding his own example, and in light of his own personal intention–based account of shared intention, Bratman observes, "Difficulties in such bargaining may, of course, lead either of us to reconsider the intention that we paint together" ("Shared Intention," 106–107). The implication is that if one of us does reconsider the intention, he (or she) may decide to exercise his rightful authority and do away with it, by doing away with his part of it.

This indicates that a shared intention on an account in terms of personal intentions is not a felicitous framework for bargaining or negotiation. If I know that you are ready and able to do away with the shared intention should you not get your way, I may be less inclined to ask for what I need, as opposed to what you are already prepared to give. Evidently, a shared intention on the plural subject account is a more felicitous framework for bargaining. It is quite robust in relation to personal desires to be rid of it.

iii. Shared Intention and Coordination Problems

Consider a "pure" two person coordination problem of the sort described by game theorists. A standard case is the interrupted telephone call: in order to reconnect, one but not both of the parties must call back. Both parties are faced with the problem "Should I call back or wait for the other person to call me back?" Only if they make choices that mesh appropriately will their resulting actions be coordinated in the fashion both desire. The parties are assumed to be such that they will act on the balance of reasons available to them, and this is assumed to be common knowledge.

In such a situation, a shared intention according to the plural subject account can solve the coordination problem. The shared intention provides each one with more secure expectations about the other than a meshing set of similar personal intentions in favor of conformity could ever provide. A commitment I understand myself to be unable to rescind without your permission is clearly more to be relied on than a commitment I understand myself free to rescind unilaterally.

In the latter case, the following considerations may confound either party: "I should do *A* if he sticks to his intention, but will he? He will if he knows I'll stick to mine, but what guarantee does he have of that? No more than I have of his sticking to his intention! So maybe he'll switch. Why should he? Well, why shouldn't he? What prevents it?"[40]

Given a shared intention, one holds the key to the other party's choice in one's own hand. All else being equal, if one has not given permission for his defection, he, being rational, will not defect.[41]

8. CONCLUSION

I began by noting three criteria of adequacy for an account of shared intention. These were not the only criteria I might have mentioned, but they are quite forceful ones. I have proposed an account of shared intention and argued that it fulfills the criteria. I have argued that shared intentions on this account are functionally important adjuncts to our lives, more fruitful in some central contexts than a set of corresponding personal intentions.

It may be helpful to summarize some key aspects of my discussion. I have argued that a shared intention is a phenomenon involving at least two agents such that:

(i) It does not necessarily involve corresponding personal intentions of these agents.

(ii) The *concept* of intention is nonetheless operative in that the agents in question are jointly committed to *intending* "as a body."

(iii) Through the joint commitment each party is under an obligation to the others to conform to the shared intention, and the others have correlative entitlements to such conformity and hence entitlements to rebuke for non-conformity.

(iv) The obligations and entitlements in question inhere in the joint commitment itself.

(v) A shared intention provides a unique type of motivational source: it provides a single motivational source for the different agents, a source that is under the control of all the agents (the underlying joint commitment cannot be rescinded unilaterally).

(vi) As a result, a shared intention is a robust framework for bargaining and negotiation, and a powerful tool for the solution of coordination problems, superior to a set of corresponding personal intentions, however closely intertwined.

In short, our intention is the intention of a plural subject in my technical sense, founded in joint commitment.

In conclusion, it seems fair to say that a joint commitment *unifies* people in a very real way. Those with a joint commitment to intend as a body are unified by that commitment, though it may be accompanied by one or more subversive individual intentions. An initial observation in this discussion was that our talk of what *we* intend suggests, on the face of it, that "something in some sense plural is unified in such a way as to count as the subject of a single intention." The plural subject account of shared intention makes something of this observation. When we share an intention it is ours: the intention we uphold together by virtue of a unifying joint commitment.

NOTES

Versions of this material have been presented in a number of places. These include an invited comment on a talk by Michael Bratman at the American Philosophical Association Central Division meeting, Louisville, Kentucky, 1992; an invited symposium talk at the American Philosophical Association Pacific Division meeting, 1993 (co-symposiasts were Bratman and David Velleman); and colloquium presentations to members of the Philosophy Program, the Graduate Center of the City University of New York, 1993, the Philosophy Department at Frankfurt University, 1993, and the Philosophy Department at King's College, London, 1996 (faculty seminar). I am grateful for the comments I received on these occasions. I would particularly like to thank Jürgen Habermas for a comment that influenced the presentation of my ideas here (June 1993). Thanks, too, to John Troyer for probing comments on sections of a late

draft. Michael Bratman and I have publicly debated what it is for *us* to intend over a
period of years, and I thank him for the seriousness with which he has in his own work
attempted to address considerations raised in relevant work of mine, in particular
Gilbert, M., *On Social Facts* (London: Routledge, 1989; reprinted by Princeton University Press, 1992). Gilbert, M., "Walking Together: A Paradigmatic Social Phenomenon," in *Midwest Studies in Philosophy,* 15, P. A. French, T. E. Uehling Jr., and H. K.
Wettstein, eds. (1990), reprinted with some revisions in Gilbert, 1996; Gilbert, M.,
"What Is It That We Do When We Intend?" invited comment, American Philosophical
Association, Central Division, Louisville, Kentucky, 1992. (Minor changes, including
the updating of some references, have been made in the original text for publication in
this volume.)

1. Cf. Velleman's idea of what a "truly 'plural subject' " would be like: "It ought to
involve two or more subjects who combine in such a way as to constitute one subject."
Velleman, D., "How to Share an Intention," *Philosophy and Phenomenological Research,*
57 (1997), 29–50.

2. I take it that this observation does not imply that there is a simple "distributive"
sense of "We intend to do A." Someone who speaks this way may be speaking ellipti-
cally, skipping the word "both," which would properly have been included had he used
words that mean precisely what *he* means. No difference is made to anything I have to
say here, however, if we allow that there *is* a simple distributive sense of "We intend
to do A."

3. Such statements as "We intend her to win a scholarship" are plausibly construed as
elliptical for something like "We intend together to bring it about that she win a scholarship."

4. Cf. Baier, A., "Doing Things with Others: The Mental Commons," in *Commonality and Particularity in Ethics,* L. Alanen, S. Heinamaa, and T. Wallgren, eds. (New York:
Macmillan, 1996).

5. See Bratman, M., "Shared Intention," *Ethics,* 104 (1993), 97–113. Bratman takes
as an overall guiding question "What do shared intentions do, what jobs do they have in
our lives?" (99) and argues, of a particular complex of intentions of the agents concerned,
that we have reason to identify shared intention with it since, roughly, it can do the jobs he
takes shared intention to do. What I shall argue, in effect, is that—from the point of view
of how we understand talk of "what *we* intend or of what *we* are going to do or are doing"
(98)—there are reasons for *not* so identifying shared intentions.

6. Some are skeptical of the possibility of any such analysis. I would hope that my
project here can then be reinterpreted in terms more congenial to such skeptics. This is not
the place for further discussion of such issues.

7. Probably the best-known competing view is that of Michael Bratman; see Bratman, "Shared Intention," and elsewhere. As Bratman observes, there are some analyses in
the same general area whose *analysanda* may not be quite the same. Bratman refers
to Tuomela and Miller (Tuomela, R., and K. Miller, "We-Intentions," *Philosophical Studies,* 53 [1988], 367–389.) and Searle (Searle, J., "Collective Intentions and Actions," in *Intentions in Communication,* P. R. Cohen, J. Morgan, and M. E. Pollack, eds. [Cambridge,
Mass.: MIT Press, 1990]). See Bratman, "Shared Intentions," 103 n17. The literature on
my specific topic and within its general area continues to grow. I do not attempt a complete bibliography here. See also Chapter 9, this volume.

8. Lewis introduced "common knowledge" into the literature. Lewis, D. K., *Conven-*

tion: A Philosophical Study (Cambridge, Mass.: Harvard University Press, 1969). For some discussion see Gilbert, M., *On Social Facts* (London: Routledge, 1989; reprinted by Princeton University Press, 1992), (especially 186–195). (See also Chapter 1 and Chapter 9, this volume. Each of these chapters presents as an example an "infinitistic" account of common knowledge. The accounts are slightly different in that one concerns common knowledge between particular individuals and the other common knowledge among "all members of a population P." The basic idea is the same.)

9. It seems that there can be cases of shared intention where the specifics of the intention are not known to all of the parties. I discuss such cases briefly in section 5 below.

10. My discussions of "shared belief" can be found in the sources: Gilbert, M., "Modeling Collective Belief," *Synthese* 73 (1987), 185–204, reprinted in Gilbert, 1996; Gilbert, M., *On Social Facts* (London: Routledge, 1989; reprinted by Princeton University Press, 1992); Gilbert, M., "Durkheim and Social Facts," in *Debating Durkheim,* W. S. F. Pickering and H. Martins, eds. (London: Routledge, 1994), 86–109; Gilbert, M., "Remarks on Collective Belief," in *Socializing Epistemology: The Social Dimensions of Knowledge,* F. Schmitt, ed. (Lanham, Md.: Rowman and Littlefield, 1994), 235–253; reprinted with some revisions in Gilbert, 1996. On "sharing in an action" see: Gilbert, *On Social Facts* (chapter 4), which examines a number of specific examples. Another article focuses on walking together: Gilbert, M., "Walking Together: A Paradigmatic Social Phenomenon, in *Midwest Studies in Philosophy*, 15, P. A. French, T. E. Uehling Jr., and H. K. Wettstein, eds. (1990), 1–14; reprinted with some revisions in Gilbert, 1996.

11. More guardedly, the relationship of a shared intention to the noted obligations and so on is on a par with the relationship of being someone's biological sister to being someone's biological sibling.

12. Michael Bratman's is a prominent example of a personal intention–based account. Bratman ("Shared Intention") appears to suppose that if there is a shared intention then there must be "intentions on the part of the individual agents to act accordingly" (111 n13). This responds to a discussion of my comment (1992) on Bratman's 1992 talk: "Shared Intention" (Gilbert, "What Is It?"). See also "Shared Intention," 98: "[Mutual promises] do not ensure a shared intention, for one or both parties may be insincere and have no intention to fulfil the promise." This will only be true if a shared intention to do A requires corresponding personal intentions.

13. Lena might not concur with this particular proposal. She might say "I think you should go on," for instance, perhaps citing Tina's greater need for exercise. In any case, the original shared intention comes to be shelved.

14. There is an analogy here with other contexts, such as shared belief. One may intelligibly dissent from what "we" believe by saying "I personally don't believe that." See Gilbert, "Modeling," for instance.

15. The two person case is special in certain ways. On this see Gilbert, M., *Living Together: Rationality, Sociality, and Obligation* (Lanham, Md.: Rowman and Littlefield, 1996), introduction, 12–13. For present purposes this need not concern us.

16. For a comparison of this formulation to some of those used in *On Social Facts,* see Gilbert, *Living Together,* introduction, 7–10.

17. For more on this see Gilbert, *Living Together,* 348–349, 358 n7 and p. 4 here.

18. See the references on "shared belief" in note 10 above. Some formulations of my

account of "We believe" are formulated in terms of what I call "joint acceptance." I take these formulations to be equivalent to the account that follows the above schema. See Gilbert, *Living Together,* introduction, 7–8.

19. See, for instance, Gilbert, *On Social Facts,* chapter 3: "This is our language"; chapter 4: "We are doing this together"; chapter 6: "This is our convention."

20. Gilbert, M., "The Author Responds: More on Social Facts," *Social Epistemology,* 5 (1991), 223–344; reprinted in Gilbert, *Living Together.* (See also Chapter 7, this volume.)

21. I first used the phrase "joint commitment" in *On Social Facts.* See especially chapter 4. In Gilbert, "Modeling," I wrote of "commitment as a body." What is important is not the phrase chosen but the intended interpretation. For more on joint commitment and references to some related discussions see Gilbert, *Living Together,* introduction.

22. This and the previous paragraph were prompted by questions from Randall Cream in my graduate seminar at the University of Connecticut, fall 1996. See also note 29.

23. In some places I have written that a joint commitment is the commitment of "two or more individuals considered as a unit or whole." I do not mean to introduce the idea of a new kind of entity, a "unit" or "whole." I could as well have written "a joint commitment is the commitment of two or more individuals considered together," which would not carry any such suggestion. The formulation in the text also avoids it. This note follows discussion with Keith Hossack, personal communication, August 1996.

24. Exactly what a violation achieves in terms of the persistence or otherwise of a given joint commitment needs careful consideration. See Gilbert, *Living Together,* introduction and chapter 16.

25. I discuss large-group plural subjects in Gilbert, *On Social Facts,* chapter 4. See also Gilbert, M., "Group Wrongs and Guilt Feelings," *Journal of Ethics,* 1, no. 1 (1997).

26. Compare the case of the deferential spouse in Gilbert, "Durkheim," 103–104, which discusses "our belief."

27. See Bratman, M., *Intention, Plans, and Practical Reason* (Cambridge, Mass.: Harvard University Press, 1987).

28. "Broadly speaking" is intended to qualify both my reference to "having reason" and the phrase "promoting the satisfaction of the intention in question," which is intentionally vague. With respect to "having reason" I take it that—all else being equal—one who while intending to do *A* did not do *A* could reasonably be seen as acting irrationally or contrary to reason in some plausible, if broad, sense. Consider this dialogue: "Why didn't you do it?" "Why should I have?" "Well, you intended to, didn't you?" On the question whether a personal *decision* gives one a reason to act in some particular way, see Gilbert, M., "Agreements, Coercion, and Obligation," *Ethics,* 103 (1993), 679–706; reprinted with some revisions in Gilbert, *Living Together.*

29. In light of the focus of the previous paragraph on personal *intentions,* I note the following. Though personal intentions may fall within the scope of the rough preliminary characterization of a "commitment" made earlier in the text of this paper, there may be relevant considerations suggesting that given a more refined account of "commitments" along the same lines, personal intentions, or some personal intentions, should not count as commitments. (I raise this question in Gilbert, M., "Intending, Deciding, and Akrasia," talk presented to the University of Connecticut Philosophy Department, 1991. That presentation amplifies a remark in Gilbert, M., "Review of *Promising, Intending, and Moral Autonomy,* by M. Robins," *Philosophical Review,* 100 (1991). This

particular issue need not concern us now. As long as standing personal intentions are generally reason-providing in some sense and commitments in general are similarly reason-providing, the analogy between personal intentions and shared intentions I am making here will hold.

30. See, for instance, Sellars, W., "Imperatives, Intentions, and the Logic of 'Ought,' " in *Morality and the Language of Conduct,* G. Nakhnikian and H.-N. Castaneda, eds. (Detroit: Wayne State University Press, 1963). For further relevant references see Gilbert, *On Social Facts,* 493 n6.

31. See in particular Gilbert, *On Social Facts,* chapter 7, 424, focusing on "We want" construed as "This is our goal"; also 493 n6. See also Gilbert, "Walking Together."

32. This was emphasized in conversation by Crispin Wright, personal communication, 1989.

33. Rosenberg suggests the propriety of some related inferences. Rosenberg, J., *One World and Our Knowledge of It* (Dordrecht: Reidel, 1980).

34. See in particular Gilbert, "Agreement." (See also Chapter 4, this volume.)

35. Evidently, if I want to be subject to a commitment that is robust in relation to *my own* change of mind, I need a joint commitment rather than a personal one. Cf. Gilbert, M., "Resisting Temptation: Plans Versus Promises," invited comment on Bratman, 1994, presented to the New York Conference on Methods, 1994. This presentation was a comment on Bratman, M., "Resisting Temptation," invited talk presented to the New York Conference on Methods, 1994.

36. A right deriving from a joint commitment may be in some sense waiveable. It is by no means clear, however, that the "waiveability" in question need involve the actual disappearance of the right. Consider the following example. Meg says "Shall we meet for lunch on Tuesday?" and Paul says "Yes" somewhat reluctantly. Meg then offers "Don't worry, you can always call me and say you've changed your mind." One plausible way of interpreting the final outcome in a situation like this is as follows: Meg and Paul have a plan to meet; their having a plan to meet involves their being jointly committed and, therefore, having the relevant obligations and rights. Meg and Paul also have a special side understanding to the effect that Meg will act as if she had no right to hold Paul to their shared plan. They may both now act as if he has the right to back out at will. Something similar may be said of a case discussed by Michael Bratman ("Shared Intention," 111), where the parties "reserve the right" to call off a joint enterprise (duet singing) at any time. Any plausible "reservation of right" of this kind is likely to be something agreed on by the parties: both may now act as if they have the right to back out at will.

37. See note 29 above on the possibility that a more refined notion of commitment might not include (all) personal intentions.

38. See Gilbert, M., "Group Membership and Political Obligation," *The Monist,* 76, no. 1 (1993), 119–133; reprinted in Gilbert, *Living Together.* See also Gilbert, "Agreements," and Chapter 4, this volume.

39. This was my drift in Gilbert, *On Social Facts,* 382, also 416. A recent example of use of the phrase "implicit agreement" to indicate something wider than would normally be referred to as a regular agreement is found in Tuomela, R., *The Importance of Us: A Philosophical Study of Basic Social Notions* (Stanford: Stanford University Press, 1995). There Tuomela proposes an "agreement" account of shared intention in some ways similar to my own.

40. For more along these lines see various of my papers on coordination problems and related matters; several of these are collected together in Gilbert, *Living Together,* part I.

41. Cf. Gilbert, 1990. On the efficacy of personal versus group principles in coordination problems, see Gilbert, M., "Rationality, Coordination, and Convention," *Synthese,* 84 (1990), 1–21; reprinted in Gilbert, *Living Together.*

3

Collective Belief and Scientific Change

Scientific change is essential to the progress of science. Is scientific change a matter of individual scientists changing their minds, or is it a matter of scientific communities changing their minds? Some may think a scientific community changes its mind if and only if all or most individual members of that community change their minds. I argue that there is a sense in which a scientific community can have beliefs and assumptions of its own: a scientific community can constitute the plural subject of beliefs and assumptions or, in an alternative formulation, have a collective belief. I argue that studies of science and scientific change need to be sensitive to the nature of collective belief. Given their internal structure, collective beliefs act as constraints on the actions and thoughts of individual members of the relevant community, and it takes more than a change of individual minds to change them. These facts may help to explain the importance of outsiders and neophytes in the progress of science.

1. WHAT IS SCIENTIFIC CHANGE?

When we are interested in scientific change, what is it precisely that we are interested in? Are we interested in how individual scientists change their minds or in how a scientific community changes *its* mind?

One problem people may have with this last, disjunctive question is that they assume that the second disjunct ultimately reduces to the first: What is it for a scientific community to change its mind? Surely it is for all or most individual members to change their individual minds. Thus if we want to find out how a scientific community changes its mind, all we need is to answer the question about individual scientists.

I propose that this reductive suggestion involves a fundamental mistake. There is an important sense in which scientific communities as such may hold beliefs. If they hold certain beliefs, then substitute new ones for them or simply cease to hold them, there is an independent question as to how this happens. That is, it is not equivalent to the question of how the individual members of the community come to change their beliefs.

In principle, all or most of the individual members' beliefs on a certain topic could change before the community's belief changed, and the community's belief might not change even if most individuals' beliefs did. Again, the community's belief could change even though most individual members' beliefs did not change. More generally, the relationship of a community or group's belief and the beliefs of the individual group members is an empirical one. It can take a variety of different forms. This is not to say that some of these forms may not be predictable.

In this paper I shall assume that, by and large, scientific communities do have scientific beliefs of their own.[1] Whether this is so or to what extent it is so is an important question for science studies since, as I shall argue, much hangs on it.

Given that a scientific community can have beliefs of its own, beliefs that change over time, I would contend that any investigation purportedly about *scientific change* should, at least for the sake of completeness, concern itself with the beliefs of the scientific community as such.

There is another, equally important reason for not ignoring what I shall call the "collective belief" aspect of scientific change, that is, changes in the beliefs of the collective that is the scientific community. That is the consequential nature of collective beliefs with respect to the behavior of individuals and, indeed, to the thoughts of individuals.

The most important consequence I have in mind is this. Even if we stick to the level of individual scientists and their beliefs, there is the question of what influences the rate of change in these beliefs and the question of who is most likely to produce new beliefs first.

What, if anything, acts as a brake on rapid change in the beliefs of individual members of a given scientific community? There may, of course, be many factors that can influence the rate of change. My proposal is that whatever is happening at the individual level, we need to factor collective beliefs into the equation. That is, the existence of a given collective belief is liable to affect who comes up with new ideas, who challenges them, and the rate at which they are (all else being equal) accepted. In order to explain this I need to say what I understand collective beliefs to be.

Naturally, it will be desirable if in so doing I can defuse any suspicion or concern over the question whether in talking about a community's own views I am improperly hypostatizing a community, or, as one might put it, improperly treating a community as a thing. Such suspicions will be defused, I take it, if I make it clear that I do not imagine a community's existence and thought to be so far removed from the individual members of the community that their states of mind are not relevant to it. This I shall, I hope, make clear. According to the conception of collective belief I put forward, collective beliefs are a matter of how it is with the individual members of the group in question. What it is not necessarily a matter of, however, is the corresponding beliefs of those members. That is, it is not the case that the group believes that *p* if and only if all or most members believe that *p*. That all or most members believe that *p* is neither necessary nor sufficient, conceptually speaking, for the group to believe that *p*. To say that, however, is not to say that a group's belief is not a matter of how it is with the members. In the clearest case, *something* will be true of all members.

Sometimes people speak of "the scientific community" as a whole. I would not dispute the sense of that; but I assume there can be smaller scientific communities or subcommunities, including those revolving around a particular speciality such as endocrinology or gastroenterology. I argue in my book *On Social Facts* that a collective belief is just the kind of thing to constitute or partially constitute a group or community of a relatively robust sort.[2] Though I shall not argue that here, it should be clear enough once I specify the nature of collective belief as I understand it.

2. COLLECTIVE BELIEF

I have been developing an account of collective belief in a number of places.[3] Starting with a particular core idea, I have gradually been elaborating on various of its aspects. I take this account to articulate a central everyday concept, a concept implicated in a range of everyday claims about *what a particular group believes* and about *what "we" believe*. As I have already indicated, my account is not "summative", that is, it does not state or imply that in order for a group *G* to believe that *p*, most members of *G* must believe that *p*.

I shall not attempt here to argue in favor of my account or against various possible alternatives of a summative nature.[4] My aim is simply to set out the account in enough detail to enable me to make clear the relevance of collective beliefs on this account of them to the understanding of scientific change.

My account of collective belief can be stated as follows.[5] There is a *collective belief that p* if some persons are jointly committed to believe as a body that *p*. These people can then accurately say of themselves that "We (collectively) believe that *p*."

The phrase "joint commitment" is a technical one, and I must explain how I use it.[6] Before doing so I should stress that I take the concept of a joint commitment to be implicit in everyday discourse and fundamental to our everyday conceptual scheme as it concerns social relations.[7] In other words, it is not a technical *concept*.

Some central features of joint commitment relevant to the present discussion are as follows. A joint commitment is the commitment of two or more people. It is not something composite, a conjunction of a personal commitment of one party with personal commitments of the others. Were it like this, one could imagine one party rescinding his or her part of the joint commitment, leaving the others with their parts intact. But it is not like this. A joint commitment is, in a sense, simple. It can only be rescinded by the parties to it acting together. Of course, any given party can act against the unrescinded commitment if he or she so desires. But then the commitment will be violated, as all of the parties will understand.[8]

One cannot be subject to a joint commitment without having the concept of a joint commitment and having exercised it. A joint commitment is created when, roughly, each of the parties has expressed his or her personal willingness to be party to it in conditions of common knowledge. That is, it is common knowledge between the parties that each of them has expressed his or her personal willingness to be a party to the joint commitment. I use "common knowledge" in roughly the sense introduced by David Lewis.[9]

There is an obvious sense in which, given a joint commitment, the parties to it are bound together. They have created a single joint commitment to which all are subject until such time as all concur in rescinding it. There is a related sense in which they have obligations and rights in relation to one another.

It is clear that by virtue of their participation in a joint commitment the parties gain a special standing in relation to one another's actions. If I fail to conform to our joint commitment, you are in a position to call me on it. For I did not merely act against a personal commitment of my own; I acted against *our* commitment. If you like, I have offended against all of the parties to the joint commitment.

Thus it may seem appropriate to say that when I am subject to a joint commitment requiring me to do certain things, *all of the parties have a right* to the relevant actions from me, and, correlatively, *I am under an obligation* to all of them to perform these actions. Clearly these are obligations and entitlements of a distinctive kind. They derive immediately from the joint commitment: once it exists, they exist also, irrespective of the surrounding circumstances.[10]

The important thing for present purposes is that once people understand themselves to be subject to a joint commitment, they understand that the other parties have a particular interest in their actions. Should they violate the commitment these others, understanding themselves to be aggrieved, may engage in action of a punitive nature.

I have argued in various places that everyday agreements, such as the agreement two people make to meet at a certain place, amount to joint decisions and that these, in their turn, involve a joint commitment to uphold a certain decision as a body. Thus intrinsic to any completed agreement are obligations of joint commitment. (See, for a brief discussion, Chapter 4, this volume.) If there is any type of joint commitment in the offing, one can expect people to behave in many ways as if they have agreed among themselves on a certain course of action, even though there has been no relevant agreement, properly speaking.

Having explained to some extent the nature of joint commitment, let me return to my account of collective belief. To repeat: there is a *collective belief that p* if some persons are jointly committed to believe as a body that *p*. What does the requirement to believe as a body that *p* amount to? It does not, as I understand it, entail that each participant personally believe that *p*. Such a condition would in any case be problematic, insofar as the idea of believing that *p* at will is problematic.

The requirement to believe as a body that *p* might be redescribed as the requirement together to constitute—as far as is possible—a body that believes that *p*. Presumably this requirement will be fulfilled, to some extent, if those concerned confidently express the view that *p* in appropriate contexts and do not call it or obvious corollaries into question. Their behavior generally should be suggestive of a belief that *p* in the appropriate contexts: if we believe that *p* as a body, the actions of each of us should reflect that fact.

Certain contextual conditions are likely to be understood. Thus, for example, members of a discussion group may in the course of one meeting form a collective belief about the merits of a certain novel. This would involve a requirement to express that belief, at least within the confines of the group. More broadly, it would require that one express that belief when acting as a member of the group. Presumably one is not always so acting. If when one was riding on a train a stranger were to ask one's opinion of the novel, it would be perfectly appropriate to reply *in propria persona,* without reference to the group's belief.[11]

As I have noted in a number of places, even in the context of the relevant group one may use such qualifiers as "Personally speaking" to preface the expression of a view contrary to the group's view. The availability of such locutions strongly suggests that a group's belief is not understood to be a belief common to all of the group's members; more generally, it strongly suggests that one's personal view is conceived as distinct from the view of a group of which one is a member. Though these locutions are available, there is likely to be some cost attached to making use of them. One thereby makes it clear that one's personal view is different from the group's view. Others may subsequently regard one with suspicion, thinking one more liable to default on the joint commitment, either inadvertently or deliberately. They may begin preemptively to think of one as an outsider, as no longer "one of us."

In sum, I propose that the concept of collective belief as I have just articulated it is an everyday concept that permeates everyday life. In what follows I shall refer to collective belief according to this account as "collective belief" simpliciter. People take themselves to participate in collective beliefs. References to what a group believes or to what "we" believe are often intended to refer to collective beliefs as opposed to a set of identical individual beliefs. Those who collectively believe something understand themselves to be party to a joint commitment to believe that thing as a body. This puts them in the following position. If they speak contrary to the collective belief without preamble, they will be regarded by both themselves and the others involved as acting out of line. More specifically, they will have violated obligations they had to the others, and the others have the standing to take other measures responsive to this situation. These could take the form of anything from a mild rebuke to complete ostracism. Even if they do not speak without preamble but make it clear that they are expressing what they personally believe, doing this only makes it clear that they are not personally in sympathy with the collective belief. That is liable to lay them open to suspicion. Hence *there is a significant initial cost* in every case of mooting an idea that runs contrary to a collective belief.

3. BUCKING THE CONSENSUS

i. "Consensus"

One term commonly used in the discussion of scientific change is "consensus."[12] Consensus is, as it were, both the end point of scientific change and its beginning. New ideas are ideas new in relation to a certain consensus. The process of change ends with a new consensus.

One who produces a new idea and proposes it as true may be characterized as "bucking the consensus." What precisely does this amount to? That depends on how the term "consensus" is construed. It is one of those terms that tends not to be defined at the outset of discussion because people assume that they and their readers understand it without explanation. The same goes for talk of "received ideas," "shared assumptions," and other such terms and phrases. The meaning of these terms is not crystal clear, however, and there is a variety of different phenomena that people could have in mind.

All of these terms could be construed in a simple summative way. There would be consensus when everyone agreed as to what was correct. Received ideas would be the ideas that all or most people had "received" or accepted. Shared assumptions would be those assumptions that all or most people made. When people are asked to give an account of these terms, their first shot is often a summative one.

Now it is up to a writer to define terms as seems appropriate. However, if terms such as "consensus" are given a summative construal, there is a danger that the phenomenon of *consensus in the sense of collective belief* will simply be overlooked. And collective belief, rather than a belief that all members of a community personally hold, has a title to be considered both the end point of scientific change and its beginning. It is a social phenomenon with a type of inbuilt stability that offers a plausible way of characterizing science itself and scientific changes and revolutions.

I am not saying that the pursuit of knowledge cannot be undertaken by an individual relatively isolated from others. Some important breakthroughs in human knowledge have taken place in this way. Yet there may be an important sense in which such breakthroughs make little impact on science. The person concerned may not be listened to; he (or she) may make no impact on the way things are done in the relevant scientific community or on what the community holds true. He may be so far "ahead of his time" that no one else knows what to make of his proposals even though he does understand them. In principle, the scientific community could be moving along a different path, and the breakthrough in question could be ignored for a long time, even forever. There has been a breakthrough in human knowledge, but there is a sense in which there has been no scientific change at all: the breakthrough in question has made no impact on the relevant scientific community.

If many or even all relevant individuals come to hold a certain view personally, this is still conceptually distinct from a change in view of the community. It is possible in principle, if unlikely, that for a certain period a widespread view is not generally known to be widespread. And even if it is known to be widespread, it still need not have attained the status of collective belief. It could be, for instance, that a single all-powerful figure needs to express his (or her) endorsement of a view before it can attain that status in a particular scientific community. This particular figure may personally believe that *p* but not yet (for whatever reason) be prepared to endorse it publicly. Others may be waiting for his endorsement before indicating their preparedness to be parties to a joint commitment to believe that *p* as a body. Until this happens, it is clear that something important has not happened: the view that *p* has not yet attained a seriously *entrenched* position within the scientific community. The community's beliefs, as such, have not yet changed at all. Generally speaking, one would, of course, expect that when most community members believe that *p,* a collective belief that *p* will soon follow.

Evidently when we talk about "science" and "scientific change" we need to decide whether we are primarily talking about the individual or the collective level of things or whether we are talking about both (in which case we need to be sensitive to the nature of both kinds of change and their impact on one another).

ii. Consensus as Collective Belief

Let us consider what bucking the consensus amounts to when "consensus" is construed as collective belief. This actually depends on what one's relationship to the collective belief is. Let us consider the situation of one who participates in the relevant joint commitment.

Suppose that Dr. Maria Bianchi is party to a joint commitment to believe that *p* along with other members of her scientific community, *S*. It may be that, in addition, all or most other members of *S* personally believe that *p*. Perhaps most of them also believe that Dr. Bianchi believes that *p*.

Let us consider first what difference these facts about what others believe might make should Dr. Bianchi come to reject the idea that *p*. It is not immediately obvious that these particular considerations are of a sort to move Dr. Bianchi in the direction of keeping her views to herself. She does not obviously have a reason not publicly to deny that *p*. The others may find her view surprising, but those who are surprised are not necessarily therefore antagonistic. Their reaction might just as well be positive. They might congratulate Dr. Bianchi on stimulating them to examine their belief that *p*.

If Dr. Bianchi is party to a joint commitment to believe that *p*, however, she has something else to contend with: she is subject to a commitment to participate with others in believing as a body that *p*. If she fulfills this commitment, she will not baldly deny that *p* when speaking to her scientific colleagues.

If she does not fulfill the commitment, she risks an appropriately negative reaction from those who had a right to its fulfillment. Even if she explicitly qualifies her denial of *p* as her personal opinion only, expressing a personal view contrary to the group view risks having others doubt her reliability with respect to the joint commitment. They now have some reason to fear that next time she will forget the qualification and come out with this heterodox opinion as if the community was not committed to anything contrary to it. Thus she risks a negative reaction whether she denies that *p* in an unqualified way or qualifies her denial as her personal opinion.

In sum, Dr. Bianchi's participation in the joint commitment requires her not to deny that *p* without qualification. Should she do this, she defaults on a commitment to which she is subject. Should she be tempted to default on the commitment, she risks negative personal consequences to which she knows she will be liable. Negative personal consequences are also predictable for a denial that *p* expressed as her personal view. In addition, it may make sense to worry about the effect her pronouncements could have on the community as a whole: perhaps its flourishing depends on its believing that *p*. Perhaps that belief is fundamental to many of its projects, and throwing it into doubt would lead to a period of crisis and even disintegration.

It is important to see how participation in a collective belief can have consequences even for one's private thoughts, inhibiting one from pursuing spontaneous doubts about the group view, inclining one to ignore evidence that suggests the falsity of that view, and so on. Fulfilling the relevant commitment may not require that one personally believes what one's group believes. Nonetheless, it is awkward to say one thing and think another. This is so for a number of reasons. One may then resist following up certain ideas. One may—consciously or unconsciously—calculate that it is not worth doing so, since by making public the likely conclusions, even characterized as one's personal conclusions, one would risk a host of negative reactions to oneself and possibly even the breakdown of one's professional group. Knowing that this is something one is not prepared to do, one may avoid pursuing any relevant thoughts, even those one suspects of having something to them.

That collective beliefs are potentially destructive of free-ranging, autonomous thought is a matter of great practical importance, not only within the confines of scientific communities. We can presume that new ideas are perennially needed for progress in all areas open to human understanding, not to speak of variety in the arts. This is not to say that collective beliefs can or should be avoided.[13] It is to say that we must be aware of their ability to trammel the growth of human knowledge, starting at the level of private thoughts and feelings. Then we can consider what can be done to minimize the problem.

iii. The Role of Outsiders and Neophytes

Who is likely to be most willing to buck the consensus in the sense of the collective beliefs of a scientific community? An obvious candidate is someone outside the community, someone not bound by the constraints of the relevant joint commitment.

People who answer to this general description fall into at least two camps. One is the person completely outside the community, someone in another field, for instance, who learns of the pressing problems in a different field—the pure mathematician who becomes interested in certain problems in physics, for instance. Another is someone who is in some sense inside the community but is not fully a member of it. Such a person may be a trainee of some kind, someone who has not yet received full "accreditation," or perhaps is not fully "established" as "one of us."[14]

In discussion, Paul Thagard has suggested that to progress, science needs new young people or outsiders.[15] This would be predictable if scientists form communities at least in part by virtue of the formation of collective beliefs. It is not so obviously predictable if scientists merely form communities of "consensus" in the sense of populations of individuals who all individually accept the same ideas. It would not be so clear why a given old-stager shouldn't simply change his (or her) mind and tell the other members of this. An old-stager who is party to the joint commitments that underlie the relevant collective beliefs will face many reasons not to express the view contrary to the belief.

Those who are not yet committed in this way will be the least constrained. Recall that what is at issue here is not mere personal commitment, like a personal decision. Rather it is participation in a joint commitment such that one is not free unilaterally to rescind the commitment or just to "drop" it. Given countervailing evidence one can drop a belief from one's personal belief system, but one cannot drop that same belief from the group belief system: no one can do that unilaterally. No one person can drop the belief from the group's belief system except with some prior authorization from the group.

4. CHANGING COLLECTIVE SCIENTIFIC BELIEFS

One can predict that the processes by which change in a scientific community's belief occurs as a result of challenge from one or another individual or subgroup will be slow and somewhat cumbersome. Precisely how such changes occur, and one belief becomes established as the collective one in another's stead, is a good question.

For a body of which I am a member to change its beliefs requires something akin to an agreement to stop believing that p together and to start believing that q instead, and this is not easy to achieve. We can investigate ways in which it might come about. One would expect that not the neophytes or fringe members but the core, established members will be most potent here. Someone may be an acknowledged "authority" in his field. Precisely what this amounts to, how one achieves this status, and how it relates to change and resistance to change in collective belief is worthy of study.

Generally scientific communities do not look to one person or body formally to decide such matters on behalf of the whole group.[16] However, the situation in medical research in the United States is of some interest in this connection. The U.S. National Institutes of Health regularly convenes Consensus Development Conferences to "evaluate available scientific information."[17] A statement is issued at the conclusion of each conference. Thus in 1994 a conference was convened to examine the claim that peptic ulcers are caused by the bacterium *Helicobacter pylori,* a hypothesis that ten years before "was viewed as preposterous."[18]

5. CERTAINTY VERSUS COMMITMENT

It may be less personal certainty on the part of scientists that prevents new ideas from being taken up quickly and more the commitments they take themselves to have, which in effect require them to turn a deaf ear to certain suggestions and make it easy for them to do so.[19] A community-wide collective belief would certainly reinforce strongly any personal inclination to reject a new hypothesis that ran counter to that belief.

Certainty may not be the best attribute of a scientist,[20] but commitment to do your part in a believing body requires behavior, attitudes, and actions that mimic those associated with personal certainty. If *we believe that p, with reasonable firmness,* then I can't express doubts in my capacity as one of us. I'm committed to being part of a body that, precisely, believes that *p* with reasonable firmness. As an individual my reasonably firm belief can simply *give way* to doubt, but as long as I believe with reasonable firmness I do *not* doubt. If I did, my belief would not be reasonably firm.

6. CONCLUSION

I have argued elsewhere that the concept of collective belief as I understand it is a central everyday concept. I take it that collective beliefs abound and that they characterize scientific communities among other types of group.[21]

The main aim of this discussion has been to argue that the philosophy and sociology of science, in particular studies of scientific change, need to consider the role of collective beliefs. Collective beliefs are inherently difficult for their members to change, and once in place they are liable to influence the thoughts, beliefs, and actions of individual scientists.

NOTES

This paper was prompted by a presentation of Paul Thagard's at the London School of Economics, March 10, 1997, regarding the bacterial theory of ulcers, a presentation based on Thagard's paper "Ulcers and Bacteria I: Discovery and Acceptance," one of two related papers that appeared in 1998 in *Studies in History and Philosophy of Science.* The second paper is "Ulcers and Bacteria II: Instruments, Experiments, and Social Interaction." Page references to Thagard are to the October 21, 1996, manuscript of those papers. Thagard reports on and analyzes the history of the bacterial theory of ulcers, first conceived of in 1983 when it was "viewed as preposterous" (I-1) and is now "widely accepted" (I-20) and possibly "on the way to medical orthodoxy" (I-24). In a brief comment during the formal discussion of his presentation I invoked a distinction between the general acceptance of a theory by individual scientists and its acceptance by a scientific community. The present paper was intended to amplify my remarks and indicate the importance of the distinction for studies of science. I thank Paul Thagard for positive comments on the first draft. Thanks also to David Papineau for comments on a later version. I should stress that this paper is not intended as a full discussion of its topic but rather as a sketch of the way in which collective beliefs (construed as in this paper) may constitute an important factor in the way science develops. It was written while I was a visiting professor at King's College London.

1. It could be that though, as I argue, there is a sense in which scientific communities can have beliefs of their own, they in fact fail to have such beliefs. I think this is unlikely: it is very natural for communities of any substantial kind to develop beliefs of their own, and the general mechanisms by which group beliefs are generated is familiar to everyone from other contexts, such as families and friendships. In addition, there is plenty of informal evidence for the existence of such beliefs in scientific communities.

2. See Margaret Gilbert, *On Social Facts* (London: Routledge, 1989), chapter 4.

3. Beginning with Margaret Gilbert, "Modeling Collective Belief," *Synthese,* 73 (1987), 185–204. For a more elaborate discussion (actually completed prior to the 1987 publication) see Gilbert, *On Social Facts,* chapter 5 (which is complemented by chapters 4 and 7). See also Gilbert, *Living Together: Rationality, Sociality, and Obligation* (Lanham, Md.: Rowman and Littlefield, 1996), introduction and chapter 14. "More on Collective Belief" is a lightly revised version of "Remarks on Collective Belief," originally published in *Socializing Epistemology,* F. Schmitt, ed. (Lanham, Md.: Rowman and Littlefield, 1994), and reprinted in Italian in G. Piazza, ed., *Esperienza e Cognoscenza* Milan: Citta Studi, 1995. This book also includes "Modeling Collective Belief."

4. The reader is referred to the discussions cited in the previous footnote, in particular Gilbert, *On Social Facts,* chapter 5, which gives lengthy consideration to summative views. See also, in Italian, G. Piazza's exposition of my views in his editorial introduction to *Esperienza e Cognoscenza* and in his article "Taylor, Gilbert, e il risveglio (sociale) del sonno dogmatico," *Fenomenologia e Societa* (1996).

5. I have formulated this account differently on different occasions. Essentially the same idea is expressible in different ways. The introduction to *Living Together,* 7–10, explains the way the different formulations I have used relate to one another. See also Gilbert, *On Social Facts,* chapter 7.

6. There is a more extensive discussion in the introduction to Gilbert, *Living Together,* 7–15. (See also Chapter 1 and elsewhere, this volume.)

7. On this see, for instance, my article "Is an Agreement an Exchange of Promises?" *Journal of Philosophy,* 90 (1993), 627–649; reprinted with revisions in *Living Together.*

8. For discussion of the consequences of such violation see the introduction to Gilbert, *Living Together,* 14–15. I there incline to the view that generally speaking violation by one or more parties renders a joint commitment voidable by the remaining parties, as opposed to immediately voiding it.

9. See D. K. Lewis, *Convention: A Philosophical Study* (Cambridge, Mass.: Harvard University Press, 1969). For further discussion along these lines see Gilbert, *On Social Facts,* 188–195 and elsewhere.

10. For discussion of the relationship of the obligations of joint commitment to another class of so-called obligations see Margaret Gilbert, "Agreements, Coercion, and Obligation," *Ethics,* 103, no. 4 (1993), 679–706; reprinted with revisions in *Living Together.* (See Chapter 4, this volume, for further exploration of the claim that joint commitment is a source of obligations and rights and also on agreements as joint commitment phenomena [see below].)

11. On the relation of collective belief to context see also Gilbert, "Remarks on Collective Belief."

12. See, for instance, Paul Thagard, "Ulcers and Bacteria II," 1996, 17.

13. See Gilbert, "More on Collective Belief," last paragraph.

14. Discussing the hypothesis that ulcers may be caused by bacteria, Thagard reports

that it "seemed crazy to many in 1983." Dr. Barry Marshall, who that year proposed this hypothesis with Dr. Robin Warren, "was relatively new to gastroenterology, having only begun specialized training in the field in 1981" (Thagard, "Ulcers and Bacteria I," 14).

15. In the formal discussion after his talk at the London School of Economics, March 10, 1997.

16. Cf. Thagard: "In most scientific fields . . . there is no central mechanism that produces a consensus"; "Ulcers and Bacteria II" 17. I do not claim that Thagard intends by "consensus" collective belief in the sense of this paper.

17. NIH World Wide Web page: http://text.nlm.nih.gov/nih/upload-v3/About/about.html, quoted in Thagard, "Ulcers and Bacteria II" 17.

18. Thagard, "Ulcers and Bacteria I" 1. Thagard reports that the panel's statement concluded that "ulcer patients with *H. Pylori* infection require treatment with antimicrobial agents." Thagard, "Ulcers and Bacteria II" 18.

19. A case that may bear this out is the Australian Gastroenterology Society's failure to accept Dr. Barry Marshall's report contending that bacteria may be responsible for ulcers early in 1983. Only eight of sixty-seven submissions were rejected. See Thagard, "Ulcers and Bacteria I" 2, 3. Marshall's contention was in conflict with more than one "prevailing belief" among gastroenterologists. Thagard, "Ulcers and Bacteria I" 14.

20. David Papineau made a similar remark in the discussion of Thagard's talk, March 10, 1997.

21. I take it that they characterize "whole" scientific communities. I assume also that they will abound within such communities. Thus I argue in *On Social Facts* that everyday conversations are a familiar breeding ground for collective beliefs. A maverick researcher will surely be encouraged if only one colleague joins him or her in believing in a novel claim, thus taking the belief to the collective level in a small way. This note was prompted by a comment from Paul Thagard.

4

Obligation and Joint Commitment

We speak of obligations in many contexts. But what are obligations? I argue that obligations of an important type inhere in what I call "joint commitments." I propose a joint commitment account of everyday agreements. This could explain why some philosophers believe we know of the obligating nature of agreements a priori. I compare and contrast obligations of joint commitment with obligations in the relatively narrow sense recommended by H. L. A. Hart, a recommendation that has been influential. Some central contexts in which Hart takes there to be obligations in his sense are contexts in which there are obligations of joint commitment. Nonetheless, different senses of "obligation" appear to be at issue.

1. INTRODUCTION: A DATUM FOR ETHICS

Suppose that you and I agree that I will make dinner and you will do the laundry. Each of us then has an *obligation* to conform to the agreement, at least in the absence of countervailing factors. Most ethical theorists would grant this much. Some would claim that it is knowable a priori.[1] It is, in any case, something of a datum for ethics. But what precisely is this datum? What in particular are *obligations*?

This is not an easy question to answer. Ethical theorists and others refer to obligations in many contexts, not only in the context of agreements.

Do all so-called obligations have the same nature? They may well have important features in common. There could still be deep differences between them. If so, what are these differences? And of what kind are the obligations of agreement? *Do* we know a priori that agreements obligate?

50

2. HART ON OBLIGATIONS

In his paper "Are There Any Natural Rights?" H. L. A. Hart suggests that the term "obligation" should be used in a more restricted way than has become common in philosophy.[2]

> Most important are the points (1) that obligations may be voluntarily incurred or created, (2) that they are *owed* to special persons (who have rights), (3) that they do not arise out of the character of the actions which are obligatory but out of the relationship of the parties.[3]

The suggestion that we construe "obligation" along the lines Hart proposes has subsequently been taken up by many authors, including John Rawls in *A Theory of Justice,* A. John Simmons in *Moral Principles and Political Obligations,* and, more recently, George Klosko in *The Principle of Fairness and Political Obligation.*[4]

Hart sees himself as objecting to a certain breadth of usage among philosophers in particular, and many philosophers continue to use the term "obligation" more broadly than he would think they should. They are not the only people to do so. Though Hart implies that this was not so when he wrote, by now at least everyday usage is similarly broad.[5]

Hart discusses a number of cases that give rise to obligations according to his criteria.[6] What he sees as the "most obvious case" is that of promises.[7] Presumably he would have no problem adding agreements under this heading.[8]

I have much sympathy with Hart's desire to draw distinctions within the broad domain of so-called obligations. In this paper I draw a distinction of my own and consider its relationship to that drawn by Hart.

The distinction I wish to draw is between what I call *obligations of joint commitment* and other kinds of so-called obligation. As I shall explain, it can be argued that making an agreement involves entering a joint commitment. This could explain the general confidence regarding the obligating nature of agreements. It could also explain the belief of some philosophers that we know a priori that agreements obligate.

I first explain what joint commitments are. I then argue that they can be said to involve obligations and correlative rights.[9] I take the relevant concept of a joint commitment to be a fundamental, if recondite, everyday concept, as opposed to a technical concept I have invented.[10]

3. JOINT COMMITMENT

A. Commitments in General

First I should say something about how I interpret the term "commitment." To cite a familiar example, I take it that a personal decision involves a commitment. If I have decided to do *A,* I am subject to a commitment to do *A.* One can bring about one's subjection to a commitment, then, without the immediate involvement of another person.

Inclinations and enthusiasms do not involve commitments. That is, I can be inclined to do *A* but not subject to a commitment to do *A.*

With respect to what a given person has reason to do, I take it that commitments "trump" mere inclinations. Suppose I decide to do *A* at some later time, and then at that later time I do not feel like doing *A.* Suppose I do not rescind my decision. Then, all else being equal, reason requires that I do *A.*

I shall not try further to specify the relevant sense of "commitment" here. I take my construal to be reasonably intuitive.

B. Personal Commitments

Before explaining what a *joint* commitment is, it will be useful to characterize what I shall call a "personal commitment." Consider a personal decision. When Anne decides to do something, she is the sole creator or author of her decision. If she wishes to rid herself of it once it is made, she is in a position to do so. She need only change her mind. There may be circumstances in which she would not be rational or reasonable to do so. She can change her mind nonetheless. One might say that she *has the authority* unilaterally to rescind her own decision.

A personal commitment, then, may for present purposes be characterized as follows. Anne is subject to a *personal commitment* if and only if she is the sole author of a commitment and has the authority unilaterally to rescind it. Personal decisions, plans, and goals all involve personal commitments in this sense.

Many of the ends one might have require the participation of two or more people for their achievement. If Anne wants her kitchen painted quickly, for instance, she will require one or more people to help her paint it. If she wants to play a game of tennis, this is not something she can achieve by her own efforts alone.

It might be thought that concordant personal commitments would suffice for the achievement of such ends. In some cases they may indeed so suffice. But one can see that they constitute a far from reliable mechanism for the purpose.

Suppose Anne's friend Ben plans to help her paint her kitchen on Tuesday and says as much to her. He might add "I'm not promising, mind you." He makes it clear that this is only his personal plan, and a personal plan, like anything involving a personal commitment, can be unilaterally rescinded by the committed person.

Anne may go ahead and plan to paint alongside Ben on Tuesday. There are now concordant personal commitments—Anne's and Ben's—in favor of painting her kitchen on Tuesday. The existence of this concordance does not alter the fact that Ben can unilaterally change his personal plan. Insofar as his commitment locks him into a course of action, he has the one and only key needed to open the lock.

A set of concordant personal commitments, then, is a far from reliable means of achieving ends whose achievement requires the participation of more than one person. As will soon be clear, there is an alternative better suited to the purpose—joint commitment.[11]

C. Joint Commitments

A joint commitment is *the commitment of two or more people.* For the sake of simplicity I shall focus here on joint commitments involving just two people.

The joint commitment of Anne and Ben is simple rather than composite. In particular, it is not composed of a personal commitment of Anne's and a personal commitment of Ben's.

The joint commitment of Anne and Ben is created by Anne and Ben together. A typical way in which this is done is for Anne to express to Ben her readiness to be jointly committed with him in some way and for Ben to reciprocate with a similar expression of his own, in conditions of common knowledge. Roughly, something is *common knowledge* between two people if it is "out in the open" as far as the two of them are concerned.[12] As both understand, the joint commitment comes into being when and only when it is common knowledge that both expressions have been made.

In this type of case each party directly expresses to the other his or her personal readiness for a particular joint commitment. For present purposes I shall assume that joint commitments formed in this typical way are at issue.

Clearly both parties to a joint commitment must have the concept of a joint commitment. Otherwise they could not mutually express their readiness *to be jointly committed.*

Each one is *committed* through the joint commitment. However, if we speak of Anne's commitment and Ben's commitment in this context, we must bear in mind that these "individual" commitments cannot exist on their own. This is because both derive from a joint commitment, and a joint commitment always holds sway over more than one person.

Neither Anne nor Ben is in a position unilaterally to rescind their joint commitment. They must rescind it together. Otherwise it cannot be rescinded.

Thus Anne can rely on the persistence of Ben's commitment to act in pursuit of some end insofar as it derives from a joint commitment. A typical way of rescinding a joint commitment is by mutual expressions of willingness that the joint commitment be at an end.[13]

Quite generally, if Anne and Ben are jointly committed, they are jointly committed to doing something as a body or, if you like, as a single unit, or "person." Doing something as a body, in the relevant sense, is not a matter of "all doing it" but rather of "all acting in such a way as to constitute a body that does it."

"Doing" is here construed very broadly. People may be jointly committed to accepting (and pursuing) a certain goal as a body. They may be jointly committed to believing that such-and-such as a body. And so on.[14]

4. THE OBLIGATIONS (AND RIGHTS) OF JOINT COMMITMENT

It can be argued that there is an important sense in which a joint commitment, in and of itself, involves *obligations* and *rights*. At its most general the idea is this. By virtue of his involvement in a joint commitment with Anne and that alone, Ben *gains a special standing with respect to Anne's actions,* and vice versa.

More specifically, without any prior analysis of the notion of an obligation or a right, it seems natural to say in this context that Ben has a *right* to Anne's conforming action and that Anne is under a corresponding *obligation* to Ben—an obligation to conform to the joint commitment. And vice versa.

It may not indeed seem to need *arguing* that a joint commitment in and of itself involves obligations and rights. What, though, if this idea does not immediately convince? In this section I sketch some relevant lines of thought.[15]

A. The Betrayal Argument

One might start with a comparison. This appeals to the idea of a betrayal and addresses the question of who is betrayed. It supports the idea that from an intuitive point of view a joint commitment gives each party a special standing in relation to the other's actions.

Consider first the case of a personal decision. Suppose Anne fails to conform to a decision of her own without first changing her mind. Perhaps she tried to conform to her decision but failed. Perhaps she forgot her decision and only remembered it when it was too late to fulfill it. She may then reflect that she has in a sense *betrayed herself.*[16]

Suppose now that Anne fails to conform to the joint commitment she is party to with Ben. It seems that here she would reflect rather that she has betrayed herself—and Ben. It would indeed be appropriate for her to apologize to Ben, to attempt to exculpate herself, and so on.

B. The Argument from the Jointness of the Commitment

One might argue that Ben has a special standing in relation to Anne because the joint commitment is *theirs*. In violating the joint commitment she is not going against a personal commitment; she is going against *their* commitment. Thus Ben is as much offended against as she is.

C. The Joint Order Argument

Is there some way of probing further into this sense of things? The following line of argument, which I call "the joint order argument," is pertinent. It speaks as much to the notion of commitment as to the notion of jointness. It has several steps, some of which could be elaborated at length. What follows is only a sketch.

The argument begins with what is essentially an intuitive point about commitments in general: there is some plausibility in representing a commitment as a special kind of order or command.[17] The order here is special in at least three ways.

First, it is issued by the addressee. Thus Anne herself issues the order that constitutes her personal commitment: *I am to do such-and-such.*[18] Anne and Ben jointly issue the order that constitutes their joint commitment: *We are to do such-and-such (as a body).*

Second, this type of order, insofar as it needs to be "pronounced," need not be *voiced.* It need only be understood or, if you like, "said-in-the-heart."[19] The relevant type of *joint* order will, presumably, be "said" in the several hearts of those who participate in its promulgation. Each will "say" it in that capacity.

Presumably in that case certain "external" conditions will need to be satisfied. Thus in the type of case on which I am focusing here, the parties will have mutually expressed their readiness to issue the order, in conditions of common knowledge. For instance (1) Anne: "Let's go to the store!" (2) Ben, in response, "Fine!"

Understanding what has transpired, the parties can act in their capacity as parties to the promulgation of the order and thus say-in-their-hearts, "We are to accept as a body the goal of going to the store." They could on occasion go on to make this manifest in some such way as this: (3) "So, we're to go to the store!" (4) "Right!" Such manifestation does not appear to be necessary for the joint promulgation of the relevant type of self-addressed order.

Third, the order is automatically legitimate in the sense of *being properly constituted as an order.* In other words, the one who issues it is necessarily in a position to give *orders* to the addressee.

In support of this claim it may be observed that my addressing *to myself* a

purported order inevitably and manifestly expresses to the issuer the addressee's acceptance of it as an order. This, it may be argued, is enough to
make my purported order a genuine or, in the relevant sense, legitimate
order.[20]

The notion of legitimacy at issue here evidently does not concern the content of the order or the consequences of the addressee's conformity. Accordingly, the legitimacy of an order in this sense need not be the last word on the
question whether to obey it.

Nonetheless, if you give me an order that is legitimate in this sense and I
fail to conform to it, I am surely at fault in relation to you. There is a sense in
which I do not give you your due or what I owe you. I owe you my conformity to your order—my *obedience.*

Suppose, then, that commitments involve orders of the special kind described.[21] It follows that should Anne not conform to her standing personal
decision she has, in a clear sense, disobeyed herself: she has disobeyed an
order that she—with perfect legitimacy—addressed to herself. She has not,
then, *given herself her due.* This would account for her feeling of self-
betrayal.[22]

Now consider the joint commitment Anne and Ben have made. Should
Anne not conform to it, she disobeys *herself and Ben.* This would account for
her feeling that she has betrayed Ben, for her sense that an apology to Ben is
in order, and so on.

Anne can reflect that the behavior in question was owed to *them* insofar
as—with perfect legitimacy—they *jointly issued* an order enjoining this behavior. If you like, she owes the behavior to Ben in his capacity as party to
the joint commitment.

According to the joint order argument, then, if Anne and Ben are the parties to a joint commitment, *each owes the other certain actions.*[23] More precisely, the participation of each in the joint commitment and that alone makes
it the case that each owes the other certain actions. In what follows I shall take
this more precise understanding for granted.

It is worth emphasizing that according to the joint order argument Anne
and Ben owe each other actions by virtue of their participation in the joint
commitment *and that alone.* Whatever bad consequences might flow from violation of the commitment, for instance, are not relevant to the issue.

*The joint commitment links Anne to Ben, and Ben to Anne, in such a way
that, immediately, each owes the other certain actions.*

D. Introducing "Obligations"

If Anne and Ben are jointly committed to doing something as a body, each
owes the other appropriate actions by virtue of their joint commitment. So
concludes the joint order argument.[24]

The point may indeed seem firm irrespective of this or any other argument. To allude to it with a single term, I shall say that a joint commitment *obligates* the parties, one to the other.

Let me now *introduce* the terms "obligation" and "right," roughly as follows. If and only if Anne and Ben are jointly committed to doing something as a body, (a) Anne is *obligated* or *has an obligation* to perform appropriate actions, and (b) Ben *has a right* to her performance of appropriate actions. And vice versa.

Ben's right is a right with respect to, or "against," a particular person, Anne, the person to whose action he has a right. Similarly, Anne's obligation is an obligation with respect, "toward" or "to" a particular person, Ben, the person with the corresponding right.

The rights and obligations in question are two sides of the same coin. If Anne violates her obligation under the joint commitment, she ipso facto fails to respect Ben's corresponding right. To say Ben has a right to Anne's performance of appropriate actions in this sense is another way of saying that Anne has an obligation toward Ben, the obligation to perform such actions. It focuses on Ben's situation in regard to Anne's performance, as opposed to Anne's situation in regard to that performance. The content of these obligations and rights is determined by determining that Anne and Ben are parties to a joint commitment with a particular content. This content may be very precise. It may also be relatively vague.

E. The Joint Abrogation Argument

In arguing for the appropriateness of speaking of "obligations" and "rights" of joint commitment, I have not yet referred to what I shall call the *joint abrogation* feature: only the parties together can abrogate, or rescind, such a commitment.[25] This feature of joint commitments is of great practical significance. Were it possible for them to exist in its absence, the obligations and rights of joint commitment would be less worthy of sustained consideration.

Imagine that—*per impossible*—people were able unilaterally to rescind their joint commitments by personally deciding to do so. Then on relevant occasions Anne could ruminate as follows: "I really don't want to do *A*. It is true that given our joint commitment I have an obligation to do *A*, and Ben has a right to my doing it. But that's of little consequence! I'll just rescind the joint commitment." She does so, and the joint commitment—and the obligation she has through it—no longer exists.

Were Ben to complain later about her not doing *A*, she could reply "I rescinded the joint commitment, so you have nothing to complain about." "How was I to know you would rescind the commitment?" asks Ben. "How were you to know that I *wouldn't*?" Anne responds. "You knew that I was perfectly entitled to do so, as you were." Their argument could perhaps continue.

Given the joint abrogation feature, the actual situation is quite different. If Ben has not concurred in the abrogation of their commitment, it remains in force. Anne violates an obligation toward him if she omits *A,* and he has a basis for complaint.[26]

What if a joint commitment could be unilaterally rescinded, but only after the other party had been *informed* of the intention to rescind? Were this the situation, Ben would be spared the kind of surprise alluded to earlier. He would still know, however, that he could be faced with the imminent rescinding of the commitment at any time—at Anne's pleasure.

The joint abrogation feature ensures that both parties have maximal security against the other's change of mind—the maximum possible given an equal security for all. The obligations and rights of joint commitment are, accordingly, importantly secure against any one party's change of mind.[27]

None of the above implies, of course, that a given party cannot simply decide not to conform to a given joint commitment and proceed to so act. But in that case this person will have failed to fulfill standing obligations, and the other party or parties will have cause for complaint.[28]

Insofar as, from the point of view of practical reasoning, commitments in general "trump" mere inclinations, joint commitments are clearly liable to play a special role in the direction of human lives. Given the joint abrogation feature, they provide a relatively stable counterblast to divergent personal inclinations in favor of whatever end is favored by the joint commitment in question.[29]

One could introduce the terms "obligation" and "right" in connection with the joint abrogation feature of joint commitments. If I am subject to a joint commitment, I am subject to a commitment of a sort I can only rescind in conjunction with one or more other people. It would evidently be quite apposite in that case to say I was "obligated" to those others and that they had "rights" over me with respect to the actions to which I was committed. These others are, after all, in a position to object to my failure to perform those actions in terms of the commitment in whose abrogation they know they have not participated. To the extent that the commitment stands, I owe them my conformity.

Once again this may not be the last word as to what I should do, all things considered. I may often have a good excuse for violating a joint commitment. To allow this, however, is not to say that my rights and obligations of joint commitment are not a significant part of my situation.

F. Summary

I have introduced, as it were de novo, the terms "obligation" and "right." I have introduced them in a specific context, that of joint commitment. More than one argument from the nature of joint commitment supports the idea of introducing special terms here. Each argument suggests that if Anne and Ben, say, are jointly committed in some way, then each has a special standing toward the other. If to conform to the commitment Anne must perform some action *A,* then one can argue in more than one way that at the same time she owes the performance of *A* to Ben.

Evidently I could have chosen terms that I invented, terms newly coined for the purpose—"blink" and "blonk," say. Why use terms that are already part of our language, "obligation" and "right"?

There are several reasons. One is etymological. The English term "obligation" derives from the Latin *"ligare,"* which means *to bind.* Clearly it is apt to refer to a joint commitment as binding together two or more parties. To use a Kantian phrase, a joint commitment *unifies their choice.*[30] This bond is indeed a sturdy one. Looked at from the point of view of the freedom of the individuals involved, it is a kind of shackle. Each is locked into it, and each has only one of two or more essential keys.

More to the point, my use of these and related terms is intended to express the following hypothesis about existing usage: the English terms "obligation" and "right" *are often used* in the context of and in response to the presence of a joint commitment. In other words, many of our so-called obligations are (in my terms) *obligations of joint commitment* rather than any other kind.

5. AGREEMENTS AND PROMISES AS JOINT COMMITMENT PHENOMENA

Suppose you and I agree that I will make dinner and you will do the laundry. Here each of the two parties to the agreement must perform one specified future act to conform to the agreement. This is a standard type of agreement.

If agreements of this type are joint commitment phenomena, this would be a prima facie reason for thinking agreements of other types are as well. Other types will include agreements that specify several acts for each party and agreements to the effect that just one person will do a certain thing.

It can be argued that our sample agreement is, in effect, a *joint decision,* involving a joint commitment to uphold as a body the decision in question.[31] More specifically, you and I would be jointly committed to uphold the decision that I will make dinner and you will do the laundry. I have argued this in detail elsewhere.[32] The core of my argument is that three salient features of our sample agreement are best taken care of by a joint commitment account of agreement.

According to the prevailing philosophical account of agreements, an agreement is an exchange of promises.[33] No promise-exchange, however, can capture these three salient features of our sample agreement and others of the same type.

First, we would normally understand that given our sample agreement and absent any countervailing factors, you have an obligation *to do the laundry* and I have an obligation *to make dinner.*[34] These obligations are understood to be *unconditional*: the natural specification of them is unconditional in form.

Second, these unconditional obligations are arrived at *simultaneously.* They are arrived at when and only when the agreement is complete.

It is possible for a promise-exchange involving at least one conditional promise to achieve a set of unconditional obligations arrived at simultaneously. Some form of conditionality is required to meet the criterion of simultaneity, as in the following exchange. I say, "On condition that you promise to do the laundry, I promise to cook dinner." So far, I have not promised to cook dinner. Rather, I have made an "externally conditional" promise whose condition has not yet been met. You reply, "I promise to do the laundry." You thus fulfill the condition governing my promise. At this point—one and the same—both of us accrue unconditional obligations: I to cook dinner, you to do the laundry.

What is impossible is for the obligations resulting from any promise-exchange to be simultaneous, unconditional, and *interdependent.* Yet it can be argued that if a promise-exchange is to mirror the structure of our sample agreement, the ensuing obligations need to have each of the three features.

Consider our sample agreement. Suppose I willfully fail to make dinner. I have thus totally failed to conform to our agreement. It seems that as far as our agreement goes you are now free not to do the laundry. It is up to you. Our obligations are interdependent in the sense that if one is, in effect, nullified, this affects the status of the other. It affects indeed the status of the agreement itself.

It is important to see that, intuitively, my willful violation *directly* affects the status of the agreement and hence of your obligation. Your freedom—as far as the agreement goes—not to do the laundry is not such that considerations of fairness or equity, for instance, need be brought in to establish it. It is a matter of *what an agreement is.*

Now suppose you have made a simple unconditional promise to me, and I have made a similar counterpromise to you: I promised to make dinner, and you promised to do the laundry. If I break my promise, this does not affect the status of your promise as a standing promise.

You could perhaps argue that your fulfillment of the promise is not required from the point of view of fairness or equity. This may be so. But this is not an argument to the effect that your promise no longer stands and hence no longer provides you with an obligation. The point, rather, is that in spite of the fact you made a promise that still stands, it is permissible, all things considered, to break that promise.

The more complex exchange involving a conditional promise discussed above also fails to provide interdependent obligations. Indeed, no promise-exchange, however complex, seems capable of simultaneously delivering unconditional, interdependent obligations to the parties.[35]

A joint commitment account of our sample agreement is better than an ex-change-of-promises model. If the agreement involves a joint commitment to uphold the relevant decision as a body, then unconditional obligations accrue to both parties simultaneously when and only when the joint commitment has been established. These obligations are a function of the joint commitment. If one party willfully violates the commitment, he or she violates something in which both parties participate, the source of the obligations of both. This would explain the judgments that one party's willful violation changes the status of the agreement and that the innocent party's conformity is now up to him or her.

What of promises? It is true that here only one person, the "promisor," has an obligation to perform an action the parties explicitly specify. Nonetheless a joint commitment account of promises also has some merit.

Consider that with typical promises there is a "promisee" who must accept the promise in order that it come into effect. Such acceptance amounts to more than a simple acknowledgment that the "promisor" has promised. It helps to constitute the promise as a promise. Further, though only the promisor has to perform a specified act, it would be untoward, all else being equal, should the promisee act so as to thwart the promisor's performance. For instance, were Anne to promise Ben she would fix his computer tomor-row, he would fail her should he deliberately deprive her of access to his computer tomorrow.

There is reason, then, to claim that both promisor and promisee take on obligations and accrue rights with respect to a given promise, something to whose creation both must contribute. These considerations, among others, support an account of promising as a joint commitment phenomenon of some kind.[36]

If agreements and promises involve obligations of joint commitment by definition, as it were, one can see why some moral philosophers (notably those known as "intuitionists") have thought, and indeed emphasized, that the fact that they obligate is knowable a priori. It is indeed knowable a priori.

What precisely is knowable a priori is, of course, the existence of an obligation of joint commitment. This may be less satisfying to the philosophers in question.

It does not appear to be knowledge of an a priori connection of certain non-moral facts (that one has made an agreement, say) with certain moral facts (that one is morally required to conform to one's agreement, all equal). Nor is it clear that it is best characterized as *moral* knowledge. That depends on the nature of morality, a thorny question.[37] That it is knowledge of *obligation* is all I argue.[38]

6. HART REVISITED

If everyday agreements and promises are joint commitment phenomena, then two central contexts where Hart would find obligations in his preferred sense involve obligations of joint commitment. In this section I focus briefly on two other contexts that have been thought to involve Hartian obligations and ask if they can plausibly be viewed as involving obligations of joint commitment.

A. Obligations of Fair Play

In a passage quoted by Simmons to introduce what he calls "the principle of fair play," Hart writes:

> When a number of persons conduct any joint enterprise according to rules and thus restrict their liberty, those who have submitted to these restrictions when required to have a right to a similar submission from those who have benefitted by their submission . . . the moral obligation to obey the rules in such circumstances is *due to* the cooperating members of society, and they have the correlative moral right to obedience.[39]

Hart sees this "very important source of special rights and obligations" as crucially relevant to the problem of political obligation.[40]

He writes, "I think political obligation is intelligible only if we see what precisely this is and how it differs from the other right-creating transactions (consent, promising) to which other philosophers have assimilated it."[41] I presume that Hart means here that other philosophers have given consent or promise-based accounts of political obligation, and this is the wrong way to go.[42]

A notable aspect of the case Hart describes is that one can argue that it will involve obligations of joint commitment. The argument runs as follows.

Suppose (1) "a number of persons" are jointly committed to pursue a certain goal as a body; in other words, I take it, the goal for a joint enterprise has been established among them, (2) they are jointly committed to accept as a body certain rules for the conduct of this enterprise, and (3) a large number of them are doing what they are obligated to do according to the joint commitments. That is, they are doing what they can to further the joint enterprise while following the rules as best they can.[43]

In this case the conforming participants in the relevant joint commitments have a right to similar behavior from those who have "benefitted by their submission." They have a right to that behavior as participants with the others in a joint commitment. Were they *not* to have fulfilled their own obligations, things would be different. But no such argument is available by hypothesis, so the conforming participants in the joint commitment have the usual rights and the usual basis for objection should any others fail to conform.

I am not saying that Hart had this particular argument in mind. As I shall note shortly, there is reason to think that he did not. Any reference to participation in a joint enterprise, however, is plausibly construed in terms of joint commitment and thus suggests a set of mutual obligations and rights that will not be undermined, at least not as long as people are acting accordingly.

Neither participation in a joint enterprise through joint commitment to pursue a goal as a body nor being party to a joint commitment to uphold certain rules is precisely the same thing as being party to an agreement. If membership in a political society involves these rather than an agreement, that is important and needs emphasis, along the lines of Hart's critique of contract theory. However, there is a precisely specifiable similarity between these two groups of phenomena, namely, their involving obligations and rights of joint commitment. This, too, will be worth emphasizing.[44]

Hart's own characterization of the situation is different: "There are of course important similarities, and these are just the points which all special rights [with correlative obligations in Hart's sense] have in common, viz., that they arise out of special relationships between human beings, and not out of the character of the action to be done or its effects."[45] What Hart says here leaves a great deal open. In principle, it seems that there could be many ways in which "special relationships" give rise to a situation in which it can be said that one person owed another some action, or (alternatively) that the other had a right to some action, and hence to a situation in which there are obligations in Hart's sense. In particular, Hartian obligations will not necessarily be restricted to situations in which there are obligations of joint commitment.

This idea is supported by other aspects of Hart's discussion of this case. He refers to the source of special rights here as "mutuality of restrictions."[46] He later argues that "in the case of mutual restrictions we are in fact saying that this claim to interfere with another's freedom is justified because it is fair."[47] In other words (in Simmons's gloss), "A beneficiary has an obligation to 'do his fair share' by submitting to the rules when they require it; others who have cooperated before have a right to this fair distribution of the burdens of submission."[48]

According to Hart, fairness in its turn is a matter of maintaining "an equal distribution of restrictions and so of freedom among this group of men."[49] Such a distribution recognizes "the equal right of all men to be free."[50]

The reference to fairness here points up an important distinction. One can distinguish between "doing one's part" or "doing one's share" and "doing one's *fair* share" in the sense of "doing what is fair."

If people understand themselves to be party to a joint commitment to accept certain rules as a body, then obeying the rules, absent special circumstances, appears to be simply a matter of doing one's part. It is what one is obligated to do through the joint commitment: the body in question will that much the less accept the rules if some of its members fail to respect them. There appears to be no need to appeal to independent considerations of fairness or equity to ground the obligation.

This suggests that Hart's criteria for obligations encompass, in principle, a different range of situations than would a criterion tying the term "obligation" to obligations of joint commitment. This is so even though in some central contexts where Hart would say there are obligations in his sense it can be argued that there are obligations of joint commitment.

B. Obligations of Gratitude

I now turn to a case that has been thought to involve obligations in Hart's sense but does not appear to involve obligations of joint commitment. Simmons, following Hart's account of obligation, allows for "obligations" of gratitude. His specification of the conditions for such an obligation is careful and complex. Roughly, one must have received a benefit that was intentionally and voluntarily granted by means of some special effort or sacrifice. The benefit must not be forced on the beneficiary against his or her will, and the beneficiary must want the benefit.[51]

If we go along with something like this set of conditions, it is not easy to see how obligations of gratitude can be construed as obligations of joint commitment. My benefiting you in the relevant way may involve us in a joint commitment, perhaps to the effect that some object that was mine to use as I pleased is now yours to use as you please. But it seems that such a joint commitment would not necessarily require any special action on the part of the beneficiary once the benefit has been received. Thus to chide someone for being ungrateful is apparently to invoke something other than a failure to fulfill obligations incurred through a joint commitment.

This may then be a case where there are Hartian obligations but no obligations of joint commitment. I say "may" because there is some question as to whether there are obligations in Hart's sense here.

Some have suggested that where those who have received benefits have obligations of gratitude toward their benefactors, those benefactors do not necessarily have rights to one's fulfillment of those obligations.[52] In that case obligations of gratitude would not have "corresponding rights" and so would perhaps fail to be Hartian obligations.

It is not clear what Hart would say about this case. Certainly there is a "prior special transaction" between benefactor and beneficiary, and each will have acted voluntarily in the matter of giving and receiving the benefit. Hart might find it reasonable to say that the beneficiary now "owed" certain acts to the benefactor, that is, acts expressive of gratitude. If so, it looks as if he might find it acceptable to talk of obligations here and hence of corresponding rights as well.

It is worth noting in this connection that Hart contemplates speaking of "obligations" when his criteria are not completely satisfied. For instance, he writes of cases involving a special "natural" relationship, such as that of parent and child.[53] These, too, are cases in which a joint commitment does not appear necessarily to be involved.[54]

For Hart, perhaps, one can reasonably speak of "obligations" when his criteria are largely, if not completely, satisfied. Hartian obligation would then be something of a "family resemblance" concept. The notion of a family resemblance may well apply, too, to the broad everyday notion of obligation whose breadth Hart decries, according to which, for instance, a passing stranger with no prior relationship to a drowning man may be obligated to try to save him if it is possible to do this without serious personal risk.[55]

7. CONCLUSION

I have argued that if there are joint commitments, there are obligations of a special sort. I conjectured that in many everyday contexts our confidence that obligations are present is responsive to the existence of a joint commitment with its special type of obligation. A case in point, which was discussed, is that of everyday agreements.

If those joint commitment phenomena are widespread in human populations, there would be a case for restricting the use of the term "obligation" to obligations of joint commitment. I do not recommend that we do this. For one thing, such a recommendation is unlikely to stem the historically broadening flow of usage, both vernacular and philosophical.[56]

It is important, though, not to confuse obligations of joint commitment with so-called obligations of other types or to confuse the type "obligation of joint commitment" with other types of obligation. I have briefly compared and contrasted obligations of joint commitment with obligations according to influential criteria proposed by H. L. A. Hart.

Hart decried the prevailing broad usage of philosophers as obfuscatory. It could be argued that Hart's criteria themselves are obfuscatory insofar as they do not bring into clear view the important class of obligations of joint commitment, obligations that are present in many of the contexts with which he deals. Rather than decry any particular usage, however, my main concern in this paper has been to argue that obligations inhere in joint commitments, obligations of a special and practically significant type.

NOTES

Versions of this paper have been read at the University of Connecticut and at the inaugural meeting of the British Society for Ethical Theory, held at Lancaster University, July 1997. I am grateful for the comments I received on these occasions. I thank Donald Baxter, Roger Crisp, Onora O'Neill, and John Troyer for reading and commenting on draft material and Christine Korsgaard for relevant discussion. Responsibility for the ideas expressed here is mine alone.

1. Cf. H. A. Prichard, *Moral Obligation and Duty and Interest: Essays and Lectures* (Oxford: Oxford University Press, 1968), 198: "Once call some act a promise and all question of whether there is an obligation to do it seems to have vanished." Prichard here focuses on promises. It seems he might equally well have said, "Once say that people have made an agreement and all question of whether they are obligated to conform to it seems to have vanished."

2. H. L. A. Hart, "Are There Any Natural Rights?" *Philosophical Review,* 64 (1955), 179, n7. The following quotation in the text is from the same passage.

3. Later Hart amplifies point (3), referring to "special *transactions* between individuals or . . . some special relationship in which they stand to each other" (Hart, "Natural Rights," 183) and to "*previous* transactions and relations between individuals" (190) (my emphasis in both quotations).

4. See John Rawls, *A Theory of Justice* (Cambridge, Mass.: Harvard University Press, 1971); A. John Simmons, *Moral Principles and Political Obligations* (Princeton: Princeton University Press, 1979); George Klosko, *The Principle of Fairness and Political Obligation* (Lanham, Md.: Rowman and Littlefield, 1992).

5. Cf. R. B. Brandt, "The Concepts of Obligation and Duty," *Mind,* 73 (1965), 374–393.

6. Hart, "Natural Rights," 183ff. He focuses on the "special rights" correlative with obligations.

7. Hart, "Natural Rights," 183.

8. He may, along with many others, assume that an agreement is simply an exchange of promises. I dispute this assumption in Margaret Gilbert, "Is an Agreement an Exchange of Promises?" *Journal of Philosophy,* 90, no. 12 (1993), 627–649; reprinted with revisions as chapter 13 of Margaret Gilbert, *Living Together: Rationality, Sociality, and Obligation* (Lanham, Md.: Rowman and Littlefield, 1996). See also the text below.

9. I first discussed joint commitment in Margaret Gilbert, *On Social Facts* (London: Routledge, 1989, second printing Princeton: Princeton University Press, 1992). See the introduction to Gilbert, *Living Together,* for a comparison of my exposition there with subsequent elaborations.

10. See Gilbert, *On Social Facts.* I there argue at length that the concept of a joint commitment is involved in our everyday concepts of group languages, social groups, social conventions, group beliefs, and other central social phenomena.

11. For related discussion see Chapter 2, this volume.

12. Many fine-grained accounts of common knowledge have been produced. The first published discussion is that in David Lewis, *Convention: A Philosophical Study* (Cambridge, Mass.: Harvard University Press, 1969). Some of these accounts have been criticized for lack of realism. For an attempt to produce an account such that common

knowledge is not "too high for humanity" and some further references, see Gilbert, *On Social Facts.*

13. The parties to a joint commitment can always initiate certain side understandings. Suppose Anne asks "Shall we meet for lunch on Tuesday?" and Ben replies "Yes" somewhat reluctantly. Anne may then offer, "Don't worry, you can always call me in advance and say you've changed your mind." One might describe the situation here as follows. Anne and Ben have a plan to meet; that is, they are jointly committed to accept a certain plan as a body. They also have a special *side understanding* to the effect that they will both act *as if* Anne is not in a position to hold Ben to the commitment—provided he calls her first.

14. I have discussed the case of belief in a number of places, beginning with Margaret Gilbert, "Modeling Collective Belief," *Synthese,* 73 (1987), 185–204, reprinted in Gilbert, *Living Together.* The introduction to *Living Together* contains an overview of this material. On goals see Gilbert, *On Social Facts,* chapter 4, and Margaret Gilbert, "Walking Together: A Paradigmatic Social Phenomenon," *Midwest Studies in Philosophy,* 15, *The Philosophy of the Human Sciences,* P. A. French, T. E. Uehling Jr., and H. K. Wettstein, eds. (Notre Dame: University of Notre Dame Press, 1990), reprinted in *Living Together.*

15. I have previously discussed this issue most extensively in Margaret Gilbert, "Agreements, Coercion, and Obligation," *Ethics,* 103, no. 4 (1993), section 3. The discussion here is significantly different. There I start by proposing a partial characterization of obligation in general, a characterization derived from reflections on the broad sweep of everyday usage: if I have an obligation to do *A,* I have a reason to do *A* that is not the "creature of my own will" in the sense that an arbitrary act of my own will was sufficient to create it and is sufficient to destroy it. I note that in contrast to personal decisions or other forms of personal commitment, joint commitments give reasons that satisfy the proposed necessary condition, reasons it seems otherwise appropriate to speak of as "obligations" (our term "obligation" comes from the Latin word "*ligare*," to bind; failure to act on joint commitment–based reasons involves breaking what is saliently a *bond.*) Here I do not attempt any initial characterization of obligations *in general.* My main aim in both discussions is to make plausible the idea that in some important contexts our talk of "obligations" (and "rights") may be responsive to the understanding that, simply, a joint commitment is present.

16. "Betrayal" may seem too strong a term for one's sense of things in some such cases. Is there not a difference between my failing to accord with a decision when this involves my acting against deeply held moral beliefs, say, and a case where nothing like this is at stake? Certainly there is a difference. Perhaps, though, there can be small betrayals. One is unlikely to react grievously to them, but one may understand them to have occurred. The suggestion in the text assumes this.

17. See, for instance, Anthony Kenny, *Action, Emotion, and Will* (London: Routledge and Kegan Paul, 1963), 218: "On our theory, to have the intention to bring it about that p, is to say-in-one's-heart 'Let it be the case that p' " and 220: "a command uttered to oneself."

18. This way of representing the order involved in a personal commitment, explicitly referring to the addressee, allows one to differentiate between the orders involved in personal commitments and those involved in joint commitments. In this it contrasts with Kenny's representation in Kenny, *Action, Emotion, and Will,* 218 (see note 17).

19. Cf. Kenny, *Action, Emotion, and Will,* note 18 above.

20. See note 21 below on what may be a necessary condition for orders that are *not* self-addressed.

21. Self-addressed orders are clearly special insofar as the orders by reference to which people learn the term "order" are addressed by one person to another (often within some background institution). It can be argued that if such an "other-addressed" order is to be more than a merely purported order, there must be a *joint commitment* that binds the issuer and the addressee, to the effect that the addressee is to do what the issuer says.

22. It may seem that nothing could count as disobedience to a self-addressed order. Would one's apparently failing to conform to one's order not show that one has in effect rescinded it? The examples in the text above of how one might fail to conform to one's decision suggest not. For instance, one might attempt to conform to one's order but fail. Thus I might order myself to leave the house at 6 P.M. but, without so intending, not leave myself enough time to make the necessary preparations. As I scurry around trying to meet my deadline, I have not yet rescinded the order. Eventually I have to admit I have failed in my attempt; I have disobeyed my order. This note was prompted by a comment from Roger Crisp.

23. Appropriate abstentions may be included under "actions" here. Insofar as the parties are always jointly committed *to do something as a body,* it appears that something will always be owing from both.

24. So also might have concluded the betrayal argument and the argument from the jointness of the commitment as these have so far been represented here. If Anne would indeed betray Ben by violating the joint commitment, she must owe him conformity to it. Similarly, if Anne's violation of the commitment that is theirs does indeed offend against Ben, she owes him her conformity. The joint order argument may make the protasis of these conditionals more persuasive. In any case, all of these arguments point to the one conclusion.

25. One might also speak of the "joint rescission" feature, "rescission" being the corresponding term in contract law.

26. "If he has not concurred." The case is not quite so simple, but for present purposes the point can stand. An important question is the outcome of one party's default. For remarks on this see Gilbert, *Living Together,* 13–15. See also the text below on the interdependence of the obligations of joint commitment.

27. Rights and obligations of joint commitment are, of course, in some sense waivable, as in the example where Anne says to Ben "You can always call me in advance and say you've changed your mind." See note 13 above. Such waivers occur, I take it, only in the context of special procedures and understandings.

28. Often people say they are sorry, but they *can't* do such-and-such after all. This, too, will not constitute the unilateral *abrogation* of a joint commitment, however precisely we should describe its significance. Quite often, of course, what is in fact at issue in such cases is preference rather than inability. It is understood that a contrary preference cannot ensure that one is let off the hook. ("I really don't want to go." "But you said you would!" etc.)

29. For related discussion see Margaret Gilbert, "Rationality, Coordination, and Convention," *Synthese,* 84 (1990), 1–21, reprinted in Gilbert, *Living Together;* and Chapter 2, this volume.

30. In *The Metaphysics of Morals,* section II ("On Contract Right"), subsection 18, (Cambridge: Cambridge University Press, 1991) Kant writes of "an act of the united

choice of two persons." I am indebted to Christine Korsgaard for referring me to Kant's discussion in this section after hearing me speak about joint commitment and obligation. Much of what I say about joint commitment in this paper and elsewhere seems to accord quite well with views Kant expresses. His key term is "common will" (also "united will") rather than "joint commitment." He argues compactly that the existence of a common will gives the parties rights of a special sort to each other's actions. He does not allude to the necessity of joint abrogation.

31. Why have the term "agreement" if one has the term "decision" and can tack on the pronominal adjective "our"? On this see Gilbert, "Agreements, Coercion, and Obligation," section 3.

32. See Gilbert, "Is an Agreement an Exchange of Promises?" See also Gilbert, "Agreements, Coercion, and Obligation."

33. For some references see Gilbert, "Is an Agreement an Exchange of Promises?" Some philosophers refer simply to "mutual promises." In discussion of the theory that agreements are "exchanges" of promises, I construe "exchange" in a broad sense: Anne and Ben exchange promises if Anne makes a promise to Ben and Ben responds with a promise to Anne. Ben's promise may be explicitly responsive to Anne's, as in "*Since* you have promised to . . . , I promise to. . . ."

34. This is not intended to imply that no other obligations are produced as well. But these are the obligations explicitly specified in the agreement.

35. For a discussion of other candidate promise-exchanges see Gilbert, "Is an Agreement an Exchange of Promises?"

36. I shall not attempt a full discussion of this idea here. I hope to pursue it in a longer study. For some further discussion see Gilbert, "Is an Agreement an Exchange of Promises?" section IX.

37. Kant, *The Metaphysics of Morals*, section II, subsection 20, makes a clear distinction between rights that stem from (or inhere in) contracts and another kind of right—a moral right?—that he says has to do with "the choice of all united *a priori*." (93) Playing on this Kantian phrase, contract right (and rights and obligations of joint commitment) could be referred to in contrast as stemming from "the choice of *some* united *a posteriori*." I discuss what may amount to the same contrast in Gilbert, "Agreements, Coercion, and Obligation," without presupposing a Kantian perspective on the moral domain. See also the text below.

38. Whether or not knowledge that one has an obligation of joint commitment is best characterized as moral knowledge, it is surely going to be knowledge of something morally *significant*. This may or may not be of some comfort to the philosophers in question. See Gilbert, *Living Together*, 297.

39. Hart, "Natural Rights," 185.

40. Hart contrasts "special rights" that have correlative *obligations* with "general rights" "which are asserted defensively, when some unjustified interference is anticipated." ("Natural Rights," 187). "You have no 'right to stop him reading that book' refers to the reader's general right. '*You* have no right to stop him reading that book' denies that the person addressed has a special right to interfere though others may have." (Hart, "Natural Rights," n13).

41. Hart, "Natural Rights."

42. This interpretation is born out at Hart, "Natural Rights," 186, "The social-contract theorists."

43. For extended discussions relating to the notion of a joint enterprise see Gilbert, *On Social Facts,* chapter 4 and, more recently, Chapter 2, this volume. For an account of social rules as joint commitment phenomena see Chapter 5, this volume.

44. I shall not attempt here to discuss the claim that membership in a political society involves one or more joint commitment phenomena, but see Gilbert, *On Social Facts,* on social groups in general and (in relation to political obligation) Margaret Gilbert, "Group Membership and Political Obligation," *Monist,* 76, no. 1 (1993), 119–133, and Chapter 6, this volume. One relevant issue is the question of large-group joint commitments. In everyday life we envisage joint enterprises involving from two to millions of people (as when we speak of a country at war). Can joint commitments be formed in large populations in which, among other things, no given member is directly acquainted with more than a relatively few other members? On this see Chapter 5, this volume.

45. Hart, "Natural Rights," 186.

46. Hart, "Natural Rights," 185.

47. Hart, "Natural Rights," 190–191.

48. Simmons, *Moral Principles,* 102.

49. Hart, "Natural Rights," 191.

50. Hart, "Natural Rights," 191.

51. Simmons, *Moral Principles,* 178–179.

52. Cf. Claudia Card, "Gratitude and Obligation," *American Philosophical Quarterly,* 25 (1988), 120: "The benefactor does not have a right to one's acting in accord with [responsibilities of gratitude] but only deserves it (or doesn't)."

53. Hart, "Natural Rights," 186–187.

54. Discussions of familial obligations need to be clear on whether they concern a biological matter or more of a social one. In speaking of a "natural" relationship, Hart appears to have the former in mind. Many joint commitments are likely to arise in the context of contacts between the members of social as opposed to biological families.

55. For comparison of this type of (commonly) so-called obligation with obligations of joint commitment see Gilbert, *Living Together,* chapter 12, especially 296–301.

56. It is possible that, historically, talk of "obligations" in English originally latched on to cases of joint commitment. See Brandt's discussion in "Obligation and Duty" of the way in which use of the term "obligation" has expanded.

5

Social Rules: Some Problems with Hart's Account, and an Alternative Proposal

Distinguished legal theorist H. L. A. Hart put social rules at the foundation of his account of law. His own influential account of them occurs in his classic treatise *The Concept of Law*. This chapter notes three problems with that account. Any account that does not deal satisfactorily with these problems is liable to appear less than adequate. The *grounding problem* requires that the existence of a social rule provide an intelligible basis for specific kinds of reaction to deviance. The *group standard* problem requires that one who issues a fiat for a group have the authority to do so. The *bindingness problem* is the problem of finding a warrant for the felt bindingness of social rules or of demonstrating the impossibility of doing so. An alternative, plural subject account of social rules is sketched. This avoids the three problems. It is, notably, less individualistic than Hart's and related accounts.

INTRODUCTION

It is generally agreed that social rules are pervasive and consequential phenomena.[1] What, though, is a social rule? I take it that a social rule is the rule of a social group.[2] Precisely what this amounts to, according to our everyday understanding, is the topic of this chapter.

Perhaps the best-known and most influential account of social rules to date

71

is the one H. L. A. Hart proposed in his now classic work *The Concept of Law*.[3] This serves as the groundwork for his celebrated account of law.[4]

Hart's account of social rules is a rich one, incorporating a variety of features. It is individualistic, in a sense to be discussed, and thus constitutes an important representative of a standard type of account of social rules.[5]

This paper starts by noting a serious problem with Hart's account of social rules. Two further problems are raised subsequently. These three problems need to be faced for a satisfactory account of social rules to be developed. A new account of social rules is then proposed. It takes care of all three problems.

This new account generally respects Hart's detailed description of the behavior and attitudes found in the context of social rules. It is not, however, individualistic in the way of Hart's account and many others.

Given this alternative account, it can be argued that there are obligations of conformity attendant on every social rule. This would explain a phenomenon observed but downplayed by Hart: the parties to any social rule have a sense of being "bound" to conform to it.[6]

1. HART ON SOCIAL RULES

i. Hart's Discussion

Hart asks, "What is the difference between saying of a group that they have the habit, e.g., of going to the cinema on Saturday nights, and saying that it is the rule with them that the male head is to be bared on entering a church?"[7] He goes on to describe a variety of features that he suggests must be present when there is a social rule. He can be construed as proposing at least a partial analysis of "the statement that a group has a certain rule" in common parlance.[8]

In his discussion of the nature of social rules in general, Hart focuses on rules of a particular and central type, and I shall do so as well. First, such rules are prescriptive. That is, they can be formulated in terms of what is "to be done." Second, they are basic or primary, at least in the sense that they do not exist by virtue of the operation of any special rule-generating rules such as "We are to do whatever Rex tells us to do."

Hart's discussion is relatively informal. A first stab at deriving a more precise account from it, without any attempt at systematization or the elimination of redundancies, might look like this.[9]

There is a *social rule in a group G* that action A is to be done in circumstances C, if every member of G[10]:
(1) regularly does A in C (this behavior need not be invariable).[11] That is,

there is a social habit in group G of doing A in C. (Call this the *regularity* feature.)

(2) has a "critical reflective attitude" to the pattern of behavior: doing A in C[12] (the *critical reflective attitude* feature).

(3) regards doing A in C as a "standard of criticism" for the behavior of members of G[13] (the *standard of criticism* feature).

(4) regards nonperformance of A in C by a member of G as a fault open to criticism [and threatened nonperformance as open to pressure for conformity].[14] The clause in square brackets is implicit in the text (the *deviance judged open to criticism and pressure* feature).

(5) criticizes any member of G who does not do A in C and puts pressure to conform on members of G who threaten not to do A in C[15] (the *criticism and pressure* feature).

(6) believes such criticism and pressure are legitimate or justified in the following sense: nonperformance of A in C by any member of G provides any member of G (either the defector or any other member) with a good reason to express criticism and exert pressure[16] (the *criticism and pressure thought justified* feature).

(7) expresses their criticisms and demands using normative language such as "You *ought* to do A now!" or "That's wrong"[17] (the *normative language* feature).

One further aspect of Hart's view of social rules may be mentioned at this point. Hart is at pains to avoid the idea that the significant internal or psychological aspect of social rules is "a mere matter of 'feelings.' "[18]

Hart has in mind feelings "analogous to those of restriction or compulsion." He goes on: "Such feelings are neither necessary nor sufficient for the existence of 'binding' rules. There is no contradiction in saying that people accept certain rules but experience no feelings of compulsion."[19]

He does allow, however, that when there is a social rule, members of the relevant group typically feel they are in some sense "bound" to behave according to the rule.[20] Though he does not make much of this and it should not be placed at the core of his account, we might add to the above list that every member of G:

(8) feels that members of G are in some sense "bound" to conform to the pattern: doing A in circumstances C[21] (the *felt bindingness* feature).

Whatever else might be said about these eight features, it is plausible to claim that they are commonly present in those contexts where we deem there to be a social rule according to our everyday understanding. It is therefore worth considering them carefully. Are there any redundancies? Are some of the listed features more fundamental than others, clearly deeper or more basic? Is the list incomplete in some way? Does it call for amplification?

ii. Eliminating Some Redundancies

It is not always entirely clear what a given feature amounts to. I shall adopt what I take to be the most plausible construals.

It will be useful to start with feature (3): group members regard a certain pattern of behavior as a "standard of criticism" for members' behavior. I take this to mean that they regard it as a standard *in relation to which members' behavior may be judged correct or incorrect.*[22]

Given this understanding of a standard of criticism, feature (2), the critical reflective attitude feature, may be construed as follows. Those with a social rule, as opposed to a social habit, have a particular *attitude* toward the relevant pattern of behavior: this attitude is "critical" in that a particular pattern of behavior is regarded as a *standard of criticism* in the above sense. It is "reflective" as opposed to being a matter of feeling or emotion.[23] Feature (2) is clearly close to feature (3) and may be regarded as, in effect, an amplification of it.[24]

We can, I think, waive special consideration of feature (4) (deviance judged open to criticism and pressure). It seems that this can be assimilated either into feature (3), discussed above, or into feature (6) (criticism and pressure thought justified), depending on how we are to understand what it is for deviance to be "open to" criticism and pressure.[25]

Features (5) and (7) involve certain actions and utterances, while feature (6) involves the belief that these actions and utterances are justified. It seems that feature (6) is the fundamental feature here, for it will presumably underpin the actions and utterances in question.[26]

iii. A Key Element in Hart's Account: Punitive Pressure

We should be clear about what feature (6) amounts to. When this feature is present, group members believe they are justified in doing more than simply *judging* deviants adversely. Indeed, they believe they are justified in doing more than dispassionately *communicating* a judgment of error. They believe they are justified in responding more strongly than this both to actual deviance, on the one hand, and to "threatened" deviance, on the other.

Hart refers to "criticism" for deviance and "pressure for conformity" if deviance is threatened. Hart implies that the "criticism" he has in mind here is a closer cousin to pressure for conformity than is a mere communication of error.

I take it that the type of "criticism" involved in feature (6) is a matter of reproofs, rebukes, and the like, directed at those who deviate from the pattern of behavior at issue. In other words, it is a matter of something that can be argued to have a *punitive* element. It constitutes a form of punishment.[27] Hart writes of "reproofs" rather than "criticisms" in his initial discussion of social rules in his introductory chapter.[28] No reason is given for writing, rather, of "criticisms" at pages 54–56. The term "criticisms" may be used simply by virtue of its greater generality.[29]

To keep the kind of criticism at issue here clearly in mind, I shall refer to it as *punitive criticism*.[30] It contrasts with what we might call *descriptive* criticism, which merely notes or points out an error. Example: "Hurrah! You've made several mistakes. I'm glad to see you are capable of that!" It contrasts also with *disapproving* criticism that is not yet reproving or punitive. For instance: "I'm sorry to disappoint you, but I can't say I approve of what you did." Another's expression of disapproval may be hurtful, but it need not be, or be seen as, punishment.

Hart stresses that where there is a social rule it will also be considered legitimate to pressure would-be deviants to conform. He speaks of "demands for compliance" in this context. Presumably any such "demands" will be "backed by threats," at least insofar as punitive criticism can be expected should the deviant act after all be performed: "Don't do that—I'm ready to reprove you if you do!"

To characterize feature (6) succinctly, I shall now say that it involves the belief that it is justifiable to meet deviance with *punitive pressure*. This is to be understood to include both punitive criticism (reproofs and the like) and such pressure as demands for conformity (backed by threats of punitive action).[31]

Feature (6) thus appears to go far beyond feature (3) as I construed it: group members regard the relevant pattern of action as a standard by reference to which members' behavior may be *judged* as correct or incorrect. For a situation to have feature (6), group members must go (much) further than this. They must believe their *imposing punitive pressure* on any of their fellows who act "incorrectly" *is justified*.[32]

Hart was right, I believe, to separate out and to stress feature (6). Any account of our everyday concept of a social rule that neither includes nor implies the existence of feature (6) will be importantly lacking.[33]

2. A STRUCTURAL FEATURE OF SOCIAL RULES

How could punitive pressure be justified in the context of a social rule? And what type of justification is at issue?

At one point Hart speaks of justification in terms of "having a good reason."[34] Now someone could have a good reason to *pressure* another to do a certain thing without being in a position to *punish* them for not doing it. What one does cannot *count* as punishment unless one has a certain standing. (One can, of course, act *in a punitive fashion* or "punishingly" without any special standing.) One who is *justified in imposing punishment as such,* then, requires the standing or entitlement to punish. In other words, to judge oneself justified in punishing is (in the first instance) to judge oneself entitled to punish.

Consider the following dialogue:

> Becky (reprovingly): "Phoebe! You've brought the cat in!"
> Phoebe: "You're telling me off—again!"
> Becky: "I should think so! We've a rule against bringing the cat in!" or "Well, you've broken one of our rules—again!"[35]

Becky's response to Phoebe appears perfectly in order from a logical point of view. That this is so suggests the following about our everyday understanding of what it is for a group to have a rule: if a given rule is the rule of a particular group, this entitles group members to impose a form of punishment on members who deviate from the rule. Becky's appeal to their rule is evidently seen to explain, in the sense of justifying, the imposition of a form of punishment (involved in reproving Phoebe or, as Phoebe puts it, "telling me off"). Any such justification presupposes an entitlement to impose such punishment.

Can we be somewhat more precise about the presumed basis for this entitlement? Consider a slightly different dialogue.

> Becky (speaking as if Phoebe has somehow *offended against her*): "You've brought the cat in!"
> Phoebe: "What's that to you?"
> Becky: "It's against our rule!"

Once again I take it that there is nothing untoward in Becky's responses, including her offended surprise.[36]

This suggests that a group's having a rule grounds a claim for each member against every member for conformity to the rule. Here Becky regards herself as having been offended against by Phoebe's nonconformity, citing their rule as the grounds for her implied claim on Phoebe.

I propose that we now add the following feature to Hart's list: [There is a social rule in group G that action A is to be done in circumstances C if every member of G]

> (6') believes that every group member *has a claim against* every other group member for the performance of A in C and a consequent *title to exert punitive pressure* on any other group member in favor of doing A in C.

In describing feature (6') I have written that every member of G *believes* certain things. Now, we ourselves have social rules, and we take it that we do not simply believe but rather *know* or (in that sense) *understand* that *these rules, in and of themselves, ground claims and entitlements of the sort in question.* Rather than alter feature (6'), I suggest that we simply add to Hart's list:

(A) The existence of a social rule in a group, in and of itself, gives group members a title to exert punitive pressure on one another for conformity to the relevant pattern in the appropriate circumstances. It does this by virtue of grounding a claim for each group member on every other group member for conformity.

(A) might be said to describe a "structural feature" of social rules. We understand that it is because of the truth of (A) that feature (6') is present when there is a social rule in some group. Members believe they have a claim on one another, and so on, because they *do* have a claim. More precisely, members know, rather than believe, these things. Analogous points can be made for feature (6).

3. A PROBLEM WITH HART'S ACCOUNT

Let us now set apart features (6) and (6') as invariably correlated with social rules that can be explained by the existence of a social rule. Once we do this, the key features remaining on Hart's original list of core features—features (1)–(7)—are (1), the regularity feature, and (3), the standard of criticism feature.

I want now to press the following question with respect to each of these features (and eventually with respect to their conjunction). Is it the case that by virtue of the presence of the feature in question, *and that alone,* members of the relevant group have a claim on other members for conformity to the pattern in question and a consequent title to exert punitive pressure for conformity in the appropriate circumstances?

I am supposing that according to our everyday understanding it is our having a given rule, *and that alone,* that grounds the claim in question. We need to ask, therefore, whether there is what I shall call a *direct* argument from one of the features in question, or from their conjunction, to the claim. No new information should be introduced.

i. The Regularity Feature

It is surely implausible to claim that feature (1), the regularity feature, itself gives members the relevant type of claim on one another for performance. As it stands, the fact that "The members of group G regularly do A in C" is not enough to give members of G a claim on one another for the performance of A in C.[37]

It is worth considering two kinds of argument that introduce additional assumptions beyond the assumption of a regularity in behavior. These assumptions invoke what may be plausible additions to the regularity feature.

The first kind of argument invokes an "entitlement to expect" conformity. With or without preamble, it supposes that (1) *Members of G have reason to believe that members of G will continue to do A in C in the future.*[38] It proceeds as follows. Given (1): (2) Members of G are entitled to expect future performance from one another. Given (2): (3) Each member of G has a claim on other members for the performance of A in C.

There is the following intransigent problem with this argument, assuming that we accept premise (1) as a plausible amplification of or addition to the regularity feature. The sense in which the argument undoubtedly shows members of G to be "entitled to expect" performance is a matter of their being entitled *to predict* that performance will be forthcoming. Such an entitlement, however, is not in itself sufficient to ground *a claim on others for their performance.*

It may well be that there is a sense of "being entitled to expect" something such that being so entitled is, in effect, being entitled to the thing itself, where this latter entitlement amounts to a claim on someone for the thing in question. It remains to be shown that those who are entitled to expect performance in the sense of being entitled to predict performance are also entitled to expect it in any other sense.[39]

The second kind of argument involves implicit appeal to a general moral principle. Various such arguments are possible. Consider the following example. This argument starts with the assumption that (1) *Members of G believe members of G will do A in C in the future.* The argument continues: (2) It is disconcerting when such beliefs about the future turn out to be false. Therefore, (3) Members of G have a claim on one another for the performance of A in C.

One problem with this argument is that it is (doubly) indirect. Whatever its plausibility, premise (2) is an empirical, psychological assumption. There is no conceptual connection between having such expectations turn out to be false and experiencing certain disagreeable feelings. One can imagine that in certain cases members of G would experience a pleasant amazement should their fellows fail to act in the predicted ways.

The argument also implicitly appeals to something like the following moral principle: (2*) All persons have a moral claim against all other persons not to be disconcerted. It appears that any argument that uses some general premise about the moral claims all persons have against all persons will be indirect from the point of view of the regularity feature or what we may now call the *expectation feature.*

Thus consider an argument making use of the assumption that all persons have a moral claim against all persons not to be put in a position where they may detrimentally rely on a reasonable but unfulfilled expectation. Given members of G reasonably believe that other members of G will do A in C in the future, this argument also concludes that members of G have a claim on one another for the performance of A in C. It, too, fails because it is an indirect argument on at least one count: it appeals to a moral principle.[40] The same can be said, evidently, of all arguments from the regularity or expectation feature that appeal to moral principles in this way.[41]

ii. The Standard of Criticism Feature

I now turn to feature (3): Group members regard a certain pattern of action as a standard in relation to which their behavior may be judged as correct or incorrect. What kind of standard is at issue?

Are correctness and incorrectness here matters of moral rightness or wrongness? Hart's few examples of social rules suggest that, in his view, this is not so. The example rule "Whatever Rex I enacts is law"[42] does not look like a moral rule and surely need not be so viewed. The example rule that "The male head is to be bared on entering a church"[43] is similar. It could apparently be understood and accepted by some person or body without the application of any moral understanding, whether or not moral ideas of some kind in fact led to its adoption.[44]

Hart's example of baring the head in church is couched in the specific form of a simple fiat: such-and-such *is to be done*. No reasons are given or obviously implied. He writes, "If a social rule is to exist some at least must look upon the behavior in question as a general standard *to be followed* by the group as a whole" (my emphasis).[45]

It seems then that we should construe regarding a pattern as a *standard of criticism* for one's group as simply regarding the pattern as a pattern that *is to be* conformed to, so that members are in error if they fail to conform to it, all else being equal. The nature of the error and the provenance of the fiat, meanwhile, are not here specified. This accords with intuitive judgments. Intuitively, there can be a social rule that is not at the same time a moral rule.[46] Something seen as a rule is, meanwhile, something seen as "to be conformed to."

Does Hart's feature (3) of itself ground mutual claims for performance, claims that entitle the claimant to exert punitive pressure in favor of conformity? The fact that I individually regard this pattern as a standard for all members of a certain group, including myself, does not seem to give me any special title to exert pressure in favor of performance.[47]

What of the presumed fact that *everyone* in our group regards this pattern as a standard? Does that directly ground the right type of claim in each member of the group? It is hard to see how a direct argument from a standard "shared" in this way can be found. Perhaps a standard "shared" or "common" in some other sense is at issue. I shall shortly argue that this is indeed so. Much more needs to be said, however, than is given in Hart's text.

I conclude that Hart's features (1) and (3) are not singly such as to directly ground the relevant type of mutual claims for performance or the corresponding rights to exert punitive pressure. Nor would they appear to be more powerful in conjunction. Hart's account of social rules is therefore problematic.

4. THREE ISSUES FOR ANY ACCOUNT OF SOCIAL RULES

My discussion of Hart so far has brought the following issue into focus: What is it about a social rule that immediately grounds claims for performance and corresponding rights to exert punitive pressure—something we believe our social rules to do?[48] Call this the *grounding* problem (for a short label). It is a problem any fully adequate account of social rules must solve.

At least two other important problems are raised by Hart's account. The first can be brought into focus by once again considering Hart's feature (3). According to Hart, when there is a social rule in a group, the individual group members personally "regard such-and-such as a standard that all should follow." I have construed this in terms of the personal endorsement of a certain fiat. This construal raises the question whether individual members of the group are conceived of and conceive of themselves as, in effect, *issuing* the relevant fiat. If so, it seems reasonable to ask: By what right or authority or title do they take themselves to do so?

Paradoxically, there is a problem here analogous to that of Hart's imaginary Rex I, who specifies what is to be done by the members of a certain population but lacks the authority to do so.[49] Hart proposes that Rex's problem (lack of authority) would be solved if there were a social rule in the relevant population precisely granting him authority to "introduce new standards of behavior into the life of the group."[50] "In its simplest form this rule will be to the effect that whatever actions Rex specifies (perhaps in certain formal ways) are to be done."[51] I propose that Rex's problem recurs at the core of Hart's account of social rules.

Suppose that all we know about the members of a population is that each member regards obeying Rex as a standard to be adhered to by the members of the population, and so on. By what right does any of them issue prescriptions for the population as a whole with respect to who may give them orders or anything else? Each can have a view on such matters, of course, but such views have an air of irrelevance. The fact that they all have the same view does not seem to make a difference. There may be safety, but it is by no means clear that there is *authority,* in mere numbers.

Rex's problem was this: How could he achieve a right to specify what is to be done for the group as a whole? Hart's solution—in terms of social rules as he characterizes them—reraises this problem at the level of social rules.[52] Assuming that social rules involve the issuing of a fiat by someone or something, we have what I shall call the *group standard* problem: Who or what can appropriately issue a fiat for a whole group?[53] To solve this problem, I believe we must go beyond the individualism of Hart's account of social rules (and of many related accounts).

Finally, there is the *bindingness* problem. Though he downplays its importance, Hart observes that in the context of a social rule people "say they 'feel bound' to act in certain ways."[54] The following question arises: Is there an appropriate basis for this feeling of being "bound"? Or must this be written off as illusory or as reflecting something other than genuinely being bound? Where there are social rules, are group members indeed bound to perform in some relevant sense, perhaps in a sense connected with the justified reprimands of others? Hart may be willing to side at least to some extent with those who take the "feelings of being bound" to be illusory, insofar as he eventually singles out a proper subset of social rules as "rules of obligation."[55]

Suffice it to say that an account of social rules that did not restrict being bound to a subclass of such rules would appear most satisfactory. When one claims that a prevalent sense of things is in whole or in part "illusory," this always leaves open the possibility that one has missed the correct explanation—unless one shows that there must be an illusion in this case.[56] The *bindingness problem* is the problem of finding a warrant for the felt bindingness of social rules—or demonstrating the impossibility of such a solution.

In the next two sections I sketch an account of social rules that surmounts each of the three problems just noted.

5. THE PLURAL SUBJECT ACCOUNT OF SOCIAL RULES

i. Joint Commitment and Obligation

In *On Social Facts* I argued at some length that underlying many of our central social or collectivity concepts is an important concept of *joint commitment*.[57] I there proposed that the concept of a social rule is one of the social concepts in question.[58]

An account of social rules in terms of an underlying joint commitment surmounts each of the three problems noted for accounts of social rules—the grounding problem, the group standard problem, and the bindingness problem. In this section I say something about joint commitment with an eye to showing in particular how this type of account takes care of the problems.[59]

I take a personal decision to be a paradigmatic case of a *commitment*. One who decides to do A is now committed to doing A, so long as his or her decision stands. A personal decision is also a paradigmatic case of a *wholly individual* commitment: as far as the concept of a personal decision goes, I can come by such a commitment alone, without the intervention of any other party. I can also revise my commitment or revoke it altogether without the involvement of anyone else. In short, a wholly individual commitment is mine to create and mine to give up. It is also mine to break: no one else can violate a wholly individual commitment.[60]

Those who are subject to a *joint* commitment may be said to have ensuing "individual" commitments in a sense: each of the individual parties will indeed be committed. But an "individual" commitment of this sort is significantly different from what I have called a "wholly individual" commitment.

A joint commitment is, precisely, joint. It is the commitment of more than one person. This has consequences for the "individual" commitments that derive from a joint commitment: I cannot be subject to such an "individual" commitment independent of all other people, and I cannot unilaterally rescind such a commitment. It stands or falls only with the underlying joint commitment, which itself can only be rescinded by *us* (the parties to it).[61]

With respect to the content of a joint commitment, in general a joint commitment is a commitment of certain parties to do something *as a body*. (It may sometimes be less awkward to speak of being jointly committed to do something *jointly* or *together*.) "Doing something" here must be interpreted broadly. I have elsewhere argued that a standard interpretation of "We believe that such-and-such" is in terms of a joint commitment to believe that such-and-such as a body.[62]

I have elsewhere used the term "plural subject" to refer to those who are jointly committed to doing something as a body.[63] They will then constitute the "plural subject" of the "doing" in question.

We should distinguish between *basic,* or "ground-level," joint commitments and *derived* joint commitments, since the conditions under which these come to be are different. Suppose we are jointly committed to accept that whatever Jones tells us to do is to be done. If Jones now tells us to do something, we presumably have a (derived) joint commitment jointly to accept that we are to do that thing. The derived joint commitment comes about on the basis of the original basic joint commitment plus Jones's telling us to do something.

How do basic joint commitments come about? Roughly, individuals must openly express their readiness to be jointly committed in the relevant way along with the relevant others.[64]

The parties to a joint commitment need not know of one another as particular individuals, though, of course, they may. One may be party to a joint commitment between oneself *as this particular person* and *another particular person or other particular people*. But one may also be party to a joint commitment between oneself and another or others *under some particular description,* such as "friend of Joe" or "person living on this island."

In many populations, particularly large ones, the parties do not know of one another as particular individuals. For instance, they know that many people live around them on a particular island, but they do not know each of these people personally or know of them as particular individuals. Nonetheless the island dwellers can participate in a population-wide joint commitment; the parties to the commitment would understand themselves to be jointly committed insofar as they are living on the island or qua island dwellers. One important aspect of this type of joint commitment is evidently that should the relevant description cease to apply to a given person, he or she will automatically be freed from the commitment.[65]

A final point about joint commitment in general.[66] A joint commitment—like any other—may be said to *require* that the participants act (or refrain from acting) in certain ways, all else being equal. However, this case has a special feature that is not present in all cases of commitment. A joint commitment is not the creation of any one of those who are subject to it, nor can it be removed at the pleasure of any one person. There is a clear sense in which the parties are *tied* or *bound* to one another with respect to their personal subjection to the requirement in question. Once the commitment is in place thanks to the action of all, each is subject to it, absent the concurrence of all (as long as it applies to them).

Let us say that one who is party to a joint commitment has an *obligation* to perform the relevant act or acts. Such an obligation is clearly an obligation of a special type. Among other things, it essentially involves at least two people, the person with the obligation and one or more others. If we call the person with the obligation the *obliger* (on the model of promisor), we may call the relevant others the *obligees* (on the model of promisee). These are the (other) people to whom the obliger is tied with respect to his or her commitment to a certain course of action. Given that we speak of the *obligations* of the obliger, it seems that we can speak of the correlative *claims* or *rights* of the obligees: they have a claim on the obliger for performance of the act in question.[67]

I suggest the sense of "obligation" (and "right") introduced here is not a novel one. Much of our everyday talk of obligations and rights is plausibly viewed as a matter of reference to a joint commitment. I include in this class the obligations of agreements and promises.[68] I have discussed elsewhere the way in which *obligations of joint commitment* differ from, for instance, the obligation to save a child from drowning if there is no significant risk to oneself.[69]

ii. The Plural Subject Account of Social Rules

I can now sketch an account of social rules, according to our everyday understanding of what such rules are. More specifically, it is an account of when a population has a rule to the effect that members of that population are to perform a certain action in certain circumstances.

I do not aim to give a full defense of this account here, to consider possible objections, or to concern myself with all possible matters of detail. I take the account to have some initial plausibility and want to show that it avoids the problems noted for Hart's account. It has merit at least to that extent and to that extent is superior to a variety of accounts more or less approximating Hart's. I am inclined to think that it or something like it is a worthy heir to Hart's account. The account—which might be dubbed the *plural subject* or *joint commitment* account—runs roughly as follows:

> There is a *social rule* if and only if the members of some population P are jointly committed to accepting as a body a requirement of the following form as a body: members of P are to do A in C. (Some reason for doing A in C may be specified, or it may not.)

If we want a somewhat shorter version, we might say, first, that members of a population P *jointly accept a requirement* if and only if they are jointly committed to accept that requirement as a body. Given that "joint acceptance" is so understood, we can now write, alternatively (and equivalently):

> There is a *social rule* if and only if the members of some population P jointly accept a requirement of the following form: members of P are to do A in C. (Some reason for doing A in C may be specified, or it may not.)[70]

Some comments are in order.

(i) Joint acceptance of a requirement as imposition of a requirement

In writing that members "jointly accept a requirement of the following form: they are to do A in C," I mean to capture the idea that such joint acceptance amounts to the imposition of a requirement. It might be more apt, then, to write that they "jointly require that members are to do A in C."[71]

(ii) Accepting (requiring) as a body

The phrase "accept (require) as a body" is just one of the possible phrases with which the relevant idea might best be indicated. One might also write "accept as a unit," for instance, or "accept as a single person." The relevant joint commitment is a commitment, if you like, to constitute as far as is possible a single entity with a certain psychological property (in this case accepting or requiring something).

(iii) *Joint acceptance versus individual acceptance*

As ordinarily understood a joint commitment jointly to accept something does not involve a commitment personally to accept what is jointly accepted. In other words, that members of a population jointly accept "We are all to do A in C" does not imply that they personally accept this.

As I have argued in discussing the group standard problem, it is not clearly *intelligible*—without some special stage setting—that a given individual personally accepts "We are all to do A in C" in the sense at issue here, that is, in the sense that he or she "requires" that we are all to do A in C. That it does make sense that as a body *we* require that *we* are all to do A in C is one way of arguing that "We require . . ." does not imply "I require."

(iv) *Social rules as a genus*

I have elsewhere conjectured that a social *convention* was a species of social rule seen by those accepting it as to be followed, period, not for some special justifying reason (which was not to say it was seen as having no justifying reason).[72] The notion of a social rule is, I take it, more general, allowing for the understanding that such a rule may have a particular type of justification.

(v) *Social rules and moral rules*

According to the account of social rules sketched here, a rule perceived as a moral rule (whatever precisely that amounts to) could be a social rule. This does not, of course, entail that moral rules, assuming there are such, are a species of social rule. Nor does it entail that the social rule we perceive as a moral rule is not indeed a moral rule; that is, we may be correct in seeing this as a moral rule, as a rule to be followed because it is morally right to do so (or something like that).

(vi) *Relation to Hart's listed features*

It is striking that this account corresponds to few, if any, of Hart's listed features. However, it can be argued that if something approximating this account is correct, then all of Hart's conditions will be satisfied, one way or another. Some of these features will be derivable more or less as a matter of logic. Others will be such that in standard circumstances one can expect them to result from the existence of social rules as characterized here.

Thus it does not follow from the fact that one is party to a joint commitment that one will conform to it. One may be swept away by blind passion or have weighty moral reasons forbidding one to conform. Nonetheless, in the absence of these things one is likely to find one has reason enough to conform. On the one hand, there is the simple fact that one is subject to a commitment. On the other hand, one knows that should one default, one has offended against other people who have the standing to rebuke one for it.[73]

(vii) Relation to the grounding problem

By virtue of the joint commitment present when there is a social rule, each member of the population in question has a claim on every other member for conformity to the rule. These claims are correlates of the obligations joint commitment creates. Each member is obligated to every member to conform to the rule. Each member has the standing or right to rebuke any member who does not conform.

The exercise of any such right will always be subject to moral and prudential constraints. In some circumstances it may not be appropriate to do anything, as when, for instance, a nonconformist could not help herself or is so sensitive that even a slight rebuke will cause her to collapse. Should one party rebuke another for nonconformity, however, his standing in the matter will be perfectly clear. That he is, in the relevant sense, *in a position to rebuke* will not be in question.

Members of the population will understand this, since all are party to the relevant joint commitment and understand the structure of such commitments. Thus the grounding problem finds a solution here.

(viii) Relation to the group standard problem

On this account, a social rule's existence is a matter of a joint commitment through which each party becomes obligated to the others to support a certain standard as a standard for the population as a whole. Here, *we* accept a standard for *us*.[74]

The proposed account is couched in terms of a "population" rather than a "social group." I have argued elsewhere that any population in which the members are linked through a joint commitment will count as a "social group" on one standard understanding of that phrase.[75]

I prefer to define a social rule in terms of a population insofar as a given population may in principle constitute a social group by virtue of having a given rule, and within the consciousness of the people concerned the extent of the group may be determined by some description such as "friend of Sally" or "person living by Lake Woebegon." In other words, they understand their rule to be the rule of the population so specified, a population they will now reasonably see as a social group in the relevant sense, given that the members are, as such, party to a joint commitment.

A joint commitment creates, in effect, a new subject of psychological attributes, a *plural* subject. These attributes are not yours or mine or mine-and-yours but rather *ours*: our beliefs, our goals, our acceptance of rules. To put the point more carefully, these attributes are attributable to the body we form by virtue of our joint commitment. That commitment unifies our agency, providing a new source of action. If you like, it constitutes a new entity.[76]

There is a holism in this account that is absent from that of Hart.[77] The holism of this account of social rules is essentially the holism of the concept of joint commitment.

(ix) Relation to the bindingness problem

A joint commitment by its nature involves obligations of a special sort and clearly could underlie a sense of being "bound" to conform to a rule. This account, then, provides a solution to the bindingness problem.

In this case one is "bound" both horizontally and vertically, so to speak: bound to others, and bound (all else being equal) to conform. One is bound (all else being equal) to conform unless and until the other parties to the joint commitment are willing to accept one's freedom.

The sense of being bound that is grounded in a joint commitment is not, clearly, a matter simply of powerful "feelings of compulsion."[78] Nor is it what some may feel is the alternative, a matter of "something external, some invisible part of the fabric of the universe guiding and controlling us in these activities."[79] It *is* grounded, but it is not grounded in the fabric of the universe. It is of our own making. If there is a type of obligation that is not of our own making, then as I see it the obligations associated with social rules are not of that type.

(x) Relation to agreements

No appeal is made in this account to an agreement. As I understand it, an agreement amounts to a joint decision, founded in a joint commitment to accept as a body a certain decision. Given this understanding, an account of social rules in terms of agreements would have some of the virtues of the account proposed. The three problems with Hart's account—the grounding, group standard, and bindingness problems—would all be solved. An account in terms of agreements would be flawed by lack of realism, however. An agreement on a rule for the group seems not to be present in many contexts in which we allow that there are social rules in the sense in question.

A joint commitment can arise more informally than an agreement can, through a more gradual process. One way in which this can happen is that someone in the relevant population speaks of "our rule."

I believe a standard interpretation of such phrases is in terms of an underlying joint commitment. In the present case, "our rule" would be interpreted as "a requirement we jointly accept." If what this person says is not rejected, the practice of so referring to the rule may spread until it is clear to everyone that everyone is ready to be party to the relevant joint commitment. The initial reference to "our rule" may be tendentious, but once this way of talking is generally accepted it may be deemed to have found a genuine basis.[80]

In any case, these uses of language do not stand alone. Other things people say and things they do will help to confirm the plural subject interpretation of "our rule." In particular, the kind of behavior Hart alludes to (the imposition and acceptance of punitive pressure) will help to confirm this interpretation, as will dialogues of the kind discussed in this chapter.[81]

CONCLUSION

Careful critical consideration of Hart's account of social rules has led to another account, the plural subject account. Hart's account brings into focus the fact that when there is a social rule, punitive pressure on deviants and would-be deviants is generally accepted as justified. From this starting point I argued in favor of the plural subject account. Punishment presupposes entitlement, and it seems that we regard our group's rules as grounding claims for performance and corresponding entitlements to punish for deviance. This argues against Hart's account of social rules and in favor of the plural subject account. If a social rule is a jointly accepted standard, we can expect many of Hart's features to be present whenever a group has a rule. Thus though this discussion rejects Hart's account of social rules in favor of an account distinct in every particular, it remains quite close to Hart's sense of social rules and, if correct, goes some way to confirm it.

NOTES

Versions of this paper have been presented to classes at the University of Connecticut, Storrs, and Princeton University (1990), at the Joint Meeting of the Department of Philosophy, King's College London, and the Department of Philosophy, Logic and Scientific Method, London School of Economics; and at Stirling University (1996). In addition to those present then, I thank Michael Cook and Arthur Kuflik for relevant discussion. I dedicate this essay to the memory of Herbert Hart.

1. Social theorists often use the term "social norm" as an alternative to "social rule." Related phenomena include (social) conventions, customs, and traditions, all of which appear to bear some relation, perhaps of subsumption, to the category of social rules. On this

see Gilbert, 1989, 403–407. I discuss social conventions (with particular reference to David Lewis's work) in Chapter 6. In the sociological classic *Suicide,* Emile Durkheim famously argued that "anomie," or the paucity of social rules, contributed to higher rates of suicide in human societies. Gilbert, *On Social Facts* (London: Routledge, 1989; reprinted Princeton: Princeton University Press, 1992).

2. Cf. Raz, Joseph, *Practical Reason and Norms* (London: Hutchinson, 1975), 52: "A social rule is a rule of a certain society or community."

3. Hart, H. L. A., *The Concept of Law* (Oxford: Clarendon Press, 1961/1994). It has been said that the "central and distinctive element of Hart's contribution to descriptive jurisprudence [is] his elucidation of the idea of a social rule and the methodology he applies in that elucidation" (MacCormick, Neil, *H. L. A. Hart* [Stanford: Stanford University Press, 1981], 43), Monographs devoted to Hart's philosophy of law include: MacCormick, *H. L. A. Hart*; Martin, Michael, *The Legal Philosophy of H. L. A. Hart: A Critical Appraisal* (Philadelphia: Temple University Press, 1987); Bayles, Michael, *Hart's Legal Philosophy: An Examination, Law and Philosophy Library* 17 (Dordrecht: Kluwer, 1992).

4. This paper will largely ignore the role of Hart's account of social rules in his theory of law. Hart makes and emphasizes a distinction between what he calls "primary" and "secondary" rules and claims "the union of primary and secondary rules is at the center of a legal system" (Hart, *Concept of Law,* 96). Secondary rules include rules enabling the promulgation of new rules by particular people or specific bodies. A simple rule of this kind would be "whatever actions Rex (some particular person) specifies are to be done" (Hart, *Concept of Law,* 56). There has been much discussion and questioning of the way Hart distinguishes between primary and secondary rules. See, for instance, Sartorius, Rolf, "The Concept of Law," *Archives for Philosophy of Law and Social Philosophy,* 52 (1966) 161–193.

5. Cf. Cotterrell, Roger, *Law's Community: Legal Theory in Sociological Perspective* (Oxford: Clarendon Press, 1995), 222–230. Cotterrell sees Hart's legal philosophy as expressive of an individualistic "imperium" conception of law as opposed to a "community" conception.

6. Hart's account of social rules in *The Concept of Law* has been discussed and critiqued from a variety of angles by numerous authors. Important criticisms and reflections are found in Raz, Dworkin, MacCormick, Sartorius, and Bayles, among others. See also Hart's own postscript to *The Concept of Law.* I do not attempt anything approximating a review of this literature here. I focus on Hart's original discussion in *The Concept of Law* and move directly to concerns of my own. Raz, *Practical Reason*; Dworkin, Ronald, *Taking Rights Seriously* (Cambridge, Mass.: Harvard University Press, 1977); MacCormick, Neil, *Legal Reasoning and Legal Theory* (Oxford: Clarendon Press, 1978); MacCormick, *H. L. A. Hart*; Sartorius, Rolf, "Positivism and the Foundations of Legal Authority," in *Issues in Contemporary Legal Philosophy: The Influence of H. L. A. Hart,* Ruth Gavison, ed. (Oxford: Clarendon Press, 1987); Bayles, *Hart's Legal Philosophy.*

7. Hart, *Concept of Law,* 54.

8. Hart, *Concept of Law,* 55. Some may wonder at the idea of characterizing Hart's project as "analytic," given his own caveats about what he thinks can be done for the concept of law itself. On reading what he writes on social rules, however, it is easy to see him as engaged in a form of semantic analysis. Thus at Hart, 9, we find: "The account which we are at first perhaps naturally tempted to give . . . is that *to say that a rule exists means only that.* . . . Plainly this is not enough, even though *it conveys part of what is meant*" (my

emphasis). And his later discussion is conducted in such terms as "there is *no contradiction in saying that* people accept certain rules but experience no feelings of compulsion" (Hart, 36; my emphasis). One way of taking his account of social rules is therefore to interpret such terms as "must" and "is enough" in terms of logical (or conceptual) necessity and sufficiency.

9. Sartorius sets out a similar (though ultimately much longer) list at 49–51. Sartorius, Rolf, "Positivism and the Foundations of Legal Authority," in *Issues in Contemporary Legal Philosophy: The Influence of H. L. A. Hart,* Ruth Gavison, ed. (Oxford: Clarendon Press, 1987). Sartorius has seven core conditions characterized as satisfied in "the normal (standard, paradigm, completely unproblematic) case of the existence of a social norm" (49). His condition 1 corresponds to my feature 1 (see the text below), his 3 to my 7, his 6 to my 8, and his 7 to my 6. His condition 2 summarizes material in Hart that he referred to earlier and corresponds to my features 2, 3, 4, and 5. His conditions 4 and 5 are conditions on preferences that he takes from the interpretation of Hart in MacCormick, *H. L. A. Hart,* rather than from Hart's text itself (see Sartorius, "Positivism," 57). Sartorius goes on to propose a total of 153 conditions, his purpose being to argue that "the concept of an accepted social rule is a cluster concept not amenable to an essentialistic analysis by way of the specification of a set of conditions which are individually necessary and jointly sufficient for its correct application" (49). Sartorius claims that none of his 153 conditions is "logically necessary to the existence of a social rule." He argues specifically for the non-necessity of his conditions 4 and 5 (51–52) and condition 1, on which see below.

10. Hart suggests that it is always possible that a minority of members exists who do not share the attitudes involved in the listed features (Hart, *Concept of Law,* 55). We can consider the account given here (in terms of "every member of G") as listing conditions for a "perfect" case of a group's having a social rule. Compare David Lewis's procedure in his discussion of convention. Lewis, David, *Convention: A Philosophical Study* (Cambridge, Mass.: Harvard University Press, 1969).

11. Hart, *Concept of Law,* 54.

12. Hart, *Concept of Law,* 56.

13. Hart, *Concept of Law,* 55.

14. Hart, *Concept of Law,* 54.

15. Hart, *Concept of Law,* 54.

16. Hart, *Concept of Law,* 54 (good reason), 55 (any member of G).

17. Hart, *Concept of Law,* 56, also 9–10.

18. Hart, *Concept of Law,* 56. This (important) negative aspect of Hart's account of social rules is emphasized in the summary in MacCormick, *H. L. A. Hart,* 29.

19. Hart, *Concept of Law,* 56.

20. Hart, *Concept of Law,* 56. Later in the book, when he focuses on what he calls "rules of obligation" (see especially 84–85), Hart seems to deny that "bindingness" is a feature or perceived feature of all social rules. See the text below.

21. Hart, *Concept of Law,* 56.

22. MacCormick has questioned Hart's use of the term "standard," arguing that Hart's account of social rules "seems almost to be circular": "We are left with the unadorned idea of a 'critical reflective attitude to certain patterns of behavior as a common standard,' but what, after all, is 'a standard'? Do we not have to account for it in much the same way as 'a rule,' or in exactly the same way?" MacCormick, Neil, *Legal Reasoning and Legal Theory* (Oxford; Clarendon Press, 1978), 285. As to why Hart writes of a "standard" rather

than a "rule" here, I suspect that this was not done (consciously or unconsciously) to mask any circularity in his account of social rules. Presumably "standard" could indeed be replaced by "rule" in this context, as long as regarding a pattern of action *as a rule* is understood to involve regarding deviance from the relevant pattern of action as in some sense erroneous. Hart's discussion of the meaning of the common phrase "they do it *as a rule*" (which does *not* imply that they regard something as a standard) may have led him to prefer the term "standard" here (see Hart, *Concept of Law*, 9, 54).

23. Hart, *Concept of Law*, 56.

24. MacCormick, *H. L. A. Hart*, 33f, argues that the term "critical" here refers—or should refer—to "an element of or relating to volition or will" (33). This element, as he understands it, "comprehends some wish or preference that the act . . . be done when the envisaged circumstances obtain. . . . Commonly such a preference may be conditional upon the pattern in question being one for which there is and continues to be a shared preference among an at least broadly identifiable group of people" (33). At 157 n50, MacCormick signifies his approval of the account of (social) conventions found in Lewis, *Convention,* which may have encouraged his reference to conditional preferences. Lewis's account of convention in terms of the underlying structure of conditional preferences he calls a "coordination problem" has drawn appreciative responses from other philosophers of law, including Postema. (Postema, Gerald, "Coordination and Convention at the Foundations of Law," *Journal of Legal Studies,* 11 [1982] 165–203.) There is a general critique of Lewis on social convention in Gilbert, *On Social Facts* (London: Routledge, 1989; reprinted Princeton: Princeton University Press, 1992), chapter 6. His coordination problem condition is taken up at 342–344. I am no more inclined to give a coordination problem account of social rules than to give such an account of social conventions. Coordination problems may often give rise to such rules, but particular rules may arise or persist in their absence. In any case, I shall proceed in terms of the understanding of Hart proposed in the text above. It may not be so far from MacCormick's proposal if taking a certain pattern of action to be a standard of criticism "relates to volition or will." It may be useful here to distinguish between "willing" in (roughly) the sense of *wishing* or *wanting* and "willing" in (roughly) the sense of *deciding* or *decreeing*. My own sense of Hart and of the facts is that a species of willing in the second sense is at issue in the case of social rules. In the quoted discussion MacCormick seems to opt for the relevance of willing in the former sense, but his most general point about a relationship to "volition or will" may reasonably be taken to cover both. (See also his *Legal Reasoning,* 285–286). In that case we are broadly in agreement. I consider at some length the special type of willing I take to be involved with social rules in section 5 below.

25. For members to regard a pattern of behavior as a standard of criticism (see feature [3]) is for them to regard deviation from that pattern as "open to criticism and pressure" in the sense that there is a basis for criticism and pressure were that legitimate. That is, *a mistake of some kind has been made.* Alternatively, regarding deviance as "open to criticism and pressure" could already involve regarding criticism and pressure as legitimate (see feature [6], discussed in the text below). Probably the latter interpretation of feature (4) is preferred.

26. Cf. MacCormick's query as to whether "expressions of demands and criticisms [are] constitutive of, or merely evidentiary of, the critical reflective attitude envisaged" (MacCormick, *Legal Reasoning,* 285). Hart distinguishes the existence of the "critical re-

flective attitude" he regards as fundamental from its "display" in overt actions and utterances, including criticisms and demands for conformity. See Hart, *Concept of Law,* 56.

27. Cf. Hart, *Concept of Law,* 10–11, where Hart refers to "informal reproofs administered for the breach of non-legal rules." Informal reproofs are seen here as the functional equivalent of legal punishment. For discussion of the punitive nature of a rebuke see Gilbert, "Durkheim and Social Facts," in *Debating Durkheim,* W. S. F. Pickering and H. Martins, eds. (London: Routledge, 1994); reprinted with revisions in Gilbert, "Remarks on Collective Belief," in *Socializing Epistemology: The Social Dimensions of Knowledge,* F. Schmitt, ed. (Lanham, Md.: Rowman and Littlefield, 1994); reprinted with revisions as "More on Collective Belief" in Gilbert, *Living Together.*

28. See Hart, *Concept of Law,* 10–11, quoted in footnote 27.

29. Given Hart's use of the phrase "standard of criticism" his writing of "criticisms" here stands to be somewhat confusing.

30. The criticisms involved in feature (5) also will include those of the punitive type.

31. Hart uses the phrase "coercive pressure" in the postscript to the 1994 second edition of *Concept of Law.* There is a distinction between "coercive" and "punitive" pressure. Punitive pressure, or the threat of it, may always be coercive. But coercion need not be, or be seen as, punitive—a form of punishment.

32. Hart has passages suggesting that feature (3) could be interpreted more along the lines of feature (6). Thus he writes that when people have the belief involved in feature (6) and express this with appropriate behavior, they "treat a regular mode of behavior as a standard of criticism" (*Concept of Law,* 55). Again, he writes of the "critical reflective attitude displaying itself" in the expression of this belief. See Hart, *Concept of Law,* 56. These statements do not *prove* that Hart's construal of feature (3) is different from mine. Believing punitive pressure is justified may *presuppose* that an error has been made, while believing that an error has been made is not yet to believe that punitive pressure from others is justified. In any case, there is an important distinction between (3) as I construe it and (6) as I construe that.

33. As is, therefore, what Hart calls the "predictive account" (*Concept of Law,* 10ff). According to this, to say a group has a rule is simply to say that the reproofs and punishments of other members are *predictable* if members deviate from a certain pattern of conduct.

34. Hart, *Concept of Law,* 54. Elsewhere he writes of our taking a given nonlegal rule as a "*reason* and *justification*" for reproofs (Hart's emphasis, 10–11).

35. Interpret Becky's use of "we" and "our" as inclusive here rather than exclusive. That is, she includes Phoebe within the "we." That it is inclusive is not self-evident from the dialogue as written; that seems equally well open to either interpretation.

36. Cf. my discussion of "offended rebukes" in Gilbert, "Remarks."

37. Compare what Hart himself says: "Habits [sc. of obedience] are not 'normative'; they cannot confer rights or authority on anyone" (*Concept of Law,* 58).

38. Is to say that "members of G regularly do A in C" already to imply that "members of G will do A in C (ceteris paribus)"? If so, then, of course, members of G have reason to believe there will be future conformity if they "know of" the existence of the "regularity." Perhaps, though, the regularity condition should be interpreted in terms of what people have done up until now. Then the legitimacy of expectations based on the satisfaction of the regularity condition is less clear. I have argued elsewhere that if we are contemplating rational agents conceived of in a particular, rather stringent way, a successful

(prior) regularity in behavior in a coordination problem does not of itself imply that there is reason to expect its continuance. Gilbert, *On Social Facts,* chapter 6. Gilbert, "Rationality, Coordination, and Convention," *Synthese,* 84 (1990), 1–21; reprinted in Gilbert, 1996. If we restrict ourselves to actual human beings, it is certainly not always true that a (prior) regularity legitimates expectations of continued conformity. There could be special circumstances that (as is known) will soon cease to produce conformity; for instance, past behavior was coerced, but the coercion is about to stop. Perhaps a prior regularity in behavior legitimates expectations of future conformity, ceteris paribus.

39. There is evidently ambiguity in the term "expect." One thesaurus notes one set of synonyms including "anticipate" and another set including "require." On the face of it, an "entitlement to anticipate" is very different from an "entitlement to require." (When "expect" is used in the "require" sense, it may retain its "anticipate" sense also. It appears, however, that the "anticipate" sense need carry with it no element of "requirement." It may simply connote what I have referred to as a "plain" expectation [Gilbert, *On Social Facts,* 347].) Ullman-Margalit, (88–89), distinguishes between what she calls "deontic" and "theoretical" expectations (my "plain expectations"). See Ullman-Margalit, Edna, *The Emergence of Norms* (Oxford: Oxford University Press, 1977).

40. It can also be argued that the conclusion of this type of argument is not in fact the desired conclusion, since it concerns the wrong type of claim or right. The type of moral premise used in this argument—alluding to the moral claims of all persons against all persons—will then generally fail to lead to the desired conclusion. I shall not pursue this argument here.

41. Including this argument from Dworkin, *Rights,* 57 ("The Model of Rules II"): "The fact that a practice of removing hats in church exists justifies asserting a normative rule to that effect—not because the practice constitutes a rule which the normative judgement describes and endorses, but because the practice . . . gives rise to expectations of the sort that are good grounds for asserting a duty to take off one's hat in church or for asserting a normative rule that one must." Dworkin is suggesting that Hart's "practice" account of social rules is incomplete as far as genuine normativity is concerned: "In fact the social practice helps to *justify* a rule which the normative judgement states." The normative judgment Dworkin has in mind is a moral judgment. By "practice" he initially refers to the whole complex of behavioral and attitudinal factors Hart associates with social rules.

42. Hart, *Concept of Law,* 56.

43. Hart, *Concept of Law,* 54, also 9.

44. This is not the place to explore what distinguishes a moral standard from other types of standards. I rely here on a certain intuitive understanding on the matter.

45. Hart, *Concept of Law,* 55. The word "standard" could presumably be replaced by "pattern" without loss of content to this sentence, since the implied normativity of the term "a standard" is made explicit by the phrase "to be followed."

46. Cf. Gilbert, 392–396, *On Social Facts,* on morality and convention.

47. The same seems to go for the fact, if it is a fact, that I *prefer* that others conform. Recall that we are eschewing appeal to moral aspects of the situation. Thus even if it could be argued that it is morally required that one conform to existing preferences, all else being equal, this would be considered extraneous to the preference condition itself.

48. Similar problems arise for other social phenomena. On shared action: Gilbert, "Walking Together: A Paradigmatic Social Phenomenon," *Midwest Studies in Philosophy,* 15, *The Philosophy of the Human Sciences,* P. A. French, T. E. Uehling Jr., and H. K.

Wettstein, eds. (Notre Dame: University of Notre Dame Press, 1990); reprinted in Gilbert, 1996. On group belief: Gilbert, "Remarks"; Gilbert, Margaret, "Modelling Collective Belief," *Synthese,* 73 (1987), 185–204.

49. See especially Hart, *Concept of Law,* 56–57.

50. Hart, *Concept of Law,* 57.

51. Hart, *Concept of Law,* 56.

52. I believe this also applies to Hart's more recent discussion of the authority of a "commander" in Hart, H. L. A., *Essays on Bentham: Studies in Jurisprudence and Political Theory* (Oxford: Clarendon Press, 1982).

53. Some would dispute the viability of any "imperative theory of norms"; in other words, they would question the assumption at issue in the text above. See Raz, *Practical Reason,* 51. I believe, however, that it can be made good. See section 5 (iii) below.

54. Hart, *Concept of Law,* 56.

55. Hart's inclination to draw a distinction between social rules that are "rules of obligation" and others may stem from his connecting at one point the notion of "bindingness" with the terms "obligation" and "duty." These can have strong moral overtones. Then, of course, it will be not just odd but wrong to claim that, for example, one has an obligation to say "You were" rather than "You was." Given the model of a group's language for which I have argued in Gilbert, *On Social Facts,* chapter 3, there *is* a sense in which the speaker of such a language is "bound" to say, for example, "You were" rather than "You was." But this is not the matter of moral obligation. This seems true to the way things are perceived. One who is learning English may have a feeling of "compulsion" with respect to saying "You were." He won't think of this as a moral obligation or as something he can't help doing, a compulsion in that sense. Rather, it may be something he finds difficult to do but knows that (as an English speaker) he is bound to do.

56. Cf. Gilbert, *On Social Facts,* chapter 3, where I argue that to criticize an intuitive doctrine as "mysterious" is nothing like the presentation of a knockdown argument against it.

57. I continue to explore the details of this concept. Some further references are given in subsequent notes.

58. Gilbert, *On Social Facts,* 405.

59. This discussion is inevitably somewhat rough. For my initial, quite lengthy introduction of this concept see Gilbert, *On Social Facts,* especially chapters 4 and 7. I have explored this idea further in subsequent writings, many of which are collected together in Gilbert, *Living Together: Rationality, Sociality, and Obligation* (Lanham, Md.: Rowman and Littlefield, 1996). See also the introduction to that book.

60. What of a father who says to his daughter "I've decided that you'll go to college"? If the daughter is not thereby committed, she does not (failing some other relevant commitment on her part) violate any commitment by failing to go to college. She does prevent the fulfillment of her father's commitment, but that is another matter.

61. I connect use of the pronoun "we" and joint commitment in Gilbert, *On Social Facts,* chapter 4. See also chapter 7.

62. See Gilbert, "Modelling"; *On Social Facts,* chapter 5; "Remarks"; Gilbert, "Durkheim and Social Facts," in *Debating Durkheim,* W. S. F. Pickering and H. Martins, eds. (London: Routledge, 1994). See also the introduction to *Living Together.* I originally wrote of "accepting as a body" in this context. "Accepting" is one synonym of "believing," and I see no obvious reason not to take it in that sense here.

63. First in Gilbert, *On Social Facts*.

64. "Openly" here is a rough way of indicating the relevant context. Something like "common knowledge" in the sense of Lewis, *Convention*, would seem to be a requirement. See Gilbert, *On Social Facts*, chapter 4, on how plural subjects are formed.

65. This is by no means a full discussion of this type of case. For further discussion of joint commitment in large groups see Gilbert, *On Social Facts*, especially 212–213; Gilbert, "Group Membership and Political Obligation," *Monist*, 76, no. 1 (1993), 119–133; reprinted in Gilbert, *Living Together*; Gilbert, "Remarks"; Gilbert, "Reconsidering the 'Actual Contract' Theory of Political Obligation," *Ethics* (1999).

66. See also Gilbert, "Agreements, Coercion, and Obligation," *Ethics*, 103, no. 4 (1993), 679–706; reprinted with amendments in Gilbert, *Living Together*; Gilbert, "Obligation and Joint Commitment," *Utilitas* 11, (1999), 143–163.

67. Hart, writing on rights, explains our talk of rights in connection with promises in terms of the promisee's having the "power to release" the promisor. Thus our intuitions in this matter have some affinity. I ground this power of release in an underlying joint commitment; Hart does not. See Hart, H. L. A., "Are There any Natural Rights?" *Philosophical Review*, 64 (1955), 175–191. On promising as a joint commitment phenomenon see Gilbert, "Is an Agreement an Exchange of Promises?" *Journal of Philosophy*, 90, no. 12 (1993), 627–649; reprinted with revisions in Gilbert, *Living Together*.

68. This is not the place to argue this, but see Gilbert, "Agreements," and Gilbert, "Is an Agreement?"

69. See Gilbert, "Agreements."

70. Cf. Gilbert, *On Social Facts*, 405. Here "members of P are" replaces "one is."

71. In Gilbert, *On Social Facts*, I stipulated that "to accept a principle of the form 'do A in C' is to subject oneself to it" in discussing social convention. In the subsequent (and intendedly derivative) discussion of social rules, I wrote of "accepting that one is to do A in C," which formulation perhaps makes it less clear that this is a matter of imposing or issuing a requirement.

72. See Gilbert, *On Social Facts*, chapter 6.

73. Sartorius, "Concept of Law," 51, argues that "contrary to what seems to be a virtually universal assumption among philosophers, it makes perfect sense to speak of a social rule as existing in a community" in which it is not generally conformed to. In his "Comment" on Sartorius, John Finnis agrees (66 n53). Finnis, John, "Comment," in *Issues in Contemporary Legal Philosophy: The Influence of H. L. A. Hart,* Ruth Gavison, ed. (Oxford: Clarendon Press, 1987), 62–75. The issue is discussed at some length by Hanina Ben-Menachem in her "Comment" on Sartorius. See also Woozley, A. D., "The Existence of Rules," *Nous,* 1 (1967) 63–79. For a related discussion of social convention in which I argue contra David Lewis that regular conformity is not a requirement, see Gilbert, *On Social Facts*, chapter 6 and elsewhere.

74. If the plural subject account of social rules is correct, it explains, in effect, how "customary rules can be regarded as imperatives issued by a society to itself," thus constituting a version of the "imperative theory of norms." The quoted words are from Raz, *Practical Reason*, 51, who there assumes the falsity of the imperative theory. This account also shows how it can be that, in Woozley's terms, "a social rule is a rule to the extent that it has the authority of society behind it." Woozley, "Existence of Rules," 72.

75. See Gilbert, *On Social Facts*, especially chapter 4.

76. Cf. Emile Durkheim, "This sui generis synthesis, which constitutes every society,"

The Rules of Sociological Method, orig. 1895. Many others might be quoted to the same effect.

77. Cf. Cotterrell, *Law's Community*, 226: "If [in the work of Hart and others with the 'imperium' conception of law] legal authority is no longer traced back to a sovereign it is still not traced to a community—to the social group as an entity whose values provide law's foundation." This citation is not intended to imply that the account of social rules I present here invokes a notion of a community's *values* specifically.

78. Cf. Hart, *Concept of Law*, 11.

79. Hart, *Concept of Law*, 11–12. John Mackie makes a similar (skeptical) characterization of the everyday conception of the way morality is grounded, which he sees as an obvious error. How can anything that is "intrinsically action guiding" be a part of the "furniture of the world"? See Mackie, John, *Ethics: Inventing Right and Wrong* (Harmondsworth, New York: Penguin, 1977).

80. See Gilbert, *On Social Facts*, chapter 4, for a lengthy discussion of the first person plural pronoun and its relationship to plural subjects. See also chapter 7 on inferences from premises of the form "We are doing such-and-such."

81. Section 2.

6

Reconsidering the "Actual Contract" Theory of Political Obligation

Many people take themselves to have certain obligations by virtue of the fact that a given country is *their* country. These are obligations, roughly, to uphold (as best one can) the institutions of the country in question. How might such a sense of things be interpreted, and how reasonable and accurate could it be? Actual contract theory answers these questions in terms of participation in an agreement. Philosophers now standardly assume that this theory must be rejected. Two reasons in particular are commonly cited, the "no agreement" objection and the "not morally binding" objection. Drawing on my account of social groups as *plural subjects* and my account of agreements in plural subject terms, I argue that there is more to be said for actual contract theory than has been thought. The "not morally binding" objection is not conclusive. As for the "no agreement" objection, though actual contract theory succumbs, a closely related plural subject theory of political obligation does not. Actual contract theory is a special case of plural subject theory. If actual contract theory is rejected, plural subject theory should be explored in its stead. Plural subject theory may be the truth in actual contract theory.

1. INTRODUCTION

a. A Sense of Political Obligation

If you cannot persuade your country, you must do whatever it orders.

Thus say the laws of Athens in Plato's imaginary speech.[1] I take it that an analogous understanding is common. More particularly, many people take

97

themselves to have certain *obligations* by virtue of the fact that a certain country is *their* country.[2]

A variety of specific obligations may be involved, ranging from buying a television license and paying income tax to participating in military operations. We may characterize them in general terms as obligations to uphold (as best one can) the political institutions of the country in question.[3] For present purposes, I shall call obligations *with this source and content* "political obligations."

I do not assume that the "sense of obligation" in question is well articulated. And while I take it that "obligation" is an appropriate term with which to capture the sense in question, I take it to be a significant task to specify carefully what "obligations" amount to in this context.

I do not say that people who take themselves to have political obligations always fulfill them. Some degree of uneasiness, however, is likely to accompany their defaults.

Is their sense of things justified? For present purposes, I shall call a theory a "theory of political obligation" if it addresses this question.[4]

b. Some Desiderata for a Theory of Political Obligation

The question calls for three related inquiries. One is interpretive or analytic. How is the understanding that there are political obligations to be interpreted? In particular, what precisely are obligations or obligations of the type in question? Then there are two inquiries relating to justification broadly speaking. One has to do with *epistemic warrant* or *reasonableness*. Is the understanding in question reasonable given the evidence available to those concerned? The other has to do with *truth* or *accuracy*: Do people actually have the political obligations they take themselves to have? A successful theory of political obligation should give convincing answers to these interrelated questions.[5]

Ideally the theory would provide a unique interpretation for the prevalent sense of political obligation such that it was both reasonable and accurate. Theories that deny reasonableness and accuracy are likely to be that much less satisfying—given that the sense of political obligation is well entrenched.[6] That is not to say that the most successful theory of political obligation may not be of this sort. The most successful theory will then simply not be as satisfying as a theory could be.

As for uniqueness, it would be most satisfying were a theory to provide an interpretation it was plausible to ascribe to all those who took themselves to have political obligations. At least on the surface, these people think the same thing, albeit in circumstances that may vary in significant respects.

c. Actual Contract Theory

In his well-known book *Moral Principles and Political Obligations,* A. John Simmons argues that the widespread sense of being politically obligated is inaccurate. Simmons reaches this conclusion through a thorough examination of a number of philosophical arguments.

An important target of Simmons and many other writers on political obligation is the argument that constitutes the hub of what I shall call the "actual contract" theory of political obligation.[7] According to this argument, to be a member of a (political) society is to be party to an agreement to uphold a particular set of political institutions. Members of any political society are therefore obligated to uphold a particular set of political institutions, those of the society whose members they are. People are obligated, then, to uphold the political institutions of their own political society or country.[8] They are not similarly obligated with respect to other countries.[9]

Actual contract theory claims that those who take themselves to have political obligations are right. They have such obligations, founded in the agreement that makes a particular country *their* country.

2. STANDARD OBJECTIONS TO ACTUAL CONTRACT THEORY

There is a standard package of objections to (actual) contract theory. Perhaps the most popular and telling objection is this: those who take themselves to have political obligations have *not* generally agreed to uphold any political institutions. The truth of this objection may seem so obvious as not to need arguing. However, some relatively detailed discussion is in place.

Most of the people in question have certainly not *explicitly* agreed to uphold the relevant political institutions. Have they perhaps *tacitly* agreed? That they have not has been argued as follows. In order that one can properly be said to have tacitly agreed, a certain type of context is necessary. For instance, one has been faced with a proposal, one clearly understands that one's silence will be taken as acceptance of the proposal, and so on. The circumstances in which a person's *silence* or *inaction* can properly be taken as his or her *tacitly agreeing* are strictly limited and are not plausibly taken to exist as required for widespread political obligations.[10]

Sometimes an *implicit* agreement is appealed to when there is neither an explicit agreement nor a tacit agreement according to conditions such as those just mentioned. Indeed, an implicit agreement may be referred to in the absence of anything that would normally count as an agreement strictly speaking.[11] One problem, then, is that it is hard to know what an implicit agreement is supposed to be.

The phrase "implicit agreement"—and related phrases—may be intended to allude to *what people would presumably agree to if asked.* Supposing we accept this construal, it is hard to be sure what normative consequences an implicit agreement has.[12] In any case, we are now talking about hypothetical rather than actual agreements and have moved beyond actual contract theory.[13]

Talk of an "implicit agreement" may not be intended to allude to a hypothetical agreement. It may be intended to suggest that something significantly *like* an agreement, something *actual,* is at issue. This, I suspect, is the correct interpretation of the many references to implicit agreements found in a variety of contexts.[14]

To evaluate the idea that something significantly like an agreement grounds political obligations, we need to clarify a number of things. What relevant phenomenon is significantly like an agreement, and in what respect is it significantly like one? Discussion later in this paper will be pertinent to this issue. For now, we may rest with the obvious point that if so-called implicit agreements are either hypothetical agreements or *not* agreements proper, appealing to them takes us beyond actual contract theory.

The objection to actual contract theory that no relevant agreement can plausibly be said to exist in most political societies—the "no agreement" objection—has obvious force. As we have seen, in its fullest form it goes beyond the indisputable claim that in actual circumstances there has been no relevant explicit agreement to address appeals to "tacit" agreements and "implicit" agreements.

In addition, there is a class of objections to the effect that either the circumstances or the content of most agreements of the relevant sort would—were they to take place—prevent them from being *morally binding.* That is, even if we allowed that relevant agreements were common—contrary to the no agreement objection—such agreements would not, in standard political circumstances, be morally binding. Hence, it is argued, they would not be a source of "political bonds."[15]

The first of these "not morally binding" objections is the most common. It alleges that an agreement to uphold the political institutions of one's country would in standard circumstances be tantamount to an agreement entered into under duress, a coerced agreement. This idea is supported by considerations such as the following. Supposing deportation, imprisonment, or social ostracism to be the expected costs of refusing to agree, these costs would be extraordinarily high for most people. Their lives would be devastated. An agreement entered into in such circumstances would be tantamount to a coerced agreement and would not therefore be morally binding.[16]

A second "not morally binding" objection runs as follows. Many laws and edicts of many states are unjust or immoral. Agreements to uphold the political institutions of such states would not be morally binding, and a sense of moral obligation based on them would be illusory. This objection jibes in spirit with the objection in terms of coercion. I am not sure it can count as a "standard" argument, but it is implicit in much of what is said on the topic of when agreements and promises are morally binding.[17]

The main standard objections to actual contract theory, then, attack the theory on two fronts. One denies the existence of an appropriate agreement. The other argues that either the circumstances or the content of many such agreements would in practice result in their not being morally binding. According to both objections, a widespread feeling of political obligation cannot be justified by appeal to actual agreements.[18]

3. PLURAL SUBJECTS AND JOINT COMMITMENT

I hold no special antecedent brief for the actual contract theory of political obligation. However, I believe more can be said in its favor than is generally thought.

As I shall argue, the "not morally binding" objection is not conclusive. The "no agreement" objection has more bite. Nonetheless, it remains possible that *something closely related to actual contract theory* can constitute a successful theory of political obligation. In support of this idea I shall sketch an alternative theory that has important affinities with actual contract theory. It is proof against both objections.

To do these things I must invoke the concept of what I have elsewhere called a *plural subject*.[19] It will be necessary to characterize plural subjects at some length.

I argued in my book *On Social Facts* that there is a central everyday concept of a social group such that social groups are *plural subjects*.[20] Any plural subject is a social group of sorts. There can be plural subjects of *belief, intention, action, language possession,* and so on.[21]

When is there a plural subject in my sense? Two or more people form a plural subject when they are *jointly committed* to doing something *as a body.* ("Doing something" is to be taken quite broadly. It includes "intending" and "believing," for instance.) I must now say what I mean by "joint commitment."

I first comment briefly on the sense—largely intuitive—in which I am using the term "commitment" here. As I understand it, one who makes a personal decision is thereby subject to a commitment in the relevant sense. To simply be attracted by a certain course of action is not yet to be committed to pursue it.

A *joint* commitment is the commitment *of two or more people.* It is not the sum or aggregate of the independent commitments of the people in question. It is a truly *joint* commitment.

When there is a joint commitment, each of the individual parties to it will indeed be committed—that is, subject to a commitment. We may therefore want to speak of the parties' "individual commitments" in this context. If we do, we must be careful to bear in mind that these "individual" commitments are subject to special constraints.

First, the "individual" commitments in question cannot exist on their own, apart from all other such "individual" commitments. They are not independent or autonomous commitments; this follows from their being severally dependent on a joint commitment.

Second, a given person cannot unilaterally rescind an "individual" commitment of this kind. What must be rescinded is the relevant joint commitment, and the parties to a joint commitment must rescind it together.[22]

How are joint commitments formed? If we look at cases involving a few people who are face-to-face, it seems that what is needed is roughly as follows. Each party openly expresses to the other his or her individual readiness to be jointly committed in a certain way. Thus Joe may ask "Shall we dance?" and Lisa may answer "Yes!" Or Joe may beckon to Lisa from the dance floor, and she may come forward to join him.

That the relevant expressions of individual readiness have been made is *common knowledge* between the parties in something like the sense introduced by David Lewis.[23] Roughly, the fact that the parties have expressed their individual readiness is out in the open between the parties.[24] I shall take it that standardly, when there is common knowledge of some fact, the parties know there is.

Joe and Lisa understand that their joint commitment is in place when and only when it is common knowledge between them that the relevant expressions of readiness have been made. In this way people become jointly committed to dancing together, and so on.[25]

Clearly an *explicit agreement* is not required in order that a joint commitment come into being. The case of Joe beckoning to Lisa and her moving forward in response, for instance, involves no explicit agreement. That case does not appear to invoke a *tacit* agreement either if a tacit agreement is a form of agreement literally speaking. It would not be correct for either party to say to the other, you *agreed*. Without entering any prior agreement, then, Lisa and Joe become jointly committed to dancing together by virtue of what they express to one another: their readiness to be so committed. They thus become the plural subject of dancing together.

In the case of Joe and Lisa the joint commitment is quickly established at a moment of which both are aware, the moment of Lisa's response to Joe. Joint commitments can also arise in a less easily "clockable" fashion. An example of a more gradual process is that of two academic colleagues who, after many ad hoc arrangements, come to understand that they are jointly committed to having dinner together after departmental meetings. This is now established as their rule or practice. That it has become so established may be perfectly clear; precisely when it became so established may be hard to determine.[26]

In cases of the face-to-face type of situation just discussed, one party expresses his or her individual readiness to the other personally. What of a population where many people do not even know of the existence of particular others?[27] An example might be the population consisting of the many inhabitants of a large island.

In such a case, members of the population can express their readiness to be jointly committed in a particular way with the other members—*whoever precisely these may be*. They need not encounter or know of every other member individually to do this. They can openly express their readiness in relation to people they do encounter, perceived not so much as particular individuals but rather as members of the population in question, as fellow islanders for instance.[28] That such expressions have been made throughout the population may become common knowledge there. Informally speaking, it may be out in the open within the population as a whole that this is so.[29]

4. JOINT COMMITMENT AND OBLIGATION

The nature of joint commitment seems to me crucial to our understanding of the notions of an *obligation* and of a *right*. I do not say that all uses of the terms "obligation" and "right" can be interpreted by reference to joint commitment. But I believe an important range of uses can be so interpreted, a range importantly relevant to political obligation.

Let me briefly explain how I see the connection of joint commitment with obligations and rights. More can be said, but I hope the following will be sufficient for present purposes.[30]

Suppose Phyllis is party to a joint commitment with Mark. Phyllis is not in a position to rescind it unilaterally; she and Mark must rescind it together. Now suppose Phyllis acts contrary to the joint commitment. She may well reflect that her act is in some sense *a betrayal of Mark*. It appears, in other words, that *by virtue of his involvement in a joint commitment with Phyllis, and that alone, Mark gains a special standing in relation to Phyllis's actions*, and vice versa.

This standing is apparently a function of the fact that the joint commitment is indeed joint; in violating it, Phyllis violates a commitment of *theirs*. By virtue of the need for them to rescind the commitment together, neither can deprive the other of this standing by simply changing his or her mind.

How might we describe this special standing? It seems natural to describe it thus: *Mark is entitled, or has a right, to Phyllis's conforming action.* Correspondingly, *Phyllis is under an obligation to Mark,* an obligation to conform to the joint commitment.

I believe that in some important contexts in which we speak of "entitlements" or "rights" and "obligations" we are, in fact, responding precisely to the existence of a joint commitment. I will discuss some of the contexts I take to be relevant here later in this chapter.

Continuing the proposed mode of description, the obligations and entitlements at issue here derive from the joint commitment alone: given that Mark and Phyllis have a joint commitment, and irrespective of other considerations, these obligations and entitlements are in place. They may be said to *inhere* in the joint commitment in that once it exists, they exist also.[31]

Someone might object that the obligations and entitlements now in question are obligations and entitlements sui generis. This may be so. We may refer to them as "obligations and entitlements of joint commitment" if this will enable us to keep their particular nature in focus.

To say that one has an obligation of joint commitment is to imply that one is obligated "to" a particular person or persons, as well as obligated "to do" something or other. I have suggested, in effect, that not to fulfill one's obligation here involves what is intuitively a form of betrayal of the person with respect to whom one is obligated.

This case contrasts with some familiar cases in which many people would speak of "obligations." Thus consider the case of Ben, a child who is drowning, and Maisie, a stranger who can easily save the child. Many would find it natural to say that Maisie has an obligation to save Ben.[32]

If Maisie fails to save Ben, has she betrayed him? At best, it is not obviously appropriate to say this. She has *wronged* him, perhaps, but one can surely wrong someone without betraying him or her. A betrayal appears to involve a special type of wrong. One might say that Maisie's connection with Ben is not of the right type to put her in a position to betray him. Relatedly, there is clearly something she has an obligation to do, but it is not clear that she is *obligated to* Ben or any other particular person in having this obligation.[33]

In speaking of the "obligations"—and "rights"—of joint commitment, then, we must be sure to note that these obligations are significantly different in character from another class of so-called obligations, the class into which Maisie's obligation to save Ben falls.[34] In discussion of any question concerning "obligations" and also interpersonal "bonds" or "ties," it is obviously important to consider precisely what we are talking about. In particular, we need to consider whether there is an implicit allusion to a joint commitment.

It is important to stress that the obligations of joint commitment are present just in case a joint commitment is itself present. Thus neither the circumstances nor the content of a joint commitment, given that it exists, affects the presence of its obligations.

With respect to circumstances, someone may object that one surely cannot obligate oneself in the face of coercion. With respect to the obligations of joint commitment, this appears not to be so. Recall that for a joint commitment to be formed it is sufficient, roughly, for the parties to express their personal readiness to be jointly committed. Quite generally, a state of readiness can be created in coercive circumstances. Thus, putting a gun to his head, a gunman may tell Jack to hand over his wallet. Realizing that the consequences of refusing are grave, Jack is now ready to hand over his wallet and could sincerely express such readiness were he called upon to do so.

Similarly, Lisa may now be ready to dance with Joe as a result of threats he has made. She may not want to dance with him, but she is ready to do so. Mutual expressions of readiness may thus lead to the creation of a joint commitment. Obligations of joint commitment necessarily ensue. It must be emphasized that *to say there are obligations (and rights) here is to focus on certain basic aspects of the structure of any joint commitment.* I take this to be one standard way of using these terms, though its precise nature has often been overlooked.

It may be that from a moral point of view a person who has been coerced into entering a joint commitment need not honor the obligations acquired through that commitment, in which case one might wonder why anyone would ever attempt to coerce another person into entering a joint commitment. One reason is that the coerced person's (accurate) sense of obligation through the joint commitment may be what drives her or his subsequent behavior.[35]

Turning to the question of a joint commitment's content, it seems people can become jointly committed to perform what are, in fact, immoral actions, just as one might personally decide to do something that was, in fact, immoral. They will then have obligations of joint commitment to perform immoral actions.

Once again, it may be that from a moral point of view these obligations need not be honored. More strongly, it is probable that they should not be honored, insofar as honoring them involves doing something immoral. This is not to say that they do not exist. If there is a joint commitment, there are obligations and rights of joint commitment.

It may be that, all else being equal, morality requires one to conform to a joint commitment and hence to respect its obligations. Among other things, not to do so would be to default on a commitment, to break an interpersonal bond, to give others grounds for complaint for violated rights, and, in so doing, to ignore a reasonable basis for reliance.

It is of course possible to allow that one is morally required to respect one's obligations of joint commitment, all else being equal, while accepting that in a particular case all else is not equal or, indeed, that further morally relevant considerations lead to the opposite conclusion. In the latter case the joint commitment and its obligations remain, though one is morally required not to respect them.[36]

One of the important places where we talk of obligations is where there are agreements and promises. Indeed, in moral philosophy a classic example of an obligation is the obligation of a promise.

In my view, both agreements and promises involve an underlying joint commitment. I have argued this at length elsewhere and proposed that an agreement is, in effect, a joint decision. More fully, it is a joint commitment to uphold a certain decision as a body.[37]

If this is so, we need not bring in considerations about the possibility of detrimental reliance and the like to conclude that agreements obligate. It will be clear that obligations are inherent in any completed agreement. These are obligations of joint commitment.[38]

5. ACTUAL CONTRACT THEORY RECONSIDERED

If I am right about agreements and about joint commitments, this has some positive implications for the actual contract theory of political obligation. In particular, one of the standard objections—the not morally binding objection—is not conclusive.

According to this objection, coercive circumstances or immoral content prevents an agreement from being *morally binding*. Many relevant agreements would thus not generate moral obligations. Whether or not this is true on some construal, if there is a joint commitment underlying (and intrinsic to) any agreement, then *obligations* of joint commitment *will* be in place *whenever an agreement is made*. The content and circumstances of the agreement will not affect this. Nor will it be plausible to argue that it is impossible to be coerced into entering an agreement or to make an immoral agreement.[39]

Thus even if many relevant agreements would be immoral or, in effect, coerced, a widespread sense of political obligation could relate to the obligations of joint commitment that are intrinsic to agreements and be accurate. As far as *this* sense of obligation was concerned, the not morally binding objection—insofar as it relates to another kind of obligation—would be *beside the point.*

Of course, supposing that, all else being equal, one is morally obligated in some sense to abide by obligations of joint commitment, it would be relevant to one's situation overall if the existence of coercive circumstances, say, meant that all else was not equal. Obviously, too, were one morally obligated, all things considered, *not* to fulfill one's obligations of joint commitment, that would be highly significant from a practical point of view. Nonetheless, the obligations of joint commitment would stand, together with the relevant type of answerability to the other parties. One's "sense of obligation" would still have a genuine basis.

What of the other standard objection to actual contract theory, the no agreement objection? This objection seems well taken. A widespread sense of political obligation could surely not be justified in the world as it is if interpreted in terms of a presumed agreement, explicit or tacit. It is surely somewhat implausible, indeed, so to *interpret* any such sense or feeling.

If we turn away from actual contract theory at this point, we should not turn too far. Actual contract theory may be on to something, albeit not a foundational *agreement*. As I suggested earlier, obscure appeals to an "implicit agreement" may be meant to allude to something importantly *like* or *akin to* an agreement, albeit *not* an actual agreement. This possibility should be investigated.

As I understand it, people who made an explicit agreement to uphold certain political institutions would produce a joint commitment with a specific type of content. That is, they would become jointly committed to uphold as a body the institutions in question. Whenever and only whenever there is a *joint commitment* with this content, there is something that generates appropriate obligations of the same type.

This suggests that we should consider the merits of a plural subject theory of political obligation. Actual contract theory is a special case of plural subject theory. It would be too hasty to abandon the general theory because we must abandon the special case.[40]

6. THE PLURAL SUBJECT THEORY OF POLITICAL OBLIGATION

Now we have some new questions. Can a widespread sense of political obligation be interpreted in terms of membership in a plural subject with an appropriate underlying joint commitment? Can a widespread sense of political obligation be justified given this interpretation? The following points are intended only to make a start in answering these questions. I cannot attempt a full answer here.

a. Considerations on the First Person Plural Pronoun

I begin with some observations on the first person plural pronoun, together with the corresponding pronominal adjective. I focus here on the English version. What I say will apply outside English-speaking populations wherever there are terms for which similar observations can be made.

Consider the pronoun "we." It is clear that people can be sensitive about its use. Jill may, for instance, take umbrage at Jack's question "Shall we go for a walk?" though she would not be concerned about "Would you like to go for a walk (with me)," "Do you feel like a walk," and the like.[41]

One explanation of such sensitivity is that "we" has spontaneously been interpreted as implying the existence of an established plural subject of the relevant sort when, according to the hearer, there is no such plural subject.[42] On the basis of such considerations, I argued in chapter 4 of *On Social Facts* that there is a central sense of "we" in which its proper referent is a plural subject.[43] I shall call this the *plural subject sense* of "we" and related terms. There is a variety of possible uses of "we" in the plural subject sense, as the following rough discussion shows.

If Jack uses "we" in the plural subject sense when the relevant plural subject does not exist, his use of "we" may be *tendentious.* He speaks as if the relevant plural subject exists, knowing it does not but hoping thereby to bring it into existence. He may assume that Jill will understand his use of "we" to be tendentious; she knows she has *not* yet expressed her readiness to be a member of the relevant plural subject. She may nevertheless decide to endorse it, thereby expressing such readiness. A plural subject will then have been brought into being by the conjunction of a tendentious with a complementary, endorsing use or acceptance of "we."

Rather than using "we" tendentiously, Jack may be using it in an *initiatory* manner. He does not mean to imply that the relevant plural subject exists but means only to express his own readiness to form one, thereby starting the process of plural subject formation. He is using "we" tentatively. Jack's initiatory "we" may be met (as intended) with a complementary closing "we" (or "us") on Jill's part, as in "Yes, let's." Jill's expression of readiness to be jointly committed establishes the joint commitment. Her closing "we" may be seen as having a double character: it both brings the relevant plural subject into being and uses "we" to refer to it.[44]

The case of Jack and Jill involves only two people. Where more than two people are involved, more than one person's matching use will be needed to complement a given tendentious or initiatory "we."

Many uses of "we" in the plural subject sense will be neither tendentious nor initiatory, and they will not be complements of these uses. They will be straightforward uses of "we" that refer to an established plural subject. Such a subject may have been established as a result of the relevant tendentious or initiatory uses of "we" being matched by their complements in conditions of common knowledge. Another possibility is one or more straightforward uses that for some reason wrongly suppose there to be an established plural subject. As long as these are "met" by the appropriate others, the relevant plural subject will be brought into being.

b. Interpretation

Consider now the question of interpretation. Can a widespread sense of political obligation be interpreted in terms of an appropriate joint commitment? It appears that it can.

Recall the datum with which I started: many people take themselves to have certain obligations by virtue of the fact that a given country is *their* country. They believe they are obligated to uphold (as best they can) a certain set of political institutions, the institutions of the country they regard as *theirs*.

Can this belief be interpreted in terms of the believers' membership in a plural subject? Clearly, *the datum that provokes the question itself suggests a positive answer.* Such an interpretation is perfectly natural given that the relevant people refer to their country as "ours." And given such an interpretation, their understanding that they are obligated makes perfect sense.

If this country is indeed *theirs* in the sense of being constituted by a joint commitment to which they are party, their understanding will indeed be correct. A joint commitment to uphold as a body a certain set of political institutions, for instance, would constitute a "political society" and a country in that sense.

c. Justification

How is the *reasonableness* of their understanding to be assessed? Let me return to the pronoun "we." There is some reason to see the plural subject reading of statements about "us" as the one that is understood to be appropriate in the absence of any special indications to the contrary. Let us assume this is so. Let us also assume, as is plausible, that the natural reading of "our country" in the plural subject sense is something like "the country whose political institutions we are jointly committed to uphold together." The natural plural subject reading of "our constitution," "our government," and "our laws" will be similar.[45]

Suppose now that it is common knowledge in a given population that in conversations, letters, and so on, everyone has intentionally and openly spoken of "our country," "our country's actions," and so on. They have spoken, more specifically, of "our constitution," "our government," "our laws." And they speak of "we" and "us" with reference to the population as a whole. They have done this without indicating that they do not wish the plural subject reading to be made.

At this point the members of the population have good reason to suppose themselves to be party to the relevant joint commitments. As is common knowledge in the population, they have all, in effect, intentionally expressed their readiness to be jointly committed in the relevant way.[46]

This may initially have been done through tendentious or initiatory or mistaken uses of "our country," and so on, but once it is common knowledge that such readiness has been expressed in *these* ways there is a foundation for everyone to use "our country" and the rest straightforwardly, referring to what is understood to be an established plural subject.

Even if we do not assume that the plural subject interpretation of "we" is the default interpretation, that a widespread use of "our country" and so on is generally intended in the plural subject sense may be supported by a variety of particular observations. That it is so supported may itself be common knowledge in a population.

For example, one member of the population may say to another "Hey! That's against the law!" in a way expressive of a complex of understandings including (1) a sense that the speaker has been in some sense offended against, (2) an entitlement to intervene, and (3) an understanding that the other will recognize this entitlement. These understandings suggest that the speaker takes there to be a corresponding joint commitment to which both members of the population are subject. The person addressed may accept what is expressed without demur, thereby suggesting that the assumption of a corresponding joint commitment is common ground.[47]

Such minute interactions—occurring on a large scale—will both confirm the plural subject interpretation of phrases and statements about "our country," and so on, and count independently as expressions of readiness to be jointly committed in the relevant way. If there is common knowledge in the population that everyone has so expressed themselves, any particular members of the population would have good reason to suppose themselves to be parties to a relevant joint commitment with other members of the population.

People will be reasonable to believe themselves jointly committed in the relevant way if these conditions or conditions approximating them obtain. Whether they are reasonable to hold this belief in a given case is an empirical matter. Whether the belief is indeed accurate in particular cases is also an empirical matter.

d. "Voluntarism"

If all this is right, it is going to be extremely significant from the point of view of understanding political behavior. The prevalence of the first person plural in the rhetoric of politicians suggests that this is well understood, at least at the pretheoretical level.

Mention of political rhetoric may raise a doubt in connection with the significance of the widespread use of such phrases as "our government," "our country," and so on, albeit in the plural subject sense. Aren't people induced to talk this way through such powerful influences as the example of parents and teachers, political rhetoric, and more general social pressure? If someone talks this way as a result, how can that amount to anything as consequential as an expression of readiness to be party to a joint commitment?[48]

Precisely how particular people come to refer to a certain country as "ours" or a particular group as "we" in the plural subject sense is one thing. What they mean when they do so refer is another. Impressed or enthused by political rhetoric, feeling the pressure of others' desire, one may express one's readiness to be jointly committed with a use of "we" in the plural subject sense. To use "we" in this sense *is* to express such readiness. One might balk at doing so, but one might not. And one might go ahead and do it anyway.[49] The option of participating in a particular plural subject may be greeted with any of a wide variety of emotions from joy to hesitation to revulsion—which may or may not be decisive with respect to what one ends up doing.

The plural subject theory of political obligation is evidently not a robustly voluntarist theory. It allows that in principle one can accrue political obligations in conditions involving strong pressure, even in conditions reasonably deemed coercive. According to the theory, then, one's being obligated is not necessarily a function of an act that is voluntary in the sense of being uncoerced.

In what sense, if any, *is* plural subject theory a voluntarist theory? If at least an endorsing or closing "we"—or other expression of readiness to be jointly committed—is needed, then one's being obligated depends in part on *one's intentionally obligating oneself.* The voluntarist nature of plural subject theory (in this sense) distinguishes it from several other theories including those that do not require one to act in any particular way, such as the theory that your political obligations are wholly determined by the context of your birth or the theory that one is obligated to obey just institutions.[50] It also distinguishes it from theories that require intentional acts, voluntary or not, but do not require an intention to obligate oneself. These include some theories that appeal to fair play or considerations of gratitude. Perhaps plural subject theory would best be referred to as intentionalist rather than voluntarist theory.

e. What Is Lost and What Is Gained by Not Invoking Agreements

Some may feel one should only be able to incur political obligations by an act—perhaps an intentionally obligating act—that is voluntary in the sense of uncoerced. This requirement would not speak in favor of actual contract theory as opposed to plural subject theory, insofar as agreements, like joint commitments in general, can be entered into in coercive conditions.

In any case, though it might be a good thing if political obligations could only be incurred through an uncoerced act, a theory of political obligation as characterized here has no obvious need to assume this is so. Such a theory focuses on a sense of obligation that many people have. The precise source of this sense is not given in advance. In particular, it is not given in advance that the source must involve an uncoerced act.

Supposing that agreements can be coerced, is there still some reason for preferring agreement-based political obligations to obligations accrued through the formation of an appropriate plural subject but without the formation of an agreement? One possible reason here concerns what might be called "premeditation."

Consider first a case that has nothing to do with agreements. On a certain morning Peter may simply get out of bed at six o'clock for no particular reason. Alternatively, he may decide the day before that he will get up at six the following morning, and at six o'clock that morning he may get up in order to conform to his decision. His getting out of bed in the latter case is premeditated: *he thought about it, indeed, resolved to do it, before he actually did it,* and he did it because he had previously resolved to do it.

Acts—including joint acts—undertaken as the result of an agreement are also premeditated. Agreements, like decisions, involve a kind of distance from the acts they require. Suppose that, according to arguments I have made elsewhere, agreements are *joint* decisions.[51] To agree to support this constitution together is, on this view, to enter a joint commitment to uphold (as a body) the decision to support the constitution together. Our fundamental joint commitment is thus not to support the constitution together but to uphold a certain decision: the decision to support the constitution together.

Given the agreement, we are entitled to think of ourselves as jointly committed to supporting the constitution together. We may now properly speak of "our constitution," implying an underlying plural subject. Thus each of us is now obligated to act in ways supportive of the constitution. An agreement, then, is a means of introducing a degree of explicitness and premeditation into the process by which political obligations of joint commitment are generated.

What is so good about premeditation? It may be argued to be a condition of actions that are "free" in an important sense. When Peter acts so as to conform to his personal decisions, he may then be said to act freely in the sense of acting in the light of his own prior demands (as opposed to those of anyone else).[52] Similarly, if Peter acts so as to conform to an agreement he has made with Betty, he acts freely in the sense that he acts in the light of a prior demand that *they* have made: and he is one of them. If you like, he is one of the "joint authors" of the demand. Acts of conformity to agreements are, in the relevant sense, self-directed.[53]

Agreement-based political obligations may, then, appear to be preferable because of the "premeditative" quality of agreements and the consequently "self-directed" nature of the relevant conforming actions. Only in this way, one may think, can political obligations be incurred in an appropriate manner.[54]

It might be a good thing if political obligations could only be incurred in a premeditated way. A theory of political obligation as characterized here, however, has no obvious need to assume this is so. It is not given in advance that the source of political obligations involves some form of premeditation. It is not even given in advance that such obligations must be incurred through the agency of those obligated, as the obligations of plural subjecthood are.

Some may feel it is a point in favor of plural subject theory, as opposed to actual contract theory, that according to the former political obligations can be incurred without premeditation. It is in this way more realistic about the processes of socialization and (as one might put it) the processes of politicization.

Note that it is not obvious that coming to use the pronoun "we" correctly in the plural subject sense presupposes prior mastery of the pronoun "I."[55] Thus plural subject theory does not obviously require self-consciousness or striving conceived of as personal to precede the understanding that one is a group member.

7. FROM ACTUAL CONTRACT THEORY TO PLURAL SUBJECT THEORY

Recall the desiderata proposed for a theory of political obligation at the outset of this discussion. Such a theory should provide a plausible interpretation of a particular understanding many people have—the understanding that they have certain obligations by virtue of the fact that a certain country is *their* country. Ideally, the interpretation should be such that it is plausible for all of those with the understanding in question. The understanding should be reasonable in the light of the available evidence and, indeed, correct.

According to standard objections to actual contract theory, it is a poor candidate theory. Most people have not entered any relevant agreement—and most people are unlikely to think they have. Thus the theory fails in relation to interpretation. In addition, even if people had made such an agreement, they would not thereby obligate themselves in standard political circumstances. Were they rightly to think they had *agreed,* their belief that they had political obligations would still not be justified.

In relation to the second—not morally binding—objection, I have argued that the obligations of agreement are obligations of joint commitment. Had most people agreed, in standard political circumstances they *would* be obligated in the way agreements standardly obligate.

The no agreement objection is more serious. It justifies rejecting actual contract theory if this is characterized in terms of regular agreements. It could perhaps be differently characterized: in terms of *agreements or whatever process might generate obligations of the same type.* If it were so characterized it would, in effect, become plural subject theory—given my understanding of agreements and the obligations of agreements.

If we stick with the characterization of actual contract theory in terms of regular agreements, then though we may reasonably reject it outright we should not ignore the fact that there is a theory with strong affinities to it—namely, plural subject theory—that avoids the no agreement objection.

An objection analogous to the no agreement objection could, of course, be formulated for plural subject theory. In most cases, it may be said, one is not party to a relevant joint commitment. But this is less easy to argue. The relevant facts, by their nature, cannot be determined so easily or in so superficial a manner.

It is on the face of it plausible to suppose that many of those who view a certain country as *ours* thereby understand themselves to be jointly committed with relevant others in a certain way. This would accord with a standard use of the pronominal adjective to refer to a plural subject. It would also help to explain why many people take themselves to have certain obligations by virtue of the fact that the country in question is their country.

A plural subject theory of political obligation, then, has some hope of giving a plausible interpretation or analysis of a widespread sense of political obligation. I do not argue that any actual set of people is, in fact, politically obligated in the way proposed. However, the more widely expressed in a given population a sense of such obligation is, the more plausible it is to take it to be justified, in terms of both epistemic warrant and accuracy. If there is indeed a widespread *sense of political obligation,* it may well be that there is about as much political obligation as there is felt to be.

It has not been my intention fully to elaborate or defend plural subject theory here. Rather, I have meant to argue for a reorientation of concern for actual contract theory in the direction of the more general theory, a theory that avoids both of the two standard objections to actual contract theory on which I have focused here.

8. CONCLUSION

Plural subject theory argues that insofar as membership in a political society is membership in a plural subject of a particular kind, then obligations (of a specified sort) do attach to membership in a political society. These are obligations of joint commitment.

Standardly, the philosophical problem of political obligation has been posed in terms of "moral obligations" or "moral bonds." Are political obligations of joint commitment moral obligations? This depends on how "moral obligation" is defined, which is something of a contentious matter.

According to the Lockean tradition in actual contract theory, moral obligations do not arise through agreements created in coercive conditions or with immoral content. In that case, political obligations of joint commitment are not moral obligations in the sense of the Lockean tradition. Nonetheless, their foundation is something that is, in my view, deeply akin to an agreement. In this important way my approach is concordant with the Lockean tradition.

One could define "moral obligation" as, or as including, "obligation one is, all equal, morally required to fulfill." Given that definition, political obligations of joint commitment may well be moral obligations.

It is important to note that, in any case, they have immediate implications for practical reasoning and motivation.[56] If citizens are obligated to one another through a joint commitment, they are subject to a commitment to do something, for instance, to uphold certain political institutions together.[57] This commitment will be in place pending the concurrence of the parties to it. One who violates the commitment offends against others, and these now have the standing to seek redress. Thus a joint commitment to uphold political institutions of joint commitment inherently involves practically significant "political bonds."

Irrespective of the specific questions of this chapter, one may reasonably inquire into the conditions under which someone is morally required, all things considered, to support and uphold the political institutions of his or her own country in particular. If this question is interpreted in terms of membership in the plural subject sense (which may often be the case in practice, if not in the context of contemporary philosophical discussion), then one will be led to ask a number of questions about the fulfillment and violation of the relevant existing joint commitments and their inherent obligations and rights. How important is it from a moral point of view to fulfill these obligations? When and why is it morally permissible to violate them? Is it ever morally obligatory to violate them, and if so, when?

These questions demand careful discussion. The claim that coerced agreements are not morally binding can be seen to belong here, amounting in effect to the claim that it is morally permissible to violate the obligations of an agreement, or joint commitment, one has entered in coercive conditions. The same goes for the claim that an agreement to do something immoral is not morally binding. Most would agree that it is morally obligatory *not* to fulfill obligations of agreement, or joint commitment, when such fulfillment would have horrendous consequences. The opposite position is liable, evidently, to have terrible results.

The claims just addressed, if true, do not imply that the obligations of joint commitment disappear in the circumstances noted. These obligations remain, for they are in a sense part of or intrinsic to the commitment. I take this to be important and also *interpretively* helpful, insofar as a "sense of obligation" may remain even in circumstances where there are strong moral reasons for deviating from the commitment, and these are recognized.

There are other important moral questions relating to joint commitments, including the following. Suppose that those living on a certain island, the "residents," contain some members who are self-styled "anarchists." The residents who are not anarchists are party to a joint commitment to support certain political institutions. The anarchists are "holdouts." They refuse to become parties to the joint commitment. What are their moral obligations, if any, in relation to the political institutions in question? Do they, all else being equal, have a moral obligation to *become* parties to the sustaining joint commitment, albeit reluctantly? Do they at least have a moral obligation to *support and comply with* the institutions in question? Is it morally permissible for them to be punished for not doing so, given that they remain holdouts?

Again, when are members of a given population morally obligated jointly to decide to set up and support a system of political institutions? Are they morally obligated to set up a particular type of system, for instance, a democratic one? Are some types of system morally proscribed?

As I have just indicated, the questions of political obligation at issue in this paper, beginning with the interpretive question, tie in with many other questions, some of which may also be referred to as "problems of political obligation." At the same time, they need to be distinguished from them. Unless this is done, the overall terrain of political obligation will remain muddy.

It could be that actual contract theory is close to the right answer to the interpretive question and hence to one important set of questions about political obligation. Other theories may answer other questions. If so, that does not detract from the interest and importance of actual contract theory or the theory I propose as its more promising successor, plural subject theory.

NOTES

This paper is one of a series of studies toward a projected monograph on political obligation. Versions of the material in this paper were presented to members of the Philosophy Program, the Graduate Center, CUNY; to the New Jersey Regional Philosophical Association; and to the American Philosophical Association Eastern Division in 1995 and to the Individual and Community conference, London University, and Reading University Philosophy Department in 1997. Thanks for probing comments to Virginia Held, Arthur Kuflik, and Jonathan Wolff, the official commentators on my APA, New Jersey, and London presentations, respectively, and to members of the various audiences for productive discussions. Thanks to Andrew Mason and Thomas Pink for further extended discussion and to A. John Simmons for his supportive interest in my work. The referees for and editors of *Ethics* made helpful comments and suggestions. Work on the penultimate version of the paper was completed while I was a visiting professor at King's College London in 1997, on leave from the University of Connecticut, Storrs. I am grateful to both institutions for their encouragement of my research.

1. Plato, *Crito, The Collective Dialogues,*E. Hamilton and H. Cairns, eds. (Princeton: Princeton University Press, 1978), 51b. Crito 51b.

2. Cf. A. J. Simmons, *Moral Principles and Political Obligations* (Princeton: Prince-

ton University Press, 1979), 3–4. See also George Klosko, *The Principle of Fairness and Political Obligation* (Lanham, Md.: Rowman and Littlefield, 1992), 5.

3. Cf. Simmons, *Moral Principles,* 5.

4. Cf. Simmons, *Moral Principles,* 3–4. The starting point for Simmons's investigations in his book is a widespread sense of political obligation seen as involving a special tie to one's own government. I take this way of initiating the discussion of political obligation from him.

5. The "method of discovery" for a theory of political obligation in this sense may start with an argument to the effect that people have political obligations and then derive its interpretive aspect from that argument: people will be said to take themselves to be obligated in the sense that they are (according to the argument) in fact obligated. There is nothing wrong with this procedure. However, a constraint on the adequacy of the theory as a whole will be the plausibility of this particular interpretation.

6. In his discussion of political obligation, Simmons focuses on the question of accuracy: Do people have the political obligations they take themselves to have? He answers "no," and one is likely to infer from what he writes that it is only errors and confusions that allow anyone to think otherwise.

7. I use the term "contract" in deference to an established use of the phrase "contract theory" that does not specifically allude to contracts in law as opposed to agreements of an everyday sort. The theory I discuss invokes an "actual" contract as opposed to a hypothetical one. The most famous contemporary invocation of a hypothetical contract is that of John Rawls, *A Theory of Justice* (Cambridge, Mass.: Harvard University Press, 1971). There will surely be variants of actual contract theory as that is characterized here. I take the following to characterize the most general theory of political obligation for which the label is clearly apposite.

8. I here assume that to have a country is to be the member of (at least one) political society: one's country is the (or a) political society of which one is a member. The terms "political society" and "country" are both somewhat vague, and I shall not attempt to make them more precise for present purposes.

9. Insofar as one could be a member of more than one political society, one would presumably be obligated to uphold the political institution of each society of which one was a member. Clearly there would then be at least the potentiality for conflicting obligations. I shall not consider this possibility further here.

10. This summary follows Simmons, *Moral Principles,* 79–82, on "tacit consent."

11. Cf. Simmons on the distinction between acts that are "signs of consent" and acts that "imply consent"; *Moral Principles,* 88ff, which I echo to some extent in the text here. I have some criticisms of the details of Simmons's discussion. In particular, his "joining a game of baseball" example seems to me to involve a member of the family to which agreements belong, albeit not an explicit agreement. The ground of the ensuing obligation is thus of a piece with the ground of the obligations of agreements proper. This is to dispute Simmons's suggestion as to how obligations would best be argued for in relation to that example (*Moral Principles*, 89). The above remark should be less obscure by the end of this chapter.

12. A similar point was made by Ronald Dworkin in relation to Rawls's appeal to what would be agreed to in Rawls's "original position." See Ronald Dworkin, "The Original Position," in *Reading Rawls*, N. Daniels, ed. (Oxford: Blackwell, 1975), 18. On Rawls's hypothetical contract see also the next note.

13. The "hypothetical" contract here appears less hypothetical in a sense than the Rawlsian contract, where both the situation of the contractors and the agreement itself are hypothetical: *were* people in the original position, and *were* a certain agreement proposed to them, they *would* enter that agreement. The idea here is rather that people are *actually* in a certain situation (they obey the laws, for instance), and *were* a certain agreement proposed to them they *would* enter that agreement. The situation of the people in question, in other words, is not different from the situation in which they would agree. They may simply not have contemplated entering the relevant agreement.

14. Such references are found in contexts other than purely philosophical ones. In theories of the family found in the literature of family therapy, for instance, the terms "agreement" and "contract" are often brought into play with (or without) one or more of a set of related prefixes ("implicit," "unstated," "unconscious"), where it is clear that neither explicit agreements nor tacit agreements of the sort Simmons suggests conditions for are what is at issue.

15. In discussing political obligations Simmons also speaks, as if equivalently, of "political bonds" and "ties."

16. Cf. A. J. Simmons, "Consent, Free Choice, and Democratic Governments," *Georgia Law Review,* 18 (1984), esp. 809–817. See also Simmons, *Moral Principles,* 77–78 ("consent must be given voluntarily"). Other references can be found in Margaret Gilbert, *Living Together: Rationality, Sociality, and Obligation* (Lanham, Md.: Rowman and Littlefield, 1996), chapter 12 (a lightly revised version of "Agreements, Coercion, and Obligation," *Ethics,* 103, no. 4 (1993), 679–706).

17. See, for instance, Simmons, *Moral Principles,* 77: "A promise to aid him in his villainy, of course, would not bind us." Simmons goes on to say: "We can sometimes succeed in obligating ourselves . . . by consent to 'autocratic and arbitrary forms of government' " (77). Perhaps a government can be "autocratic and arbitrary" (a phrase Simmons borrows from Rawls), though conformity to its edicts did not yet constitute aiding it in its "villainy."

18. Other objections to actual contract theory have been made. Those noted in the text above are the ones most commonly found in discussions critical of actual contract theory, including those found in political philosophy textbooks. I focus on these in this paper.

19. Originally in Margaret Gilbert, *On Social Facts* (London: Routledge, 1989; reprinted Princeton: Princeton University Press, 1992). See the text below. The most recent published discussion is in the introduction to Gilbert, *Living Together.* See also "What Is It for Us to Intend?" chapter 2. I continue to refine my understanding and exposition of this central notion.

20. See especially chapters 4 and 7.

21. On belief see, for instance, Gilbert, *On Social Facts,* chapter 5, and *Living Together,* chapters 7 and 14; on action see *On Social Facts,* chapter 4, and *Living Together,* chapter 6; on language possession see *On Social Facts,* chapter 3, and *Living Together,* chapter 10; on intention see Gilbert, "What Is It for *Us* to Intend?"

22. Evidently, if I want to be subject to a commitment that is robust in relation to *my own* change of mind, a joint commitment will serve my purposes well. Cf. my "Resisting Temptation: Planning versus Promising," manuscript 1994, comment on Michael Bratman, "Planning and Temptation," *Conference on Methods,* New York, New York, 1994. Bratman's paper has since been published in revised form in *Mind and Morals,* Larry May and Marilyn Friedman, eds. (Cambridge, Mass.: MIT Press, 1996).

23. See David Lewis, *Convention: A Philosophical Study*, (Cambridge, Mass.: Harvard University Press, 1969), reprinted by Basil Blackwell; Stephen Schiffer, *Meaning* (Oxford: Oxford University Press, 1972) (Schiffer writes of "mutual knowledge").

24. I shall not attempt to fix on a more precise account of common knowledge here. But see Gilbert, *On Social Facts*, 186–195, also 212–213 and elsewhere.

25. "To dancing together": this is a natural way to put things. In accordance with my sense of the matter, a more perspicuous if more cumbersome characterization would be something like the following: Joe and Lisa are jointly committed to accepting as a body the goal of partnering each other in a dance.

26. Cf. Gilbert, *Living Together*, 367. On social rules see Gilbert, *On Social Facts*, chapter 5, especially 403–407; and Chapter 5, this volume.

27. Cf. Benedict Anderson who, in a much cited phrase, characterizes nations as "imagined communities" "because the members of even the smallest nation will never know most of their fellow-members, meet them, or even hear of them, yet in the minds of each lives the image of their communion." Benedict Anderson, *Imagined Communities*, rev. ed. (London: Verso, 1991), 6.

28. That this is going on could be made clear in some such way as this: "You live on this island, don't you. . . . Well, then . . ."

29. Cf. Gilbert, *On Social Facts*, 212–213. I could know that *everyone on a particular island,* say, had provided the relevant expression without knowing with respect to *a given individual person on the island* that he (or she) had provided such an expression. This would happen if I did not *know of* that individual. I could then have *no* knowledge about *him* in particular. I would naturally make use of my knowledge about everyone were I to meet him.

30. For additional discussion see Gilbert, *Living Together,* chapter 12, relevant sections. I go into the matter further in Chapter 5, this volume.

31. The rights deriving from a joint commitment may be in some sense *waiveable*. It is not clear that the "waiveability" in question must involve the actual disappearance of the right. Consider the following example. Meg asks "Shall we meet for lunch on Tuesday?" and Paul replies "Yes" somewhat hesitantly. Meg then offers "Don't worry, you can always call me and say you've changed your mind." The final outcome in a situation like this may be representable in some such way as the following: Meg and Paul have a plan to meet; their having a plan to meet involves their being jointly committed to uphold the relevant plan together and therefore having the relevant obligations and rights. In addition, Meg and Paul have a side understanding constituted by a joint commitment to uphold as a body the decision that *they are to act as if* Paul has the right to back out at will (given that he informs Meg first). Something similar may be said of a case discussed by Michael Bratman ("Shared Intention," *Ethics,* 104 [1993], 111), where the parties "reserve the right" unilaterally to call off a joint enterprise (duet singing) at any time. Any plausible "reservation of right" of this kind is likely to be something explicitly agreed on by the parties. It could, of course, initiate a *convention* so that it became unnecessary in particular cases explicitly to bring up the side understanding in question.

32. Some philosophers have argued for a restriction of the term "obligation" to cases that would *not* include this one. See in particular H. L. A. Hart, "Are There Any Natural Rights?" *Philosophical Review*, 64 (1955), 175–191. Vernacular usage, however, leans in the direction of using "obligation" here. See R. B. Brandt, "The Concepts of Obligation

and Duty," *Mind,* 374–393, on the way in which use of the term "obligation" has developed over time.

33. Cf. Brandt, "Concepts," who argues, not without proper caution with respect to some of his examples, that "there are uses of 'obligated' and 'obligation' in connection with which it would be absurd to identify an individual to whom the obligation is owed" (379).

34. For further discussion see Gilbert, *Living Together,* chapter 12. In the *Metaphysics of Morals,* 274, Kant makes a distinction among rights that appears to correspond quite closely to what I argue for here. I hope to discuss Kant's remarks in another place. I thank Christine Korsgaard for drawing them to my attention after hearing me discuss my own ideas.

35. For more on the topic of coercion and joint commitment see Gilbert, *Living Together,* chapter 12. I argue that an agreement crucially requires the formation of a joint commitment (290–296) and that coercive circumstances do not rule out the formation of an agreement so understood (301–303).

36. Simmons makes a similar point about obligations as he understands these in *Moral Principles,* 10. He says that obligations do not provide "conclusive reasons" for acting, meaning that to say *one has a certain obligation does not of itself close the discussion.* There could be other considerations that make it the case that one should not fulfill one's obligation. Given no other relevant considerations, an obligation is presumably a sufficient reason for acting, hence conclusive in *that* sense.

37. See in particular Gilbert, *Living Together,* chapter 13. This is a lightly revised version of "Is an Agreement an Exchange of Promises?" *Journal of Philosophy,* 90, no. 12 (1993), 627–649. See also *Living Together,* chapter 12 and Chapter 3, this volume. I argue that given certain features of typical everyday agreements (more precisely bilateral executory agreements), such agreements cannot be constituted by a pair of exchanged promises, as is often thought. A joint commitment to uphold a certain decision as a body has the features in question. Typical promises, too, can be argued to involve an underlying joint commitment.

38. This way of looking at agreements and promises provides a new perspective on many discussions relating to obligations in ethics. See Chapter 5, this volume.

39. On the prima facie implausibility of arguing that an agreement cannot be coerced see Gilbert, *Living Together,* 286–288. The same seems to go for immoral agreements (can't thieves agree as to where to hide their booty?). I argue that an ambiguity in talk of "voluntariness" may be responsible at least in part for a contrary judgment on the matter of coerced agreements. With respect to immoral agreements, philosophers have tended to see them as "nonbinding" and therefore as perhaps impossible (insofar as all genuine agreements are "binding"). Compare the quotation from Simmons in note 17 above. Something similar has been said of coerced agreements also. But once one construes the "binding" nature of agreements as the binding nature of joint commitments, this tendency appears to be misplaced. This is, of course, not to say that immoral agreements (or coerced agreements) are "binding" in *another* sense. Such agreements may be neither *morally* binding (in some relevant sense) nor—in estimable legal systems—*legally* binding.

40. In some places I have suggested that plural subject theory is a "form of" actual contract theory. This could be misleading. Clearly plural subject theory is the more general theory; actual contract theory is a special case of plural subject theory—assuming my understanding of the nature of agreements.

41. Cf. Gilbert, *On Social Facts,* 175ff. (the restaurant case).

42. "Of the relevant sort": Given that the parties are talking together, must they not already constitute a plural subject? Perhaps so, but the appropriateness of proposing that *we* go for a walk together may seem to require more than this as a basis. Going for a walk together may appear to be a thing of a saliently different kind from having a casual conversation. Someone who has established his or her readiness for the latter may reasonably feel they have not established it for the former. Cf. Gilbert, *On Social Facts,* 177–178.

43. See in particular pp. 167–199; see also 214–219 (on the formation of social groups).

44. Cf. Gilbert, *On Social Facts,* 217.

45. I shall shortly consider what happens if we waive the first assumption. I will not for present purposes question the second.

46. As noted earlier, I am assuming that those with common knowledge of some fact will know of that common knowledge. In Gilbert, *On Social Facts,* 195, I note the plausibility of that assumption, given the particular account of common knowledge proposed there.

47. Cf. Chapter 4, this volume, which argues for a plural subject interpretation of the notion of a social rule by reference to the specific type of criticisms liable to arise in the context of a social rule.

48. Cf. A. John Simmons, "Associative Obligations," *Ethics,* 106 (1996), 247–273, 264: "Of course we identify ourselves with 'our' countries, 'our' governments, and 'our' fellow citizens. We have typically been taught from birth to do so . . . but none of . . . these ways of speaking . . . seems, considered by itself, in any way inconsistent with denying that we are morally bound by political obligations to our countries of residence." In writing of our being "morally bound" Simmons may mean to appeal to a type of obligation that is not at issue in the discussion in the text here. Nonetheless, a parallel worry may arise regarding joint commitment.

49. Suppose one knows that if one does not say "our country," and so on, one will be thrown into jail or worse? The secret police are all around. If in such a context one speaks of "our country" in the plural subject sense, can this betoken a genuine readiness to commit and be the basis for ascribing participation in a joint commitment? Note that one is asking not what is betokened by a *mere utterance of the words* "our country" but of their utterance, given *a certain understanding.* One might compare the case of saying "I promise" in similar circumstances. One may while promising know full well that one plans not to fulfill one's promise. One may despise the person who compels the promise. Yet under what circumstances can one properly deny that one promised at all? To echo Wittgenstein: "Can I *say* 'I promise' and *mean* 'I don't promise?'" That seems hard. Perhaps one could understand there to be inverted commas around one's uttered "our." One would then not be using "our" in the plural subject sense but rather "quoting" it as used in that sense. Using terms in such an "inverted commas" sense may be possible. However, this use is properly marked by a change in intonation or delivery of the terms—an overt difference the secret police might notice and hence probably to be eschewed. None of this implies, of course, that anyone who becomes subject to a joint commitment in such extreme circumstances is morally bound, all things considered, to uphold the commitment. Nor does it imply that people in this position are going to lack strong motivations to act against it.

50. It may be argued that, standardly, people are "born into" a particular political soci-

ety, and by virtue of this fact alone they have the appropriate political obligations. Cf. John Horton, *Political Obligation* (Atlantic Highlands, N.J.: Humanities Press International, 1992), chapter 6; see also Ronald Dworkin, *Law's Empire* (Cambridge, Mass.: Harvard University Press, 1986), on "associational obligations."

51. See note 37 for references.

52. Cf. T. Pink, *The Psychology of Freedom* (Cambridge: Cambridge University Press, 1996).

53. This point appears to stand even for coerced agreements, insofar as it is the agreement that is coerced, not the act that is done to conform to the agreement. See the discussion of the agreement to marry in Gilbert, *Living Together*, 301–303. It seems to follow that one can be "forced to be free" in the following sense: one can be forced to enter an agreement; that agreement being in place, one is free in the sense that one is in a position to act freely in the sense of the text. If one can be forced *to act in the light of an agreement one has made,* then one can be forced to act freely. There is no need to pursue this issue further here or to consider the relationship of the points made so far with the famous passage in Rousseau's *Social Contract* (Indianapolis, Ind.: Hackett Publishing Company, 1983) (first published in 1792) (chapter 7, last paragraph), in which he writes of forcing people to be free.

54. Cf. Simmons, *Moral Principles,* 70 "The feature that promises, contracts, and the giving of consent share is that they are all deliberate undertakings." I don't say that Simmons has in mind precisely the feature of premeditation noted here.

55. Cf. Gilbert, *On Social Facts,* 432.

56. Cf. Simmons's discussion of "positional obligations," which do not have such implications in his view; *Moral Principles,* 16–23.

57. On commitments as providing reasons for action, see Gilbert, *Living Together,* 288 and 306 n13.

7

Collective Remorse

Remorse is an important response to wrongdoing. Among other things, it can be a vital precursor to forgiveness and an important basis for reconciliation. Can a group feel remorse over its wrongful acts? If so, what does group remorse amount to? I consider three accounts of group remorse. Two are aggregative. The first of these takes group remorse to involve an aggregation of cases of personal remorse. Three versions of this account are considered. A crucial problem is that no one, on this account, has to feel remorse over an act of the group. The second aggregative account invokes what I call "membership remorse": a member's remorse over his or her group's act. I argue for the intelligibility of such remorse in light of doubts from Karl Jaspers and others. I propose, however, that generalized membership remorse does not suffice for the remorse of a group. Finally, I present the plural subject account of group remorse that I prefer. I call the phenomenon characterized in the account "collective remorse" and argue for its practical importance.

1. INTRODUCTION

As she discovered after the fact, Irene Anhalt's father had been a high-ranking member of the Gestapo in Nazi Germany. In a memoir addressed to him she writes: "I still could not give up my hope that you would feel remorse." Later she describes his deathbed scene: "With infinite effort, as if you already had to call up the words from another world, you spoke: 'It was wrong of the Spaniards to murder the Incas and steal their land.' My throat tightened with tears as I answered you: 'Yes, Daddy—thank you.' "[1]

Moral theory has a tendency to focus on the right and the good rather than on the wrong and the bad. This is not surprising. What we need, it would seem, is instruction as to how to act rightly, not on how to act wrongly.

Yet in the world we live in there is much wrongdoing. Anyone concerned with the right and the good must consider how we should respond to wrongdoing, as perpetrators, victims, and observers.

In this essay I focus on one possible response to wrongdoing. The response in question is remorse. It is not a particularly predictable response.[2] But if and when it does occur it is liable, as Anhalt's story shows, to have significant positive consequences in terms of the feelings of those other than the perpetrator and their relationship to him or her.

Anhalt's father referred not yet to the Nazis or Nazi Germany but rather—as a first step, perhaps—to the Spaniards: "It was wrong of the Spaniards to murder the Incas and to steal their land." This raises the question of wrongdoing by groups and the appropriate responses to that. Insofar as a group can act wrongly, can *it* subsequently feel remorse over its wrongful act?

What could the remorse of a group amount to? This is the question I explore in what follows.

2. REMORSE

a. Remorse in General

To feel remorse over one's act, one must at a minimum judge that one has done something seriously wrong. The term "remorse" suggests that the wrong is definitely more than a mere peccadillo. Regret might suffice for trivial matters. Remorse would be too strong in such a case.

I shall assume that remorse involves a judgment of serious *moral* wrongdoing. That one judges one's act to have been *morally* wrong may or may not be essential to remorse as such. Many instances, however, clearly involve such a judgment.

This does not yet distinguish feeling remorse over one's act from feeling guilt over it. One difference between these two may be that one who feels remorse could always sincerely exclaim, "Would that I had not acted so!" This may not be true of one who feels guilt.[3]

For present purposes I shall assume that we are concerned with altogether *well-founded* remorse. That would mean at least that it is not founded on a mistake about what, if anything, one has done. Nor does it depend on a false judgment to the effect that what one did was seriously morally wrong. It may be that remorse over one's act involves a judgment of one's blameworthiness. In that case well-founded remorse would involve no mistake on that score.

b. Consequences of Remorse

If one truly feels remorse over what one has done, this is liable, when recognized, to find a response in others. There may be a sense that one has undergone a major transformation, a transformation deep enough for something approaching forgiveness to take place.

The reason for this sense of transformation is clear. Remorse is liable to involve a fundamental change of perspective: one did a certain thing without hearkening to any doubts one might have about it. When one feels remorse it is as if, when it is too late to avoid the action, one finally hearkens to such doubts, perhaps *having them* for the first time. Were the original situation to repeat itself now, one is apparently now so disposed that one would not perform the action.

On this account of it, one who experiences true remorse is clearly liable to act differently in the future. Thus it may reasonably provoke not just backward-looking forgiveness but a renewal of forward-looking trust.

c. Remorse and Relationships

Given its connections to forgiveness and the restoration of trust, remorse is clearly of great importance where what is at stake is *a relationship* between a perpetrator and a victim, a relationship that either may or must continue in some form or other.[4] Some such relationships are relationships between groups—for instance, nations, different factions within a nation, and families. Can groups feel remorse over what they have done?

3. IS GROUP REMORSE POSSIBLE?

a. Skepticism about Group Emotions in General, and an Initial Response

It may be argued that a group or collectivity cannot feel remorse because remorse is an emotion, and groups cannot have emotions of their own. Their individual human members can, of course, have emotions of *their* own, but *groups* cannot. Why might one think this?

Emotions, it may be argued, essentially involve *feelings,* which are somewhat on a par with *sensations.* An example of such feelings would be the so-called pangs of remorse. Let us call feelings with this "sensation-like" quality "feeling-sensations." It may be proposed that nothing that is not a living organism can have feeling-sensations.

One response to this type of argument might be that it is not clear that emotions essentially involve feeling-sensations. It may be questioned, more specifically, whether to feel remorse is essentially to feel anything of the nature of pangs, twinges, and so on. I have supposed that remorse centrally involves a judgment of serious wrongdoing plus a thought of the form "Would that I had not done that!" Such a thought encapsulates, one might say, a desire not to have acted in such a way. Might this judgment and this desire not be the central core and essence of remorse?[5]

The skeptic about collective emotions might respond that even if it is correct, this last proposal requires that emotions are properties of *minds*. And there are no group minds. Hence there can be no group emotions.

Whatever we think of these skeptical arguments, what are we to make of the fact that people often quite comfortably say things like "Our family mourns the loss of a dear friend," "The whole department is in a state of shock," and "The nation views with great remorse what happened in those years"? People ascribe a whole range of emotions to groups, including remorse. What do these ascriptions mean? Alternatively, what are people talking about when they speak this way?

In what follows I shall understand by "a group's remorse" whatever it is that people refer to when they speak in those terms. Let us now pursue the question: What is it for a group to feel remorse over what it has done?[6]

b. Skepticism about a Group's Action, and an Initial Response

The skeptic about group remorse in particular may observe that this raises the question whether a group as such can act. One of the founders of sociology, Max Weber, asserted, indeed, that "there is no such thing as a collective personality which 'acts.' "[7]

Weber may have had in mind the fact that for him action was defined in terms of what he calls "subjective meaning."[8] It may seem to follow that groups as such cannot act. If we take this line, we have a problem similar to that of denying the possibility of group emotion.

There is a problem because people talk all the time as if groups act: "The USSR invaded Afghanistan," "The department elected Jack chair," and so on. Are they referring to some actual situation, and if so, what are the components of that situation? What, in other words, do the group actions of common parlance amount to?

I shall at first proceed on the basis of two rough assumptions about group actions. I take it that many group actions conform to these assumptions. They thus help to define a *standard type* of group action.

I shall assume, first, that when a group acts, one or more members of the group *contribute directly* to the group's action. For example, someone's flying over enemy territory may be a direct contribution to his group's act of war making.

I shall assume, second, that some members of a group that acts may *not* directly contribute to the group's action. Thus a university department may elect Jack Jones chair, though one member of the department, Peg, is on leave abroad and does not know the election is being held. Though Peg did not contribute directly to the group's action, she can properly say *of the department* "We elected Jack."

In relation to a given action of a group, I shall call the members who directly contribute to the action "active" members and the rest "passive" members. The distinction between active and passive members may be hard to characterize precisely, but the examples here fall clearly enough on one or another side.

It is now time to appraise some candidate accounts of group remorse. I shall consider three such accounts.

4. GROUP REMORSE I:
THE AGGREGATED PERSONAL REMORSE ACCOUNT

The first account is what I call the aggregated personal remorse account. It involves a sum or aggregate of states of personal remorse. By *personal remorse* I mean an individual person's remorse over an act of his or her own.

This account runs roughly as follows:

> *A group G feels remorse over its act A* if and only if each active member of G feels remorse over an act or acts of his or her own and taken together these acts comprise all of the members' acts that contributed directly to the group's act A.

For instance, an officer may feel remorse for having ordered the killing of a group of civilians, and each of his men may feel remorse for following his orders and killing several people. According to the account, the group comprising this officer and his men satisfies the conditions for feeling remorse over the group's act of killing the civilians.

This account has some attractive features. The state of affairs it takes to be a group's remorse is clearly a possible one. No "mysterious" entities, such as a group mind that operates independently of the minds of the group members, are posited. It is clear that only individual human minds are involved. In addition, insofar as some individual members of a group did morally repugnant things, their personally feeling remorse would appear to be desirable. Among other things, it is likely to lead to better things in the future.

In spite of these advantages, several things suggest that this account must be rejected. For one thing, according to the account each of the relevant people must feel remorse over his own action or actions, and that is all. But it is supposed to be saying what it is for a *group* to feel remorse over *its* act. Here no one is even focusing on an action of the group.

In response to this concern, the original account could be amended to run something like this:

A group G feels remorse over its act A if and only if each active member of G personally feels remorse over having directly contributed to the group's act A.

In this case there is a sense in which all of the relevant people are, indeed, *focusing on* an action of the group. No one yet, though, feels *remorse over* an action of the group. Each of the relevant members' remorse is over an action of his own, namely, his contribution to the group's action, as such.

This account also shares the following problem with its predecessor. Perhaps very few people directly contributed to the group action in question. Now suppose these people feel remorse over their contributions as such. It would surely seem odd to say, just for that reason, that *the group* felt remorse over its action. Yet if these few do feel remorse, the conditions laid down in the amended account are satisfied.

We could try amending the account again to include remorseful feelings on behalf of the passive members over having acted in such a way as to be associated, *as group members,* with the act in question. Then we would have something along the following lines:

A group G feels remorse over its act A if and only if each member of G feels remorse *either* over his or her direct contribution *or,* for those not directly contributing, over his or her association with the group's act A.

A problem here is that it may not be *reasonable* for the various passive members to feel remorse of this kind. Some may have had little choice, for instance, regarding their membership in this particular group. Some may personally have fought against the performance of the group act as best they could. And so on.

When all or most of the passive members reasonably do *not* feel personal remorse over anything they have done relating to their group membership or to the group's act, can there be no group remorse over the group's act? That is at least not obvious, but the newly amended account makes it true by definition.

Suppose that, as may sometimes be the case, every group member *is* personally remorseful over his or her *contribution to* or *association with* the group act. This situation still involves no remorse over the group's act itself.

It seems, then, that both the original aggregated personal remorse account and two variants on it are problematic. The two variants both require that the personal remorse bear some relation to the group's act, but none involves remorse over the group's act itself. In addition, all seem to give the wrong result for the case in which there are few active members and they are the only group members to feel personal remorse in relation to the group's act. On the first two accounts, which both refer to the active members only, *there will be group remorse* solely by virtue of the personal remorse of these few, which seems wrong. On the third account, which requires all members to feel personal remorse over their participation or association with the group's action, *group remorse is ruled out by definition*. This, too, seems wrong.

5. GROUP REMORSE II:
THE AGGREGATED MEMBERSHIP REMORSE ACCOUNT

Is there any other type of account available? In particular, is there an account that does not appeal to the remorse of particular group members over their personal contributions to or association with an act of the group? At this point what I shall call the *aggregated membership remorse account* may suggest itself. It runs roughly as follows:

> *A group G feels remorse over its act A* if and only if the members of *G*—both active and passive—personally feel remorse over act *A*.

Does it make sense for *any* individual member of a group personally to feel remorse over the *group's* act? Common experience suggests that it does. Reflecting on what her group has done, Sarah may think remorsefully, "We did a terrible thing!" referring precisely to what *her group* did and not to what she personally did. She is not likely to question the intelligibility of her emotional response.

That does not mean its intelligibility cannot be questioned. In *The Question of German Guilt,* philosopher and psychiatrist Karl Jaspers movingly recounts his own similar responses to the acts of his country but worries that in so responding he has "strayed completely into the realm of feeling" without the warrant of reason.[9]

Before pursuing this question, let me give the emotional response at issue a label. I shall call it "membership remorse." It is (more fully) a group member's remorse over the act of a group of which he or she is a member.

What does the present account of group remorse seem to have in its favor? Some of its attractions are as follows.

First, there is here—finally—remorse over the group's act itself. Second, on this account a group could in principle feel remorse even when, reasonably, only a few members felt personal remorse over either personal contributory actions or association with the group. For what is required is that members feel membership remorse, not personal remorse. Precisely which and how many members feel personal remorse—if any—is not relevant to the issue of group remorse on this account.

Third, insofar as membership remorse is intelligible at all, it will apparently be appropriate for all members to feel it in relation to a relevant action of the group's. Its appropriateness, in other words, is not restricted to active members or to any other special category of member. It concerns what the group has done, not what the member has personally done. Hence the conditions postulated by the account are not themselves unfeasible for a group of reasonable people even when most members have no reason for remorse over actions of their own.

Is membership remorse intelligible? Can it indeed be appropriate for both active and passive members in relation to a candidate group action? What of someone who did not know the action was taking place at the time? Or someone who protested the action, or . . . ?

One can argue that there need be no exceptions among group members with respect to the intelligibility of group remorse. The argument I have in mind appeals to a relatively fine-grained model of group action. This will be useful not only in relation to the evaluation of the aggregated membership remorse account but for other purposes of this chapter as well.

6. GROUP ACTION REVISITED

I now sketch an account of group action that goes beyond the assumptions I have been operating with so far. It allows us to grant intelligibility to the idea of membership remorse. I first introduced this account of group action in my book *On Social Facts* in 1989.[10] I have been elaborating it since and continue to do so. The core of this account is the following necessary condition on group action:

> For a group to act or (initially) to have its own goal for action, group members must be *jointly committed* to accept the relevant goal *as a body.*

What is it to accept a goal as a body? I understand this somewhat as follows. For two people to accept a goal as a body is for them, *as far as is possible,* to constitute through their several actions (including their utterances) a single "body" or person who accepts that goal. To put it somewhat quaintly, these two people must attempt as best they can to constitute as far as they can a four-handed, two-bodied person who (single-mindedly) has that goal.

The type of commitment appropriate to something like accepting a goal as a body is a *joint* commitment.[11] One way to understand what a joint commitment amounts to is to compare and contrast it with a *personal* commitment.

Consider first a personal decision, which is, I take it, a form of personal commitment.

Suppose Mike decides to vote for candidate *C* in the election. One way of thinking about this decision is as embodying a special kind of order or command: a *self-addressed* command. Mike, in effect, commands himself to vote for candidate *C*. He is the sole author of the command; he is also in a position to rescind the command unilaterally by, as we say, "changing his mind." Until he does so, however, the command stands, and if he fails to vote for candidate *C* he can be criticized in light of it.

This "self-addressed" command model of personal commitment can be extended to cover joint commitment also. A joint commitment—as I understand it—is not a sum of personal commitments but a truly joint commitment, the commitment of two or more people. These two or more people constitute the author of the relevant command, and no one is in a position unilaterally to rescind it. The parties must rescind it together.[12]

Given this understanding of joint commitment one can argue that one who defaults on a joint commitment offends against the other parties. They have a clear ground for calling the offender to account, and to rebuke or impose other forms of punitive pressure on him or her.[13]

All joint commitment has the same general form: for some predicate @, people jointly commit *to @ as a body*. People enter joint commitments by mutually expressing their willingness to be jointly committed in the way in question with the relevant others. This is how the relevant joint order is issued. Thus Harry may ask Frank "Shall we meet at six?" If Frank replies "Sure, that'd be great," they now have a joint commitment, indeed, an explicit agreement.[14]

In a large group where people do not know one another personally, they must openly express their willingness to be jointly committed with others of the relevant type. For instance, each might openly express his or her willingness to be jointly committed in some way with others living on a certain island. The commitment in this case might be to abide "as one" by a certain rule of the road or as a body to accept certain people as arbiters in their disputes. It must be apparent that all of the relevant expressions have been made.[15]

The existence of these expressions should, indeed, in all cases be "common knowledge" in roughly the sense introduced by David Lewis in his book *Convention.*[16] Informally speaking, one might say there is common knowledge in a group *G* that *p* if and only if the fact that *p* is "out in the open" in *G*.

Going back to group action, we can say:

> A group G performed an action A if and only if, roughly, the members of *G* were jointly committed to accepting as a body the relevant goal *X,* and *acting in light of this joint commitment,* relevant members of *G* acted so as to bring *X* about.

For instance, you and I may be jointly committed to accepting as a body the goal of having the house painted by virtue of the painting activity of each of us. Subsequently we may both act in the light of our commitment, coordinating our behavior in such a way that our goal is reached. It can then be said that we (collectively) painted the house.

Acting in the light of a joint commitment will often involve the parties in a variety of side agreements or in carefully monitoring one another's behavior or both. The initial joint commitment need not specify a procedure for its satisfaction.

For present purposes it is important to note that members of G may be jointly committed to accepting a certain goal as a body without all knowing or even conceiving of the content of the commitment. This can happen if there is a "ground-level" joint commitment allowing some person or body to make decisions, form plans, and so on, on behalf of the jointly committed persons. Thus an established leader and his or her henchmen may formulate and carry out a plan in the group's name, and the members properly say of the group as a whole, "We did it."

7. GROUP BLAMEWORTHINESS

Does remorse over an act imply the blameworthiness of that act? I have not taken a position on this issue here. But if the answer is positive, it seems that feelings of membership remorse can only be fully intelligible if the idea of a blameworthy group makes sense. Many theorists have supposed it does not, or at least they have supposed the unintelligibility of what they refer to as "collective guilt." As they conceive of it, this seems to amount to much the same thing as group blameworthiness.

It is not clear that this skepticism is warranted. Some pertinent points follow.

I take it as a good axiom to respect the intelligibility of common pretheoretical thoughts so far as is possible. Thus if remorse implies blameworthiness, the existence of membership remorse itself suggests the intelligibility of a group's blameworthiness, as it suggests its own intelligibility.

The idea that a group may indeed be blameworthy is also supported by the way people talk outside the context of membership remorse. Outsiders frequently say such things as "Switzerland must take the blame for the current crisis," suggesting that in our everyday conception of things groups can be worthy of blame.

Is there an intelligible basis for speaking of the blameworthiness of a group as such? Insofar as this requires a collective or group agent, I have suggested satisfiable conditions of group action. The framework of analysis I have used in relation to group action can also be applied to such things as group belief, including a group's moral belief. Thus I argued in *On Social Facts* that according to our everyday conception, a group as such believes something if and only if the members are jointly committed to believe that thing as a body.[17]

One can, then, make sense of the idea that a group did something it took to be wrong. It also makes sense to distinguish between the coerced and the uncoerced actions of groups. A group may "cave in" to external pressure—or it may act in disregard of such pressure or in its absence. Thus a group can do something it knows to be wrong without being pressured into it.

If in spite of these things a group for some reason cannot be considered blameworthy for its act, and if membership remorse implies the group's blameworthiness, then membership remorse will be that much less intelligible.[18]

8. MEMBERSHIP REMORSE AND THE REMORSE OF A GROUP

Leaving aside the intelligibility of a group's blameworthiness (in favor of which I have argued), the joint commitment account of group action supports the intelligibility of another aspect of membership remorse. That is its suggestion that the group's members all bear some relevant relation to the act of their group.

The joint commitment underlying a group act, on this analysis, provides such a relation. The remorseful person may be linked to his (or her) group's act not by any directly contributing act of his own but rather by his participation in such a commitment. This provides an intelligible basis for, if you like, his *identification* with the group as agent in this case. It allows him to say, with point, "We did it"—as opposed to "They did it" or "Some of us did it."

Some authors appear to see a person's identification with a group's act as self-justifying. In other words, if I identify with a group's act, there is no issue as to whether this identification is justified.[19] I see such identification as, on the contrary, raising the question of justification.[20] And I see participation in an appropriate joint commitment as sufficient justification. Identification has also been brought forward as a ground of political obligations.[21] Here, too, it remains seriously obscure how identification is supposed to do the necessary work of justification.[22]

If Jane—with justification—feels remorse over an act of her group, she may feel no remorse on her own account. She may know that she has acted honorably in the matter of the group action. She may have attempted to stop it or been ignorant of it without culpability for that ignorance. She is still tied to the group and its action by virtue of her participation in the underlying joint commitment.

She can therefore intelligibly think not only that "We did it" but "We should not have done it!" and "Would that we had not done it!" and "We must never do that again!" And she may feel an accompanying pang of remorse. Given its context, this might reasonably be called "a pang of membership remorse."

Suppose now that we grant that those who express membership remorse are doing something that is fully intelligible and that may be entirely appropriate even for those with no personal culpability. Should we accept the membership model of group remorse? I suggest not.

Note first that this account, like the previous ones, is an aggregative account. What is aggregated here is the (membership) remorse of the individual members. It is not remorse over their own acts, or what I have been calling "personal remorse." Rather it is remorse over the group's act. Still, on the ground, so to speak, we have what is clearly a number of *separate subjects of remorse* rather than one undivided subject of remorse—the group.

Another point, briefly, is that in principle this aggregated membership remorse could be hidden from public view. Each group member may think that he (or she) alone feels remorse. He may therefore not express his remorse openly but suffer it secretly. Once one brings this possibility out, the idea that we should say that the group feels remorse in this case is likely to seem even more suspect.

One could posit common knowledge of the generalized feeling of membership remorse. This, however, does not overcome the first problem. We will then have common knowledge that a set of individuals, the members of group G, feel membership remorse. What of the group as such? There still seems to be a gap between what we have here and something we can with clear aptness refer to as the remorse of a group as such.

It is worth pointing out that this new common knowledge condition can be fulfilled without anyone having publicly expressed remorse. In addition, there may be serious barriers to such public expression. Imagine that in this group the members are jointly committed together to uphold the view that the group can do no wrong. Unless something is done about this joint commitment, it stands as a barrier to anyone's saying that the group has indeed done something wrong.[23]

In this situation group members may constantly speak to one another as if the group's act, *A,* was perfectly fine, properly justified. This may be the continuing tenor of public discourse. All may realize that they risk rebukes in the name of the joint commitment should they speak otherwise without qualification. And few may wish to risk even the use of the legitimate qualifier "I personally" as in "I personally feel that we acted badly when . . ."[24] Though this does not amount to outright subversion of the joint commitment, it could be seen as inherently subversive; hence one risks being seen as disloyal to the group even if going only so far.[25]

In the case as it has now been described, it would surely be reasonable to say that *the group* did not yet feel remorse over its act *A,* though the members individually felt membership remorse over *A,* and this was common knowledge within the group. One might be reluctant to give up the aggregated membership remorse account, perhaps in its common knowledge version, if no alternative was available. There is an alternative, however, to which I now turn.

9. THE PLURAL SUBJECT ACCOUNT OF GROUP REMORSE

a. The Account

I now come to the account of group remorse that I favor. It is perhaps predictable given all that has gone before. I call it the "plural subject" account. It runs thus:

A group G feels remorse over an act A if and only if the members of *G* are jointly committed to feeling remorse as a body over act *A.*

Following what was said earlier, the joint commitment of the parties is (more fully) *to constitute as far as possible by their several actions, including utterances, a single body that feels remorse.* I say that people who are jointly committed to doing something as a body constitute the *plural subject* of the "doing" in question. Thus I call this the plural subject account of group remorse.[26]

There is no doubt that the phenomenon characterized by this account is possible. One who takes it to exist is not committed to the existence of any dubious entities. The existence of a joint commitment is a function of the understandings, expressive actions, and common knowledge of the parties.

b. Pangs of Remorse in the Context of Group Remorse

Here is a possible worry about this account. Are what I have been calling "feeling-sensations" part of the phenomenon in question? If not, can it really be remorse?

Let us first consider the case of remorse in general. Can one who does not feel pangs of remorse really feel remorse? Contrary to the drift of the questions, the correct answer may be affirmative.

Consider the case of an individual human being. When I say to you "I feel great remorse" must I be saying something false unless there are pangs or the like in the background? On the face of it, I need not be saying something false. Note that some apparently equivalent expressions do not use the term "feel" at all: "I am full of remorse"; "I am truly remorseful."

If this is right, a joint commitment to constitute with certain others, as far as is possible, a body that feels remorse would not require the production of associated pangs of remorse. Nor would it require that one attempt to produce such pangs.

Be that as it may, pangs of remorse are presumably common accompaniments of remorse in an individual human being. Witness the commonplace nature of the phrase "pang of remorse." Is group remorse, on this account, a type of remorse essentially devoid of these natural accompaniments of remorse in an individual human being?

Against this idea, consider the following. Suppose one is intentionally conforming to a joint commitment to constitute with certain others, as far as is possible, a body that feels remorse. One's conformity is likely to involve one in saying such things as "What we did was truly terrible," "Would that we hadn't done that!" and so on. In saying such things and acting accordingly in light of one's joint commitment, one may experience certain associated "pangs."

It is worth considering how best to describe these pangs. Are they associated most directly with one's personal remorse, with one's membership remorse, or with the remorse of the group itself?

By hypothesis, the pangs in question are directly responsive to the group's remorse rather than to any remorse of one's own. Had the group not come to feel remorse, one might never have felt this way. And one's feeling this way may not correspond to any judgments one has made in one's heart with respect to the group's act or to any associated act of one's own.

The pangs in question, then, may best be described as pangs of remorse associated with the group's remorse or, more succinctly, as "pangs of group remorse." That there can be pangs of group remorse in this sense does not fly in the face of common sense, reason, or science. There is no suggestion that there are pangs of remorse experienced within some kind of collective consciousness that exists independent of individual human minds. Pangs of group remorse, in the sense envisaged, exist in and through the experiences of particular group members. Nonetheless, this way of labeling them makes sense.

This is an intriguing line of argument. Whatever one makes of it, for reasons already given the plausibility of the plural subject account of group remorse does not hang on its conclusion—namely, that on that account there is some likelihood of plausibly so-called pangs of group remorse.

I propose that if we are faced with a case of group remorse according to the plural subject account, it is more apt for the title of "group remorse" than the phenomena captured by any of the aggregative or summative accounts considered. It alone brings remorse to the collective level. I propose further that standard everyday claims to the effect that we collectively feel remorse are well interpreted in terms of this account. To make it clear that I am talking about group remorse according to the plural subject account, I shall in what follows refer to it, exclusively, as "collective remorse."

Collective remorse does not rule out personal remorse for one's personal role—and in many cases it will be entirely appropriate to feel such remorse. It does not, however, entail personal remorse for one's personal role—and in many cases it will not be appropriate to feel such remorse.

What I have called "membership remorse" is a person's remorse over the actions of his or her group. This is expressible as "I feel remorse over what my group has done," as opposed to "I feel remorse over what I have done." Evidently, I can feel membership remorse in the absence of collective remorse. Indeed, such membership remorse can be widespread without collective remorse being present, as in the case imagined earlier.

It is possible, too, that there can be collective remorse without membership remorse. In other words, I might be able correctly to avow "We feel remorse over our act" without being able correctly to avow "I personally feel remorse over our act." Perhaps I have not reached my own decision on the matter, though I was willing to be jointly committed with the other members of my group to feel remorse as a body.[27]

Clearly, though, there are likely to be de facto connections between membership remorse and collective remorse. If membership remorse is widespread, it is presumably apt to give rise to collective remorse, though it may not do so in special circumstances. If, by virtue of my participation in the prevailing collective remorse, I regularly allude to the wickedness of what we have done, express the wish that it had not happened, and so on, I may well come to reflect privately on the group act in question. I may myself judge it to be evil, myself wish that we had not acted so. In other words, I may come to experience membership remorse, my own remorse over what we have done.

10. REMORSE AS A BEGINNING

Remorse may seem at the end of the day too passive a basis for the reconciliation of victims and persecutors—and of two parties each may have played both roles at some time in their relationship. Yet it is unlikely that without remorse such reconciliation can take place.

Given the existence of remorse, one can expect that perpetrators will go on to perform relevant acts, for instance, to provide restitution or compensation for victims or (in the case of groups) to make relevant changes in their constitution or their laws. Refusal to engage in such acts, when appropriate, will throw doubt on the claim of remorse, if it does not actually refute it.

Thus collective remorse according to the plural subject account is liable to lead to important reconciling actions. When people understand that they are jointly committed as far as is possible together to constitute a single body that feels remorse, they will understand that their remorsefulness (as a body) calls for them to carry out appropriate actions.

I hazard that without collective remorse, where appropriate, intergroup relationships are likely to remain stuck at a level of continuing defensiveness and hostility. Periods of calm are likely to erupt into war over and over again. Collective remorse and collective forgiveness may be required for any genuine reconciliation and any lasting peace.

NOTES

Versions of this paper were presented in November 1997 to the Philosophy Department at the University of Connecticut, Storrs; to my undergraduate class in philosophy of social science at the same university; and to an international conference on War Crimes at the University of California, Santa Barbara. I also used some of this material in a presentation at the University of Illinois, Urbana-Champaign, in December 1998. I received many useful and stimulating comments on those occasions. I am particularly grateful to Thomas Fote and Jerry Shaffer. Thanks also to Anthony Ellis for written comments and to James Robertson for lending me the book in which I found Irene Anhalt's essay. The subject is a rich one, and this paper only begins to explore it.

1. Irene Anhalt, "Farewell to My Father," in *The Collective Silence: German Identity and the Legacy of Shame,* Barbara Heimannsberg and Christoph J. Schmidt, eds., trans. C. O. Harris and G. Wheeler (San Francisco: Jossey-Bass, 1993), 48.

2. People will often remark of someone who has done some dreadful thing, "He showed no remorse." Sometimes they say this with a degree of incredulity, as if they are thinking, "How could he not feel remorse for *that*?" Presumably, though, the more horrible an intentional act, the less one would expect the perpetrator to feel remorse. The very performance of such an act suggests that the agent lacks moral perspicacity; yet some such perspicacity is necessary for remorse.

3. Thus Herbert Morris: "A person who feels guilty may not be disposed to say, 'I'm sorry' or 'Forgive me'; he may not feel sorry about what he did. . . . He may be neither contrite nor repentant. . . . We need only think of the young boy who disobeys his father and who, while feeling guilty, also looks upon himself with more respect. He feels guilty but prefers being damned to renouncing his act." Herbert Morris, "Guilt and Suffering," *Philosophy East and West,* 21 (1971), 107–108.

4. Irene Anhalt's case and others like it may fall under this rubric in a rather special way. Anhalt would seem to have had several motives for her persisting hope for her father's remorse. She clearly wished her father finally to embrace the values she held dear; this would be a precondition of his remorse and would be liable to give rise to it. She may have felt his remorse would benefit him in that he would at last see true and judge himself accordingly. She evidently also felt it would benefit her in allowing her to experience more positive feelings toward him. Among other things, she would presumably be able both to understand and to respect him more. She seems also to have felt his actions cast a shadow on his family, including herself. In that case she may have sought a basis for her own act of forgiveness. As has often been claimed, it is not clear that anyone other than someone's

victim can have the standing to *forgive* him or her. Here Anhalt would not be forgiving her father in the name of his primary victims, but she might have a basis for forgiveness nonetheless.

5. Jerome Shaffer has contemplated an analysis of emotion that takes beliefs and desires as essential to emotion in general, though not exclusively so. See his article "An Assessment of Emotion," *American Philosophical Quarterly* (1983), 161–172. The possibility of an analysis purely in terms of beliefs and desires is mooted at p. 171. I thank Professor Shaffer for bringing this article to my attention in the context of this essay.

6. As will appear from considerations to be advanced later, this is not the only kind of remorse a group might feel. But this question is fine for present purposes.

7. Max Weber, *Economy and Society,* 1, G. Roth and C. Wittich, eds. (Berkeley: University of California Press, 1978) (from the posthumous German original, 1922), p. 14.

8. For discussion of the nature of subjective meanings in Weber's sense see Margaret Gilbert, *On Social Facts* (London: Routledge, 1989), chapter 2.

9. Karl Jaspers, *The Question of German Guilt,* trans. E. B. Ashton (New York: Capricorn, 1947), 80–81. I discuss this passage in more detail in "How to Feel Guilt: Three Different Ways," presented at the conference Guilt, Shame, and Punishment at Columbia University School of Law, March 8, 1998, in honor of Herbert Morris.

10. See especially Gilbert, *On Social Facts,* 154–167. See also Chapter 8 here.

11. For relatively extensive discussions of joint commitment see Margaret Gilbert, *Living Together: Rationality, Sociality, and Obligation* (Lanham, Md.: Rowman and Littlefield, 1996), introduction, and Chapter 1, this volume.

12. I elaborate on the "self-addressed command" interpretation of commitment and joint commitment in Chapter 4.

13. In Chapter 4, this volume, there is a related argument that those who are party to a joint commitment have inextricably associated obligations toward and rights against the other parties.

14. An explicit agreement is not required for the formation of a joint commitment; see Chapter 1, this volume, and elsewhere. I take it, though, that everyday agreements are joint commitment phenomena. An agreement may be characterized as a joint decision, a joint decision as constituted by a joint commitment to uphold a certain decision as a body. See Margaret Gilbert, "Is an Agreement an Exchange of Promises?" *Journal of Philosophy,* 90, no. 12 (1993), 627–649.

15. For further discussion of the large-group case see, for instance, Chapter 6, this volume.

16. David Lewis, *Convention: A Philosophical Study* (Cambridge, Mass: Harvard University Press, 1969); reprinted by Basil Blackwell. For further discussion and references on common knowledge see Gilbert, *On Social Facts,* chapter 4. See also Chapter 1, this volume.

17. I have discussed collective belief in a number of places; see Gilbert, *Living Together,* 7–8, for a brief overview of these discussions. See also Chapter 3, this volume.

18. See Chapter 8, this volume, for a discussion of philosophical skepticism about collective guilt and the relationship of such skepticism to an account of collective guilt along the lines sketched here.

19. See, for instance, Herbert Morris, "Nonmoral Guilt," in *Responsibility, Character, and the Emotions: New Essays in Moral Psychology,* Ferdinand Schoeman, ed. (Cam-

bridge: Cambridge University Press, 1987), 239–240; John Horton, *Political Obligation* (Atlantic Highlands, N.J.: Humanities Press International, 1992), 151–154.

20. For further remarks on the appeal to identification see Margaret Gilbert, "Group Wrongs and Guilt Feelings," *Journal of Ethics,* 1, no. 1 (1997), 65–84.

21. See, for instance, Yael Tamir, *Liberal Nationalism* (Princeton: Princeton University Press, 1993): "Our obligation to help fellow members derives from a shared sense of membership." On the need for some grounding to a "shared sense of membership" (in a distributive sense of "shared") see the discussion in Gilbert, *On Social Facts,* 146–152.

22. Cf. A. John Simmons, "Associative Political Obligations," *Ethics,* 106 (1996) 247–273: "Identification with a political community or with the role of member within it is not sufficient for possessing political obligations" (264). Simmons goes on to envisage that one might "cast identification as a sort of consent," rightly seeing this as an additional move, wrongly (I would say) seeing it as tantamount to a reassertion of the "voluntarism that the identity thesis was originally advanced to replace" (265). For some explanation of why I say "wrongly" here, see Gilbert, *Living Together,* Chapter 12 and Chapter 6 here.

23. See the discussion of collective belief in Chapter 3, this volume.

24. On the permissibility of the use of such qualifiers in the context of an established group belief see Gilbert, *On Social Facts,* chapter 5, especially 288–292, or the similar discussion in Gilbert, *Living Together,* 200–203.

25. Cf. Chapter 3, this volume.

26. I introduced the phrase "plural subject" with the meaning I am giving it here in Gilbert, *On Social Facts,* chapter 4.

27. Compare the discussion in Gilbert, *Living Together,* 206–207, of reasons why one might be willing to participate in one's group's belief that such-and-such though not personally believing that such-and-such.

8

The Idea of Collective Guilt

People often speak of the guilt of one group or another. They speak, that is, as if groups can act in a culpable fashion. Philosophers have been skeptical of the possibility of genuinely collective guilt. Either it is nothing more than the personal guilt of all or most group members, or it is hard to see what it could amount to. Part of the trouble stems, I conjecture, from a problem in understanding how it can be that a group as such can act. I set forth an account of group action and argue that groups as such can freely do what they know to be wrong. This may suffice to allow for genuinely collective guilt or blameworthiness. I go on to argue that the existence of collective guilt, so understood, has no implications either way for the personal guilt of the members. In particular it implies neither that all group members bear some personal guilt in relation to the act in question nor that none of them do. The question of who bears personal guilt depends on the facts of the particular case. I explain why, in spite of this, the existence of collective guilt is of considerable practical importance.

1. INTRODUCTION: THE PRACTICAL IMPORTANCE OF MORAL RESPONSIBILITY

Human history resonates with the names of groups in conflict. In the course of these conflicts atrocious acts are often committed. If we are to avoid such horrific events, we need to know who or what is responsible for them.

There are two relevant kinds of responsibility, causal and moral. If I have some degree of moral responsibility for something, then I am at least in part causally responsible for it. But moral responsibility goes beyond causal responsibility.

Moral responsibility is the responsibility of *agents,* that is, of those who do things intentionally. If I bear some degree of moral responsibility for the breaking of a certain glass, then either I broke the glass intentionally or, roughly, I intentionally did something I expected to lead to its breaking, such as telling my assistant to break it.

If we know that a certain agent is morally responsible for some bad action, a variety of responses may then be appropriate. These include calling the agent to account and urging the agent to recompense or at least apologize to the relevant people or groups. Such responses may help in various ways to prevent such actions from occurring in the future.[1]

2. COLLECTIVE GUILT STATEMENTS

Sometimes a government issues an apology on behalf of a nation. It implies that the nation is blameworthy, that it is guilty of some improper action.

It is not only the leaders of nations who speak of collective guilt in the sense of collective moral responsibility.[2] Newspapers and everyday conversations are full of statements implying the guilt of one group or other. Thus one might read or hear, for instance, "The union is to blame for the strike" or "Our family acknowledges its guilt in the matter."

Though such statements and avowals are common in everyday life, it has been said that "the problem of collective guilt" is "one of the *murkiest* and *least explored* topics in moral philosophy."[3] The problem of collective guilt is the problem of whether there is any such thing as collective guilt.

3. PHILOSOPHICAL SKEPTICISM ABOUT COLLECTIVE GUILT

Both philosophers and other theorists have expressed skepticism over the very idea of collective guilt. Philosophical skepticism can take one of two main forms. To explain what these are, I shall use a hypothetical example.

Imagine that a certain nation wages an aggressive war in which thousands of people are killed. I shall call this nation Badland. Now suppose someone claims that Badland is guilty of these deaths.

i. The Reductionist Critique

The first form of skepticism construes this as the claim that *every single citizen of Badland is personally guilty in relation to these deaths*.[4] It may immediately be observed that when the claim that Badland is guilty is so understood, it is unlikely to be *true*. Many citizens are likely to be morally blameless in relation to the wars their nations undertake. Some citizens may not know the war is taking place, others may attempt to stop it, and so on.

In spite of this, the claim that Badland is guilty *could* be true on this construal. And it is perfectly intelligible.

The philosophical skepticism about collective guilt to which this construal gives rise may be expressed as follows. If what we refer to as Badland's guilt is simply the personal guilt of each of Badland's citizens, then in an important sense there is no such thing as *collective* guilt. That is, there is no such thing as the guilt of *a group itself* as opposed to the personal guilt of the group's members.[5]

I shall call the first form of skepticism about collective guilt *the reductionist critique*. It stems from the thought that so-called collective guilt *reduces to,* or is simply a matter of, the personal guilt of a group's individual *members.*

ii. The Antiholist Critique

The second form of skepticism takes a different view of the claim that Badland is guilty of the war deaths. Rather than taking this as a claim about the personal guilt of all of Badland's citizens, it takes it at face value; to claim that Badland is guilty is precisely to claim that the *nation* is guilty, the nation as opposed to any or all particular citizens.

The argument then proceeds as follows. It is hard to see what it could be for a group to bear guilt, that is, a group itself *as opposed to any or all of its members.* After all, what *is* a group over and above its individual members? What could it be for a *group* to act as opposed to some or all of the group's members acting? As the great sociologist Max Weber roundly stated, "There is no such thing as a collective personality which 'acts.' "[6]

On this view, to speak of collective guilt smacks of "holism." That is, it treats groups as if they were wholes or real units, as things that exist in their own right. To speak this way—it is argued—is philosophically suspect, if not simply unintelligible.

I shall call this form of skepticism *the antiholist critique*. It takes collective guilt to require that groups are in some sense "wholes" or real units, an implication it finds doubtful at best.[7]

4. A POSITIVE APPROACH TO THE IDEA OF COLLECTIVE GUILT

I believe both the reductionist and the antiholist critiques misrepresent collective guilt. To put it more carefully, I believe there is a viable idea of collective guilt that does not reduce to the idea that all group members are personally guilty. Indeed, it has no implications with respect to the personal guilt of the group's members. It is holistic but not, I believe, in an unacceptable way.

To argue this I first ask what it is for an individual person to be morally responsible for doing something bad. I then argue that groups can be morally responsible in much the same way. Finally, I consider the connection between personal and collective guilt. I should add the appropriate caution that much more can be said on all of these topics than I shall venture here.

5. PERSONAL MORAL RESPONSIBILITY

When is an individual person morally responsible for a bad act? Let us approach this question informally and intuitively.

Think of the times when you feel it is right to take the blame for something. Perhaps you agree that you can properly be blamed for ignoring your best friend Jane at the party you both went to last weekend. You knew a lot of people at the party and Jane didn't. She had asked you to introduce her to some people, and you'd said you would. In the event, you were having such a good time you decided to ignore her. Jane left early, feeling you had let her down.

What are the crucial features of this case? First, *you did something,* you (knowingly) ignored your friend. Second, in ignoring your friend *you acted freely,* at least in the sense that no one forced you to ignore her. Your uncoerced decision to ignore her is what led you to do so. Third, *you knew it was wrong* to ignore her. Or, perhaps more sparingly, it was wrong, and that's what you believed.

In this case, then, you freely did something wrong, something that, moreover, you believed to be wrong. This seems to sum up the intuitive basis for saying you are to blame for what you did or are morally guilty in this matter.

6. THE MORAL RESPONSIBILITY OF GROUPS: PRELIMINARIES

What, then, of groups? Can groups as such be morally responsible in the way individual people can? This seems to break down into three questions. First, can a group act or do things? Second, can a group act freely in the sense of being uncoerced? Third, can a group as such believe a certain act is wrong or immoral?

First, then, *can* groups act or do things? Well, we talk about groups doing things all the time. I spoke earlier of a nation, Badland, starting a war. Starting a war is surely an action. So is declaring war and invading another country's territory, both ways in which a country might start a war. We also talk about groups believing and knowing things. And we talk about them being coerced or uncoerced.

Philosophers and other theorists have, though, seen a problem here. They have questioned what these ways of talking amount to and whether they really make sense.

The problem is reflected in the critiques of collective guilt I have discussed. The reductionist critique suggests that a group's action is nothing but a collection of the actions of the individual group members. The antiholist critique suggests that a group's act—were one to occur—would be something other than this, something whose possibility is hard to accept.

One can see where these divergent conceptions of group action come from. On the one hand, it may be hard to see what a group's action could be if it is not simply the sum of the actions of individual group members. On the other hand, to say that a group acts appears to make a claim about something other than individual group members. In short, it seems to make a claim about the group itself. If we agree that a group's act is indeed a *group's* act as opposed to the act of any individual people, we may despair as to the very intelligibility of group action.

It seems, then, that we need an account of a group's action before we can decide whether a group as such can be morally responsible. We also need to know if it makes sense to speak of a group's action as free as opposed to coerced. And we need some purchase on what it is for a group to believe something, in particular what it is for a group to believe something is morally wrong.

In the following section I present in some detail the account of group action I prefer. I then argue that it makes sense to distinguish between coerced and uncoerced actions on this account. Finally, I present more briefly a related account of a group's belief. Putting these together I construct an account of collective moral responsibility that I consider in the light of the philosophical concerns outlined above. I take some care clearly to articulate the central elements of the account but do not attempt to repeat the reasoning that led me to believe these represent the way these things are understood in everyday life.[8]

7. GROUP ACTION: A PHILOSOPHICAL ACCOUNT

i. Introduction

How does a group do something? Must everyone in the group contribute to the group's action with some relevant action of his or her own? That seems doubtful, since it seems that in some cases only officials, for instance, are involved. But can it be enough for one or more officials to do something? How can the actions of those people amount to the action of the group rather than, purely and simply, their personal actions?

The following general account of a group's action draws on a number of previous discussions of my own. It will not assume any knowledge of those discussions.[9]

ii. Walking Together

Consider three people who are out on a walk together. We can think of them as constituting a small group. They could be referred to as the "walking party" or the "group of walkers."[10] What is it for people to be out on a walk together? One might guess at first that it was enough for them to be walking along side by side, each with the intention of continuing this way for a certain period of time. But this is fairly clearly not enough. Three people could meet these conditions but just happen to be walking along in tandem, with similar intentions.

What is lacking in this case? Some readers may know the rhetorical question raised at one point in the Bible: "Shall two people walk together except they have agreed?"[11] I say this is rhetorical because it seems to imply that an agreement is a prerequisite of walking together. In my view, something like this is right.

Typically, when people go for a walk they make some sort of arrangement first. This may be very casual and informal. For instance, one person asks the other two "Shall we go for a walk?" and the others nod or say "Sure" or whatever. Or one person may be out walking and two others come up to him and ask "May we join you?" The first person indicates that they may.

Now, in these cases the parties do enter into an agreement. Each could later say "We agreed to walk together." But people can end up walking together without an agreement proper being in place. Consider the following case. A man is leaving his house on a walk and his wife, realizing what is happening, says "Just a minute, I'll join you." He doesn't say anything but waits for her. Soon she reappears with her coat on, and they go out together without further discussion.

I don't think one can say these people *agreed* to walk together, even though clearly the right understanding was set up by what transpired between them. One might speak of a "tacit agreement" here, but since we've already decided there was no agreement we will need to explain what a tacit agreement amounts to. Indeed, if we want a certain depth of understanding, we need to know in any case what an agreement amounts to.

iii. Joint Commitment

I believe that what goes on in both types of cases—and others, too—is the formation of what I call a joint commitment.[12] The idea of a joint commitment can be understood by reference to the idea of a personal decision through which someone becomes personally committed to a course of action.

If I decide to go to the beach, for instance, I commit myself to going to the beach. It's true that I can change my mind, but while the decision stands I am committed. I now have reason to go to the beach. All else being equal, I should go to the beach.

The idea of a joint commitment is the idea of a commitment *of two or more people*. It is not a set of personal commitments, one for each of the parties. It is rather the commitment of them all. It applies to each of the parties and can only be rescinded by their concerted action. While it stands, each has reason to conform to it.

In chapter 4 of my book *On Social Facts* I argued that, intuitively, the parties to any joint commitment thereby constitute a social group in a central sense. The joint commitment binds the participants together. It can be argued to create a "real unity" of sorts, providing the basis for an innocuous form of holism.[13]

Joint commitments are commitments to do something as a body, where "do" in this context is construed very broadly so as to cover psychological attributes in general. Thus people can be jointly committed to espousing a certain goal as a body or to believing that such-and-such as a body, and so on. When persons X and Y are jointly committed in some way, I say that they constitute a *plural subject*. If they are jointly committed to believe that p as a body, say, they form a plural subject of belief.

For present purposes, it is important to mark a particular distinction among joint commitments. We can distinguish between ground-level and derived joint commitments by virtue of their mode of production. In order to produce a ground-level joint commitment to espouse a certain goal, the parties must, roughly, mutually express their readiness to enter this commitment. A derived joint commitment is arrived at less directly, as when the parties have first produced a joint commitment to allow a certain person to make certain plans for them. When the designated person announces the relevant plans, the parties may then be said to have a derived joint commitment to accept those plans as a body.

iv. The Role of Joint Commitment

Why have joint commitments? What are they good for? A joint commitment is a very useful tool for several people, all of whom wish to advance toward a particular goal.

Suppose three people personally wish to enjoy one another's company on a walk. Each could personally decide to pursue this goal as best possible, perhaps telling the others of his or her decision. But they will all do better if they enter a joint commitment to pursue the goal together or *as a body*. In that case at least two important things are achieved.

First, the goal in question is shared in the sense that each of the parties is subject to a commitment to aim at it. Second, none of the parties is at liberty unilaterally to give up this commitment. Thus each has some security, in doing and planning to do his or her part, that the others will be acting accordingly. If all cease personally to want the goal to be achieved, they may rescind the joint commitment together. They are therefore not stuck with it irrespective of all their wishes.

There is, of course, an obvious cost involved, which is that if one of the parties ceases to want to go on walking, he (or she) cannot unilaterally remove any commitment to doing so. He can always act contrary to the commitment, but then it will have been violated and the other parties have a basis for complaint. This lack of personal freedom is simply the other side of the coin of the security in relation to others' actions that a joint commitment provides.

In my view, when people speak of "our" goal or "our" intention, what is at issue is often not a goal each party personally espouses but rather a goal they are jointly committed to pursuing as a body. Given that we have a goal in this joint commitment or plural subject sense, each of us has reason to reach that goal, coordinating as best he can with the others involved.

v. Group Action: A Rough Account

I have now provided the background tools for the following rough general account of group action.

> *There is a group action* if and only if the members of a certain population are jointly committed to pursuing a certain goal as a body, and in light of this joint commitment relevant members (perhaps not all) successfully act so as to reach the goal in question.

This formulation highlights the fact that what makes a group action in this sense is not simply the acts of the members who help to bring the goal about. The underlying joint commitment plays a crucial role. It is *in light of* that commitment that the relevant members act, or must act, if we have a clear case of a group action.

This account allows for a group to act without all members of the group knowing what is happening. All members of the population may be party to a ground-level joint commitment to accept as a body that a particular person or group is to set goals for the population as a whole and to organize the implementation of these goals. The person or group established as the one to set the group's goals may formulate and implement a plan in the group's name without most members knowing about it or participating in its implementation. After the fact, all of the parties to the relevant ground-level joint commitment are in a position to say of the group as a whole "We did it." The ground-level joint commitment constitutes the act in question as the group's act.

Those who can say "We did it" include not only members who were ignorant of the action or simply failed to participate in its implementation but also those who knew of the action and protested against it. It should not be thought that such protesters must inevitably lose the intimate connection to a group action that participation in a constitutive joint commitment provides. Both protesting individuals and protest groups can and standardly do protest in their own name. Their reasonable intent may be to start a debate or initiate change within the larger group rather than to sabotage the group's effort or destroy the group.[14]

8. FREEDOM OF GROUP ACTION

Given the proposed account of group action, can we distinguish between group actions that are free in the sense of uncoerced and those that are not? We can certainly describe cases that fall clearly enough on different sides of the relevant divide. Consider the following imaginary scenarios.

The inhabitants of the island of Demos have determined that one of their number, Polemia, will set goals for them as she sees fit and will see to it that these goals are implemented. In other words, the Demotians are jointly committed to accepting as a body the goals Polemia sets for them and to supporting as a body her efforts to make sure these goals are carried out. It is an era of peace and tranquillity. The neighboring islanders either keep to themselves or are friendly and cooperative. Polemia decides it would be good if the inhabitants of Demos had more leisure, and she sets for them the goal of attacking Pathos—one of the neighboring islands—subduing the inhabitants, and bringing them to Demos to be slaves. She has no trouble organizing a successful attack on Pathos.

From the foregoing description, it seems reasonable to describe the Demotian attack on Pathos as a free or uncoerced action. There were, importantly, no external agents putting pressure on the group in favor of the group action through pressuring Polemia or in any other way.

Things could have been different. Polemia might have seen no value in attacking Pathos, and the very idea might not have entered her head. Not, that is, until she received a message from the mainland telling her that unless the Demotians attacked Pathos and enslaved its inhabitants, Demos would be attacked and ravaged. No one would be left alive. In this circumstance, had Polemia set for the Demotians the goal of attacking Pathos, she would have done so under duress, and it would be implausible to consider the Demotian attack a free or uncoerced action.

It is not essential to either case that there be a single person who sets a group's goal. Taking the coercion case first, the inhabitants of Demos (a small island) might have set their goals by coming together in a parliamentary session and deciding things by majority vote. With the external threat from the mainland hanging over them, they might well have decided to attack Pathos to avoid their own destruction. It would seem fair to say that had they so decided, they would have done so under duress.

Supposing that there was no external threat or pressure of any kind, the Demotians might simply have decided to attack Pathos through their usual process of debating and voting. In this case, absent further relevant information, the subsequent attack could be considered a free action on the part of the people of Demos.[15]

9. GROUP BELIEF

I now turn briefly to group belief.[16] My account of group belief follows the approach to group action that I have outlined. It runs as follows:

There is a group with a belief if and only if the members of a certain population are jointly committed to believe something as a body.

I take this joint commitment to require that the people in question must, at a minimum, express the relevant belief to one another when, roughly, they are interacting as members. One or more of them may not personally have the belief. If they wish to *express* the contrary belief, however, they must do so using some qualifier such as "personally," as in "Personally I don't think we can afford to maintain such a large army in peacetime."

A group's beliefs can, of course, include moral beliefs of greater or lesser generality. Thus a group may believe it is morally wrong to wage an aggressive war, that it is morally acceptable to engage in a particular war, and so on.

10. COLLECTIVE MORAL RESPONSIBILITY

Here, then, is an account of collective guilt in the sense of collective moral responsibility. Taking as read the above accounts of the relevant terms, a group bears guilt for an action performed if, acting freely, it did something wrong, something that it believed to be wrong.

If we accept this account, we are not forced to say that given collective guilt, each member of the group in question is personally morally blameworthy. To decide on personal guilt, we need to know precisely who did what, why they did it, and what they knew of its moral status.

Similarly, we are not forced to deny that any of the individual members bears guilt. Some may indeed be personally guilty. Again, it depends on what a given individual did, why he (or she) did it, and what he knew of its moral status. A leader may have understood that the war was immoral, a follower might not have, or vice versa. And so on.

This account appears to have avoided, then, the Scylla of the reductionist critique and the Charybdis of the antiholist critique. A central aim of this essay was to show that this is possible.

11. THE IMPORTANCE OF COLLECTIVE GUILT

At this point someone might wonder, What is the point of saying a particular group is worthy of blame if this has no implications for the guilt of any particular individual members? What difference can it make?

If we know that the conditions on collective guilt I have specified are fulfilled, we clearly know a great deal, whether or not we know which individual members of the group, if any, bear some guilt in the matter. This knowledge may affect different people or groups differently, but for many it will be reasonable to take some action on the basis of it.

Perhaps I am a member of the group and see that it is likely to continue to act culpably. If this is a realistic option, I may decide to leave the group, not wishing to be associated any further with such wrongdoing. I would rather think of such a group as "them" than as "us."

If leaving is not a realistic option, I may decide to work for change within the group. If it is feasible for the group to disband, I might attempt to bring that about. If I do none of these things, I may at least come to accept that my group is not perfect and that a certain humility in relation to its actions is in order.

If a group has acted badly enough or badly enough in relation to others, outsiders may decide they have to act. Perhaps they will simply make public their recognition of the offending group's blameworthiness, hoping this will effect some change or some reparatory action. Perhaps they will cease to interact with the group in selected ways or in all ways. Perhaps they will decide they have to engage in more active aggression to stop the continuance or repetition of the culpable group's offenses.

Suppose one accepts that there can be collective guilt without personal guilt or with little personal guilt among group members. One is perhaps more likely then to adopt a humane posture toward the group members of a blameworthy group failing any cast-iron evidence of personal evil.

Both insiders and outsiders are likely to reflect on the character of a group that is guilty of moral wrongdoing. They may address the possibility of relevant change, such as change in the group's values or goals.

A group that is guilty may be capable of a change in character. If this is what is needed to improve its actions, it will be well if its members are able to come to grips with its character and to work for the necessary changes. It will be useful, as a prompt to this, if both individual members and the group itself are able to acknowledge with remorse that the group has indeed acted culpably.[17]

In short, the idea of collective moral responsibility seems not only to be theoretically respectable but of great practical importance. If so, it is important that it receive a warmer welcome from philosophers than it has in the past.

NOTES

Thanks to Keya Maitra for helpful comments on a draft of this essay. Thanks also to lively and perceptive audiences at Providence College (April 1998) and the University of Illinois, Urbana-Champaign (December 1998). This essay is adapted from my contribution to a festschrift for Burleigh Wilkins.

1. The fact that moral responsibility allows for such responses provides a well-known tool for manipulative souls. In (once) common parlance one person may attempt to "lay a guilt trip" on another, even when there is no appropriate basis for the ascription of moral responsibility. Though trumped-up charges of guilt may sometimes work, one assumes that genuine charges are more likely to be effective. At least they are susceptible of justification.

2. In what follows I shall generally interpret "collective guilt" in this way.

3. Burleigh Taylor Wilkins, *Terrorism and Collective Responsibility,* (London: Routledge, 1992), 19, my emphasis. I shall not attempt to review or explore here the details of Wilkins's interesting and sensitive discussion of collective guilt in the pages that follow the quoted passage (19–27). Central points of agreement are our desire to take the idea of collective guilt seriously and our connecting it with something that might be referred to as "solidarity." ("Solidarity" also features in relevant recent writings of Joel Feinberg and Larry May.) Nor shall I attempt any detailed literature survey or discussion of the literature in the present paper. The aim of my discussion is rather to sketch a relatively precise account of collective guilt that appears to be proof against a variety of philosophical doubts (see section 3 below).

4. Cf. H. D. Lewis, "Collective Responsibility," *Philosophy,* 23 (1948); reprinted in *Collective Responsibility,* Larry May and Stacey Hoffman, eds. (Lanham, Md.: Rowman and Littlefield, 1991). See also Daniel Goldhagen, *Hitler's Willing Executioners,* foreword to the German edition (New York: Abacus, 1997), 481.

5. One may think the so-called guilt of Badland must be a matter simply of the personal guilt of Badland's citizens, because one *assumes* there is no such thing as the guilt of a group as such. Either assumption can lead to the other, though the latter could lead to a variety of different construals of Badland's guilt. For instance, it could be construed as

a matter of the personal guilt of those citizens directly involved in developing and implementing the nation's war aims.

6. See Max Weber, *Economy and Society,* I. G. Roth and C. Wittich, eds., p. 14.

7. An alternative formulation might speak of the involvement of "reification," treating groups as things in their own right, indeed as agents in their own right.

8. For that see Margaret Gilbert, *On Social Facts* (London: Routledge, 1989; reprinted Princeton: Princeton University Press, 1992), chapters 4, 5, and 7 in particular.

9. A central reference is Gilbert, *On Social Facts,* chapter 4. Other references are given in later notes.

10. I discuss this example in detail in "Walking Together: A Paradigmatic Social Phenomenon," *Midwest Studies in Philosophy,* 15, *The Philosophy of the Human Sciences,* P. A. French, T. E. Uehling Jr., and H. K. Wettstein, eds. (Notre Dame: University of Notre Dame Press, 1990); reprinted in my book *Living Together: Rationality, Sociality, and Obligation* (Lanham, Md.: Rowman and Littlefield, 1996).

11. Amos 3:3. This is a translation from the original Hebrew and may not capture its every nuance.

12. For some other types of case see Chapter 1, this volume.

13. See Margaret Gilbert, "Sociality, Unity, Objectivity," presented as an invited talk at the World Congress of Philosophy, Boston, 1998, to appear in the conference proceedings.

14. For more on the situation of protesters in particular see Gilbert, *Living Together,* 380–383. This considers both the specific requirements of a joint commitment and the implications of one person's default on a joint commitment in which many participate.

15. One relevant question, which I shall not pursue at this time, is to what extent and in what contexts, if any, coercion exercised within the group affects the freedom of the group's act. As long as we assume we are considering cases where there is no such coercion, this issue need not arise. Fabio Maldonado-Veloza raised this issue in my graduate philosophy of social science seminar at the University of Connecticut, Fall 1998.

16. Extended discussion of the account of group belief that follows in the text can be found in several places, including Gilbert, *On Social Facts,* chapter 5, and *Living Together,* introduction and chapters 7 and 14. See also Chapter 3, this volume.

17. See Chapter 7, this volume, for discussion of what it is for individual group members to feel remorse over their group's action and what it is for a group itself to feel remorse over its act.

9

In Search of Sociality— Recent Developments in the Philosophy of Social Phenomena

This paper reviews some of the growing body of work in the analytic philosophy of social phenomena, with special reference to the question whether adequate accounts of particular social phenomena can be given in terms that are *individualistic* in a sense that is specified. The discussion focuses on accounts of what have come to be known as shared intention and action. There is also some consideration of accounts of social convention and collective belief. Particular attention is paid to the need to explain the association of certain rights and obligations with the phenomena at issue.

Interest in the nature of social phenomena is increasing among analytic philosophers. There are clearly articulated rival theories of a variety of particular social phenomena. The importance of this topic for many other areas of philosophy—including epistemology, philosophy of science, ethics, and political philosophy—is rapidly becoming salient.

The nature of social phenomena in general is part of the agenda, as it was for the pioneering and philosophical sociologists Max Weber, Emile Durkheim, and Georg Simmel.[1] My book *On Social Facts* starts from the question "Which are the social phenomena?"[2] Having developed an account of a "plural subject" (see below), I argue that plural subject phenomena are the paradigmatic social phenomena.[3]

Discussion of the nature of social phenomena in general continues.[4] In large part, however, contemporary philosophers have directed their attention to particular social phenomena, with the most intense focus on what has come to be known as shared intention and action.[5] Such work is, of course, highly pertinent to the more general question. My own conclusion on that question was arrived at through sustained and independent examinations of, in particular, group languages, shared action, social groups, social convention, and collective belief.

My discussion here concentrates on the most prominent work on shared intention and action. It touches more briefly on collective belief and social convention.[6] Investigation of each of these topics, among others, is liable to provide some help with a persistent question about human sociality that I shall call the question of individualism versus holism.

The terms "individualism" and "holism" have been used by a variety of authors to characterize a variety of positions. To explain the particular question I have in mind, I turn to a well-known account of social convention. David Lewis proposed this account[7] and it continues to attract attention, endorsement, and critique.[8]

Lewis's discussion of convention exemplifies the kind of careful, indeed painstaking work that can go into philosophical accounts of particular social phenomena. His account of convention runs roughly as follows. There is a convention in a population of P of doing action A in circumstances C if and only if the members of P (1) regularly do A in C, (2) expect other members of P to do A in C, (3) prefer any given member of P to do A in C if the others do A in C, and (4) prefer any given member of P to do an alternative action, B, in C if everyone else does B in C. Lewis calls a situation in which this structure of preferences obtains a "coordination problem."[9]

Lewis adds that it must be "common knowledge" in P that (1) through (4) obtain. His account of common knowledge has aroused much interest and discussion, including alternative proposals.[10] This is not the place to dwell on the details. Suffice it to say that a popular account of common knowledge runs as follows. It is common knowledge that p in a population P if and only if (1) everyone in P knows that p, (2) everyone in P knows that (1), (3) everyone in P knows that (2), and so on, ad infinitum.[11]

Lewis's account of convention is *individualistic* in at least the following sense: it appeals only to the personal actions, beliefs, preferences, and so on—"actions" for short—of particular human individuals. Further, those with the convention themselves appeal only to such personal actions in their thought about each other. There is no essential appeal at any level to the actions of anything composed of two or more human individuals. For present purposes a *holistic* account of convention or any other social phenomenon may be understood as one that fails to be individualistic in the above sense.

The question of individualism versus holism I have in mind is this: Can adequate accounts of sociality and particular social phenomena be given in terms that are individualistic in the sense just sketched? Obviously a pertinent question is whether Lewis's account of social convention is an adequate one. I take that up later. First, I address shared intention and action with the question of individualism versus holism as a guide. I focus on relevant work by

Annette Baier, Michael Bratman, Raimo Tuomela, and John Searle, along with my own.

Michael Bratman, well known as a theorist of intention, has proposed what looks like an individualistic account of shared intention.[12] Shared intentions are reported or expressed when we speak of "what we intend or of what we are going to do or are doing."[13] There are several proposals on offer as to the nature of shared intention in this sense.[14]

Bratman's proposal runs as follows. We intend to J if and only if (1) (a) I intend that we J and (b) you intend that we J; (2) I intend that we J in accordance with and because of 1a, 1b, and meshing subplans of 1a and 1b, and you intend similarly; (3) (1) and (2) are common knowledge between us.

How is "that we J" to be construed in "I intend that we J" (see Bratman's condition 1)? To my knowledge Bratman does not go into this, but there is reason to think he has an individualistic construal in mind. Consider his central example of painting the house together. I shall take it that he construes my intending that we paint the house together as something like this: my intending that the house be painted by virtue of my actions along with complimentary actions of yours.

How plausible is Bratman's proposal? As he notes, I have argued that "in an important sense of 'acting together' each participant has associated nonconditional obligations to act and nonconditional entitlements to rebuke the other for failures to act."[15] If this is so, are Bratman's conditions on shared intention sufficient?

In a related discussion, Bratman appeals to Scanlon's moral principle of fidelity to argue for the presence of (nonconditional) obligations in many (but not all) of the situations in which his proposed conditions on shared intention hold.[16] He claims to have thereby identified "an important phenomenon that includes shared intention *and more*."[17]

As I have argued, I do not see nonconditional obligations as part of shared intention and more but of shared intention simpliciter.[18] I explain my own account of these obligations shortly. It will be useful first to turn to John Searle's discussion of what he refers to as "collective intentionality."[19]

Searle's target is not so much shared intention as the personal state of mind appropriate to participation in a shared intention. He writes: "Most empirically minded philosophers think that collective intentions [shared intention?] can be reduced to set of individual intentions together with sets of beliefs and especially mutual beliefs."[20] He opposes such philosophers, arguing specifically against the carefully constructed account by Tuomela and Miller of what they call "we-intentions."[21]

Searle's positive proposal is strikingly uncomplicated: "The thought in the agent's mind is simply of the form 'We are doing so and so.'" This thought, Searle contends, is not reducible to a thought about what "I" am doing, and so on. He also formulates his proposal in terms of a similarly nonreducible

"We intend that we perform act A." One who has this thought, Searle notes, may be mistaken. "I do indeed have a mistaken belief if I have a collective intention [i.e., think 'We intend that we perform act A'?] that is not in fact shared [i.e., those others to whom I refer do not think the same way?]."[22]

It is not clear precisely how Searle would flesh out an account of shared intention, given that it is at least necessary that the participants all think (with respect, presumably, to the same people) "We intend that we perform act A." In any case, given this necessary condition, Searle's account of shared intention would appear to be holistic according to the characterization of holism proposed above; "we" comprise several individuals, and an intention is irreducibly ascribed to "us" by each of the participants.

We might now distinguish between "internal" holism and "external" holism as follows. One is an internal holist about shared intention (for instance) if, roughly, according to one's account of shared intention the *participants* in such an intention irreducibly ascribe an action (in the broad sense indicated) to something they together constitute. One is an external holist if one's account of shared intention itself irreducibly ascribes an action (in the broad sense indicated) to the participants in a shared intention.

Is Searle an external holist? It seems not, for it appears he would say there is a shared intention just in case the participants personally think "We intend." This account does not itself irreducibly ascribe an action to anything composed of two or more human beings, though the participants appear irreducibly to ascribe an action to something they together constitute, namely "us."[23]

This would seem to accord with Searle's sense that what is wrong with the accounts he criticizes is that they "think collective intentionality can be reduced" to a set of "I intends" in the minds of individual human beings. His alternative is rather to reduce collective intentionality to a set of "We intends" in the minds of individual human beings. For *them* to intend is for *each of them* to think a particular thing.[24]

It is not clear how, on this account, one is to explain the obligations and entitlements I have argued to be inevitably associated with shared intention and action. Nor is it clear how to explain that, as I have also argued, those who take themselves to be acting together in the relevant sense inevitably understand themselves to have these obligations and entitlements.[25] If we are out on a walk together, say, and you start to walk so fast that I cannot keep up, I will understand that I am entitled to complain.

Searle makes the point, noted earlier by Sellars, that those participating in shared or collective action may form intentions expressible in terms of what "I intend" on the basis of what they understand *our* intention to be.[26] Thus I may form the intention to cover the net because *we* are trying to win this doubles tennis game and my covering the net is the best way to do this, given what you are doing. Assuming that our intention is not itself composed of (among other things) some relevant intention of mine, one can ask what it is that allows intentions of mine to be derivable in this way from intentions of ours.[27]

My own proposal regarding the nature of shared intention and shared action invokes what I call "joint commitment.[28] Those who are acting together understand themselves to be parties to a commitment of this kind, which may be characterized as a "commitment of the whole." It is not a conjunction of the personal commitments of the various parties but the commitment of all.

In a simple case involving two people who are face-to-face, the parties first mutually express their personal readiness to be jointly committed to some "cause" such as espousing a certain intention as a body. As they understand, when and only when both have expressed this readiness is the joint commitment in place. As they understand further, neither party can rescind the joint commitment unilaterally. Nor can either one rescind any "part" of it, since it does not have parts. It binds them together in the service of the cause in question until they concur in dissolving the bond they have created.

I have argued that the concept of a joint commitment underlies an important concept of obligation, the concept, if you like, of *an obligation of joint commitment.* In brief: if one violates a commitment that is *joint,* one is evidently *answerable* to the other parties. Or—as one might put it—given a *joint* commitment, one is *obligated* to conform to the commitment; one is obligated *to* the other parties, who have corresponding *rights against* one to the action in question.

This argument for the existence of these obligations does not have the usual form of a moral argument but is rather an argument *from the structure of joint commitment.* It may thus be best not to think of these obligations as included in the class of moral obligations.[29]

According to my account of shared intention, people share an intention if and only if they are jointly committed to espouse a certain intention as a body.[30] Therefore they have associated obligations and rights of joint commitment with respect to one another, including derivative entitlements to rebuke anyone who violates the joint commitment.

Is this account holistic? The parties to a shared intention must be, and understand themselves to be, jointly committed in a certain way. In a broad sense of "action," then, they must ascribe an action to something composed of two or more individuals: the joint commitment is a commitment of two or more individuals. Thus the account appears to be internally holistic. It would seem that it is externally holistic also. Again, the joint commitment is a commitment of two or more individuals. It is the foundation of what I call the "plural subject" they form, in this case the plural subject of an intention. In my technical terminology, people form a plural subject of X-ing if they are jointly committed to X as a body.[31]

In Tuomela, *A Theory of Social Action*, Raimo Tuomela put a notion of "we-intention" at the center of his account of shared action. Each participant in a shared action must have the relevant we-intention.[32] Tuomela notes that according to his account, "the concept of 'we-intention' is *explicitly definable* essentially in terms if I-intentions and I-beliefs."[33]

According to that account, roughly: A member *Ai* of a collective G *we-intends* to do *X* if and only if (i) *Ai* intends to do *X* (or his part of *X*), given that (he believes that) every (full-fledged and adequately informed) member of *G* . . . will . . . do *X* (or his part of *X*); (ii) *Ai* believes that every (full-fledged and adequately informed) member of *G* . . . will . . . do *X* (or his part of *X*); (iii) there is a mutual belief in G to the effect that (i) and (ii).[34] On the face of it, this account is neither internally nor externally holistic.

Tuomela, in *The Importance of Us*, introduces the "underlying assumption that we-intentions are formed in a process involving the making of an explicit or implicit agreement (or at least believed agreement)."[35] In response to the charge that making an agreement is itself a shared action so that an explanation of shared action in terms of agreements is circular, Tuomela explains his understanding of "agreements" as follows:[36] "From the factual or nonnormative point of view—shared we-intentions involve the acceptance of a joint conduct plan" where what this amounts to is that "each of the participants intentionally accepts the plan." Thus the "agreements" fundamental to we-intentions and shared action, according to Tuomela's "agreement view," are conceived of individualistically.[37]

It is not surprising, then, that like Bratman, Tuomela appeals to Scanlon's moral principle of fidelity to argue that obligations arise in the context of shared action on his account of it.[38] There is a problem here, raised in connection with Bratman's account: it may not be plausible to suppose that this principle applies in all cases of shared action in Tuomela's sense, while intuitively all shared action appears to involve obligations—of some kind.

Annette Baier has objected to the "individualistic bias" she finds in recent philosophical work on shared intention and action.[39] She questions the assumption that the first person singular is more basic than the first person plural.[40] She proposes rather that doing things with others is more basic than doing things alone.

To say this is not yet to explain what doing things with others amounts to. One can still ask, for instance, "Is there some structure underlying shared intention that can render intelligible derivations of a personal intention from what we intend?" One can ask again whether it is possible to explain the accountability those acting together perceive themselves to have to one another. A joint commitment account of "We are doing A" can explain both the perceived mutual accountability of those who intend or act together and the intelligibility of the derivations in question.[41] I take this to be a strong merit of such an account.

This is all I shall say here about the ongoing debate on the nature of shared intention. I now turn briefly to a related issue that is also the subject of growing attention.

What is it for *us* to believe something? A clearly individualist account was proposed somewhat in passing by Quinton in his essay "Social Objects": for us to believe that *p* is for all or at least most of us to believe that *p*.[42] I argued against this account in Gilbert, *On Social Facts*, and also against two embellishments of it.[43] Among other things, these accounts cannot explain associated obligations and rights, including the right to rebuke one of us for saying the opposite of what we think without preamble. In their place I have proposed a plural subject account of collective belief. This was perhaps the first extended philosophical discussion of the topic of collective belief.

Frederick Schmitt has built upon the plural subject account of collective belief in work on collective justification.[44] The account has received critical attention from Raimo Tuomela, among others.[45]

The topics of collective belief and knowledge have taken their place among the central topics of the newly labeled philosophical subfield of social epistemology.[46] They are also highly pertinent to the philosophy of science.[47]

I now return to the topic of social convention. In spite of its elegance, it can be argued that Lewis's account is radically inadequate.[48] None of his conditions are necessary; nor are they jointly sufficient for the presence of social convention.

I argue in Gilbert, *On Social Facts*, for a plural subject account of social convention. According to this account people are parties to a social convention when they are jointly committed to accept as a body a rule of the fiat form. This account explains the mutual reprimands and apologies parties to a social convention are apt to make in the presence of deviant behavior without appeal to any moral reasoning.[49] In addition, it explains why conformity and expectations of conformity are likely to arise in the presence of social convention, though they are not necessarily present. I have made similar proposals about some important social phenomena that have received much attention from ethical, political, or legal theorists: agreements, promises, social rules, and law.[50]

This is not to say that self-perpetuating regularities in behavior of the type Lewis discusses may not arise when humans are gathered together and need to coordinate their actions. It is to say that we can transcend our individualistic perspective on coordination problems and the like and to argue that we do so when we enter agreements or together create social conventions, rules, and laws, creating a framework for the rational solution of these problems.[51]

It is to be hoped that philosophical explorations of shared intention, collective belief, social convention, and other central social phenomena will continue. Such investigations are an important means to understanding the human condition, including the rights and obligations with which we are endowed and by which we are constrained.[52]

A key question, as I see it, involves the nature and source of the rights and obligations associated with acting together and a variety of other social phenomena. In answer, must we turn to a moral principle such as Scanlon's principle of fidelity, in the manner of Bratman and Tuomela? Or are these rights better understood as inherent in the jointness of a joint commitment—or in some other way? The debate on this question connects with another, the question of individualism versus holism. Are the best accounts of the paradigmatic social phenomena internally holistic, externally holistic, or both? Or can we after all give plausible accounts that are purely individualistic? In other words, is social *union* more apparent than real? What kind of *togetherness* is there in acting together?

NOTES

1. For commentary on relevant writings of each of these see Gilbert, M. *On Social Facts.* London: Routledge, 1989; reprinted Princeton: Princeton University Press, 1992. (Chapters 2, 5, and 4 contain discussions of Weber, Durkheim, and Simmel, respectively.)

2. As did Gilbert (1978), though with different results. See Gilbert (1991), section VI. Gilbert, M. *On Social Facts.* Ph.D. dissertation. Oxford: Oxford University, Bodleian Library collection, 1978.; Gilbert, M. "More on Social Facts: Reply to Greenwood." *Social Epistemology,* 5 (1991), 233–234.

3. For further discussion of this position, see Gilbert, "More on Social Facts"; Gilbert, M. "Concerning Sociality: The Plural Subject as Paradigm." In *The Mark of the Social,* J. Greenwood, ed. Lanham, Md.: Rowman and Littlefield, 1997.

4. See, for instance, Greenwood, J. "The Mark of the Social" (review of Margaret Gilbert, *On Social Facts* 1989). *Social Epistemology* (1990); Greenwood, J. ed. *The Mark of the Social.* Lanham, Md.: Rowman and Littlefield, 1997. The latter includes essays from authors in a variety of fields including philosophy.

5. Though see Greenwood, *Mark of the Social,* which returns to the topic. On "shared" intention and action see below.

6. Social phenomena not discussed here include group emotions. See, e.g., Gilbert, "More on Social Facts, Remorse," Chapter 7, this volume.

7. Lewis, D. K. *Convention: A Philosophical Study.* Cambridge, Mass.: Harvard University Press, 1969.

8. The more recent literature on Lewis includes Robins, Gilbert, chapter 5, Miller, Collin, and Millikan. Robins, M. *Promising, Intending, and Moral Autonomy.* Cambridge: Cambridge University Press, 1984. *On Social Facts*; Miller, S. "On Conventions." *Australasian Journal of Philosophy* (1992).; Collin, F. *Social Reality.* London: Routledge, 1997; Millikan, R. "Language Conventions Made Simple." *Journal of Philosophy* (1998).

9. Following Schelling, who suggested that what he calls "coordination games" underlie the stability of institutions and traditions. Schelling, T. *The Strategy of Conflict.* Oxford: Oxford University Press, 1960, 91. For some problems with Lewis's characterization of a coordination problem see Gilbert, M. *Living Together: Rationality, Sociality, and Obligation.* Lanham, Md.: Rowman and Littlefield, 1996.

10. See also Schiffer, S. *Meaning.* Oxford: Oxford University Press, 1972; Aumann, R., "Agreeing to Disagree," *Annals of Statistics,* 4 (1976), 1236–1239.

11. For discussion see Heal and Gilbert. Heal, J. "Common Knowledge." *Philosophical Quarterly,* 28 (1978), 116–131; Gilbert, *On Social Facts.*

12. Cf. Bratman's comment that his approach is "broadly individualistic in spirit" (112). Bratman, M. "Shared Intention." *Ethics,* 104 (1993), 97–113.

13. Bratman, "Shared Intention," 98.

14. Perhaps the sense in question needs a little more specification. The emphasis on "we" is meant, I take it, to indicate that the intention or action in question is ours *collectively* as opposed to *distributively.* Precisely what it is for an intention or action to be ours collectively is the question at issue. When I write of "shared intention" in what follows I mean shared intention in this collective sense.

15. Bratman, "Shared Intention," citing Gilbert, M. *On Social Facts.* London: Routledge, 1989; reprinted Princeton: Princeton University Press, 1992; Gilbert, "Walking Together."

16. Bratman, M. "Shared Intention and Mutual Obligation." *Cahiers d'Epistemologie,* no. 9319 (1993), 13–21; Scanlon, T. "Promises and Practices." *Philosophy and Public Affairs,* 19 (1990), 199–226.

17. Bratman, "Shared Intention and Mutual Obligation," 21.

18. See Gilbert, *On Social Facts,* 161–164. See also Gilbert, M. "Walking Together: A Paradigmatic Social Phenomenon." In *Midwest Studies in Philosophy,* 15, *The Philosophy of the Human Sciences,* P. A. French, T. E. Uehling Jr., and H. K. Wettstein, eds. Notre Dame: University of Notre Dame Press, 1990.; Gilbert, M. "What Is It for Us to Intend?" In *Contemporary Action Theory,* 2, *Social Action,* G. Holmstrom-Hintikka and R. Tuomela, ed. Kluwer, 1997. (The last article focuses on shared intention specifically; the former discussions focus on shared action or acting together and appears as Chapter 3 here.)

19. Searle, J. "Collective Intentions and Actions." In *Intentions in Communication,* P. R. Cohen, J. Morgan, and M. E. Pollack, eds. Cambridge, Mass.: MIT Press, 1990; in a less detailed passage Searle, J. *The Construction of Social Reality.* Free Press, 1995.

20. Searle, "Collective Intentions," 404.

21. This article represents some revisions of Tuomela's account on which see the text below. Tuomela, R. *A Theory of Social Action.* Dordrecht: Reidel, 1984. Tuomela responds to Searle's criticism of Tuomela and Miller in Tuomela, R. *The Importance of Us: A Philosophical Study of Basic Social Notions.* Stanford: Stanford University Press, 1995. 427 n6. This contains its own sustained discussion of "intentional joint action," discussed in the text below.

22. Searle, "Collective Intentions," 407–408.

23. Cf. Velleman, D. "How to Share an Intention." *Philosophy and Phenomenological Research,* 57 (1997), 29–50. (abstract). Velleman's thoughtful article brings the theory of intention in Searle to bear on ideas in Gilbert, *On Social Facts.* Searle, J. *Intentionality.* Cambridge: Cambridge University Press, 1983.

24. Searle, J., *The Construction of Social Reality.* Free Press, 1995.

25. See, for instance, Gilbert "What Is It for Us to Intend?" 67.

26. Searle, "Collective Intentions," 403. See also Sellars, W. "Imperatives, Intentions, and the Logic of 'Ought.' " In *Morality and the Language of Conduct,* G. Nakhnikian and H.-N. Castaneda, eds. Detroit: Wayne State University Press, 1963.

27. For Searle's proposal in this regard see "Collective Intentions," 412–413. I return to this question in the text below.

28. Other authors have used this phrase, and definitions differ. See, for instance, Levesque, H. J., P. R. Cohen, and J. H. T. Nunes. "On Acting Together." In *American Association for Artificial Intelligence, Proceedings,* 1. Cambridge, Mass.: MIT Press, 1990. 96ff.

29. For further discussion see Gilbert, M. "Agreements, Coercion, and Obligation." *Ethics,* 103, no. 4 (1993), 679–706.

30. On "as a body" see, for instance, Gilbert, *Living Together,* 348–349, 358 n7.

31. Cf. Gilbert *Living Together,* 8–9.

32. Tuomela, *Theory of Social Action,* 11.

33. Tuomela, *Theory of Social Action,* 119.

34. Tuomela, *Theory of Social Action,* 35.

35. Tuomela, *Importance of Us,* 127.

36. Tuomela, *Importance of Us,* 425–426 n2.

37. For a comparison of Tuomela's "agreement" view and my joint commitment account of shared action see Gilbert, Review of Tuomela, *The Importance of Us, Ethics,* 1998.

38. Tuomela, *Importance of Us,* 421–422 n9.

39. See Baier, A. C. "Doing Things with Others: The Mental Commons." In *Commonality and Particularly in Ethics,* L. Alanen, S. Heinamaa, and T. Wallgren, eds. New York: Macmillan, 1996; Baier, A. C. *The Commons of the Mind.* Chicago: Open Court, 1997. The former work contains sustained discussions of the work of Bratman and Searle in particular.

40. I am one of the targets she names. But see Gilbert, *On Social Facts,* 432: "One who has the capacity to be a group member and act as such may yet lack the capacity to act as a singular agent."

41. On the intelligibility of these derivations see Gilbert, *On Social Facts,* 424; Gilbert "Walking Together."

42. Quinton, A. "Social Objects." *Proceedings of the Aristotelian Society,* 75 (1975).

43. Gilbert, *On Social Facts.*

44. Schmitt, F., ed. *Socializing Epistemology: The Social Dimensions of Knowledge.* Lanham, Md.: Rowman and Littlefield, 1994; see also Piazza, G. "Taylor, Gilbert, e il risveglio (sociale) de sonno dogmatico," *Fenomenologia e Societa,* 1996.

45. See Tuomela, R. review of Gilbert, *On Social Facts* 1989. *Philosophia* (1990), 331–338; Tuomela, R. "Group Beliefs." *Synthese* (1992). An alternative account is detailed in Tuomela, *Importance of Us.* See also, Corlett, A. *Analyzing Social Knowledge.* Lanham, Md.: Rowman and Littlefield, 1997.

46. For collections of essays helping to define the relevant area see Schmitt (1994), and Piazza (1995). There is also the journal *Social Epistemology,* edited by Steve Fuller. Schmitt, *Socializing Epistemology.* Piazza, G. ed. *Esperienza e Cognoscenza.* Milan: Citta Studi, 1995.

47. As I argue in Gilbert, M. "Collective Belief and Scientific Change;" *Fenomenologia e Societa* 21 (1998): 32–45 (Chapter 3 here). See also Greenwood, "Mark of the Social."

48. See Gilbert, *On Social Facts,* chapter 6, for a lengthy critique.

49. Hart (1991) emphasized this "mutual reprimands" aspect of social rules. As I

understand them, conventions are a type of social rule. Hart, H. L. A. *The Concept of Law.* Oxford: Oxford University Press, 1961. See Gilbert, *On Social Facts*, 403–407.

50. On agreements and promises see in particular Gilbert, *Living Together,* chapter 13.

51. On the need for such a framework in coordination problems see Gilbert, "Rationality." Some suppose that one may transcend the individualistic perspective more easily. Cf. Hurley, S. *Natural Reasons.* Oxford: Oxford University Press, 1989. 136–170. For discussion see Sugden, R. "Thinking as a Team: Towards an Explanation of Nonselfish Behavior," in *Altruism,* E. F. Paul et al., eds. New York: Cambridge University Press, 1993.

52. Here is one place where the philosophy of social phenomena meets moral and political philosophy. See Gilbert, *Living Together,* chapter 15; Simmons, A. J., "Associative Obligations." *Ethics* 106 (1996), 247–273. There are, of course, other ways of making that connection. See, for instance, Pettit, P. *The Common Mind: An Essay on Psychology, Society, and Politics.* Oxford: Oxford University Press, 1993.

Bibliography of Related Works by the Author

Works listed include all those referred to in this book but not those essays included in it. Where applicable, original publication details for the essays in this book are to be found in the front section titled "Sources."

BOOKS

On Social Facts. London: Routledge, 1989 (in the series *International Library of Philosophy*). Reprinted Princeton: Princeton University Press, 1992.
   Living Together: Rationality, Sociality, and Obligation. Lanham, Md.: Rowman and Littlefield, 1996. [LT]

ARTICLES

"Game Theory and *Convention.*" *Synthese,* 46, no. 1 (1981), 41–93. [LT]
   "Agreements, Conventions, and Language." *Synthese,* 54, no. 3 (1983), 375–407. [LT]
   "Notes on the Concept of a Social Convention." *New Literary History,* 14, no. 2 (1983), 225–251. [LT]
   "On the Question Whether Language Has a Social Nature: Some Aspects of Winch and Others on Wittgenstein." *Synthese,* 56, no. 3 (1983), 301–318. [LT]
   "Coordination Problems and the Evolution of Behavior." *Behavioral and Brain Sciences,* 7, no. 1 (1984), 106–107.
   "Modeling Collective Belief." *Synthese,* 73 (1987), 185–204. [LT]
   "Rationality and Salience." *Philosophical Studies,* 55 (1989), 223–239. [LT]
   "Folk Psychology Takes Sociality Seriously." *Behavioral and Brain Sciences,* 12, no. 4 (1989), 707–708. [LT]
   "Fusion: Sketch of a Contractual Model." In *Perspectives on the Family,* R. C. L. Moffat, J. Grcic, and M. Bayles, eds. Lewiston: Edwin Mellen Press, 1990. [LT]

"Rationality, Coordination, and Convention." *Synthese,* 84 (1990), 1–21. [LT]

"Walking Together: A Paradigmatic Social Phenomenon." In *Midwest Studies in Philosophy,* 15, *The Philosophy of the Human Sciences,* P. A. French, T. E. Uehling Jr., and H. K. Wettstein, eds. Notre Dame: University of Notre Dame Press, 1990. Reprinted in Chinese translation in *Sociology Today,* 1992. [LT]

"Wittgenstein and the Philosophy of Sociology." In *Ludwig Wittgenstein: A Symposium on the Centennial of His Birth,* S. Teghrarian, A. Serafini, and E. M. Cook, eds. Wakefield, N.H.: Longwood Academic, 1990.

"More on Social Facts: Reply to Greenwood." *Social Epistemology,* 5 (1991), 233–344. [LT]

"Collective Belief." In *A Companion to Epistemology,* J. Dancy and E. Sosa, eds. Oxford: Basil Blackwell, 1992.

"Group Membership and Political Obligation." *Monist,* 76, no. 1 (1993), 119–133. [LT]

"Agreements, Coercion, and Obligation." *Ethics,* 103, no. 4 (1993), 679–706. [LT]

"Is an Agreement an Exchange of Promises?" *Journal of Philosophy* 90, no. 12 (1993), 627–649. Reprinted in *Pragmatics: Critical Assessment,* Asa Kasher, ed. London: Routledge, 1997. [LT]

"Norms." In *Blackwell Dictionary of Twentieth Century Social Thought,* W. Outhwaite and T. Bottomore, eds. Oxford: Blackwell, 1993.

"Durkheim and Social Facts." In *Debating Durkheim,* H. Martins and W. Pickering, eds. London: Routledge, 1994.

"Remarks on Collective Belief." In *Socializing Epistemology: The Social Dimensions of Knowledge,* Frederick Schmitt, ed. Lanham, Md.: Rowman and Littlefield, 1994. Translated into Italian and reprinted in *Esperienza e Cognoscenza,* Gianguido Piazza, ed. Milan: Citta Studi, 1995. [LT]

"Sociality as a Philosophically Significant Category." *Journal of Social Philosophy,* 25, no. 3 (1994), 5–25.

"Me, You, and Us: Distinguishing Egoism, Altruism, and Groupism." Comment on target article by D. S. Wilson and E. Sober. *Behavioral and Brain Sciences,* 17 (1994), 621–622.

"Social Epistemology and Family Therapy." *Esperienza e Cognoscenza.* Translated into Italian by Gianguido Piazza, ed. Milan: Citta Studi, 1995.

"Group Wrongs and Guilt Feelings." *Journal of Ethics,* 1, no. 1 (1997), 65–84.

"Concerning Sociality: The Plural Subject as Paradigm." In *The Mark of the Social,* J. Greenwood, ed. Lanham, Md.: Rowman and Littlefield, 1997.

"Social Norms." In *Routledge Encyclopedia of Philosophy,* E. Craig, ed. London: Routledge, 1998.

"In Search of Sociality." *Philosophical Explorations,* 1, no. 3 (1998), 233–241.

Critical study of *Moral Relativism and Moral Objectivity* by G. Harman and J. J. Thomson, forthcoming in *Nous.*

"Sociality, Unity, Objectivity," forthcoming in the *Proceedings of the 1998 World Congress of Philosophy.*

"Joint action," forthcoming in the *International Encyclopedia of the Social and Behavioral Sciences,* N. J. Smelser and P. B. Baltes, eds. Oxford: Elsevier.

"Philosophy and the Social Sciences," forthcoming in the proceedings of the 11th Annual Meeting of the Society for Logic, Methodology, and Philosophy of Science, Cracow, Poland, 1999.

BOOK REVIEWS

Review of W. Wallace, *Principles of Scientific Sociology, Ethics* (1987).

Review of M. Robins, *Promising, Intending, and Moral Autonomy, Philosophical Review* (1991).

Review of L. May and S. Hoffman, eds., *Collective Responsibility: Five Decades of Debate in Theoretical and Applied Ethics, Canadian Philosophical Reviews* (1993).

Review of P. Pettit, *The Common Mind, Mind* (1994).

Review of C. Bicchieri, *Rationality and Coordination, Philosophical Review* (1996).

Review of R. Hardin, *One For All, Philosophical Review* (1998).

Review of Tuomela, *The Importance of Us, Ethics* (1998).

Review of A. Baier, *The Commons of the Mind, Ethics* (1999).

Comprehensive Bibliography

This bibliography does not include works by the author. Numbers in square brackets refer to the chapters in which the work is cited.

Anderson, B. *Imagined Communities,* rev. ed. London: Verso, 1991. [6]

Anhalt, I. "Farewell to My Father." In *The Collective Silence: German Identity and the Legacy of Shame,* B. Heimannsberg and J. Schmidt, eds.; tr. C. O. Harris and G. Wheeler. San Francisco: Jossey-Bass [7]

Aumann, R. "Agreeing to Disagree." *Annals of Statistics* (1976). [9]

Baier, A. C. "Doing Things with Others: The Mental Commons." In *Commonality and Particularity in Ethics,* Alanen, L. S. Heinamaa, and T. Wallgren, eds. New York: Macmillan, 1996. [2, 9]

———. *The Commons of the Mind.* Chicago: Open Court, 1997. [9]

Bayles, M. "Hart's Legal Philosophy: An Examination." *Law and Philosophy Library,* 17. Dordrecht: Kluwer, 1992. [5]

Ben-Menachem, H. "Comment." In *Issues in Contemporary Legal Philosophy: The Influence of H. L. A. Hart,* R. Gavison, ed. Oxford: Clarendon Press, 1987.

Brandt, R. B. "The Concepts of Obligation and Duty." *Mind,* 73 (1985), 374–393. [6]

Bratman, M. *Intention, Plans, and Practical Reason.* Cambridge, Mass.: Harvard University Press, 1987. [2]

———. "Shared Cooperative Activity." *Philosophical Review,* 101 (1992), 327–342. [9]

———. "Shared Intention." Paper presented to the American Philosophical Association, Louisville, Kentucky, 1992. [2]

———. "Shared Intention." *Ethics,* 104 (1993), 97–113. [2, 6, 9]

———. "Shared Intention and Mutual Obligation." *Cahiers d'Epistemologie,* no. 9319 (1993), 1–28. [2, 9]

———. "Planning and Temptation." Invited talk presented to the New York Conference on Methods, 1994. [1, 2, 6]

———. "Planning and Temptation." In *Minds and Morals,* L. May and M. Friedman, eds. Cambridge, Mass.: MIT Press, 1996. [1, 2, 6]

————. "I Intend That We J." In *Contemporary Action Theory,* G. Holmstrom-Hintikka and R. Tuomela, eds. Dordrecht: Kluwer, 1997. [9]

————. *Faces of Intention.* Cambridge: Cambridge University Press, 1999. [1]

Card, C. "Gratitude and Obligation." *American Philosophical Quarterly,* 25 (1988), 120. [4]

Collin, F. *Social Reality.* London: Routledge, 1997. [9]

Corlett, A. *Analyzing Social Knowledge.* Lanham, Md.: Rowman and Littlefield, 1997. [9]

Cotterrell, R. *Law's Community: Legal Theory in Sociological Perspective.* Oxford: Clarendon Press, 1995. [5]

Durkheim, E. *The Rules of Sociological Method,* tr. W. D. Halls. New York: Free Press, 1982; from the 1895 French original. [1]

Dworkin, R. "The Original Position." In *Reading Rawls,* N. Daniels, ed. Oxford: Blackwell, 1975. [6]

————. *Taking Rights Seriously.* Cambridge, Mass.: Harvard University Press, 1977. [5]

————. *Law's Empire.* Cambridge, Mass.: Harvard University Press, 1986. [6]

Finnis, J. "Comment." In *Issues in Contemporary Legal Philosophy: The Influence of H. L. A. Hart,* R. Gavison, ed. Oxford: Clarendon Press, 1987. [5]

Gavison, R., ed. *Issues in Contemporary Legal Philosophy: The Influence of H. L. A. Hart.* Oxford: Clarendon Press, 1987. [5]

Goldhagen, D. *Hitler's Willing Executioners.* Foreword to the German edition. New York: Abacus, 1997. [8]

Greenwood, J. "The Mark of the Social." (Review of Gilbert, 1989), *Social Epistemology* (1991), 221–232. [9]

————, ed. *The Mark of the Social.* Lanham, Md.: Rowman and Littlefield, 1997. [9]

Hart, H. L. A. "Are There Any Natural Rights?" *Philosophical Review,* 64, (1955), 175–191. [4, 5, 6]

————. *The Concept of Law.* Oxford: Clarendon Press, 1961/1994. [5, 9]

————. *Essays on Bentham: Studies in Jurisprudence and Political Theory.* Oxford: Clarendon Press, 1982. [5]

Heal, J. "Common Knowledge." *Philosophical Quarterly,* 28, (1978), 116–131. [9]

Holmstrom-Hintikka, G., and R. Tuomela, eds. *Contemporary Action Theory,* 2, *Social Action.* Dordrecht: Kluwer, 1997. [9]

Horton, John. *Political Obligation.* Atlantic Highlands, NJ: 1992. [6, 7]

Hurley, S. *Natural Reasons.* Oxford: Oxford University Press, 1989. [9]

Jaspers, K. *The Question of German Guilt,* tr. E. B. Ashton. New York: Capricorn, 1947. [7]

Kant, I. *Metaphysics of Morals.* Cambridge: Cambridge University Press, 1991. [6]

Kenny, A. *Action, Emotion, and Will.* London: Routledge and Kegan Paul, 1963. [3, 7]

Klosko, G. *The Principle of Fairness and Political Obligation.* Lanham, Md.: Rowman and Littlefield, 1992. [6]

Levesque, H. J., P. R. Cohen, and J . H. T. Nunes. "On Acting Together." In *American Association for Artificial Intelligence, Proceedings,* 1. Cambridge, Mass.: MIT Press, 1990. [9]

Lewis, D. *Convention: A Philosophical Study.* Cambridge, Mass.: Harvard University Press, 1969 (reprinted by Basil Blackwell). [1, 3, 6, 7, 9]

Lewis, H. D. "Collective Responsibility." *Philosophy,* 23 (1948). Reprinted in *Collective Responsibility.* vol. 23, L. May and S. Hoffman, eds. Lanham, Md.: Rowman and Littlefield, 1991, 3–18. [8]

MacCormick, N. *Legal Reasoning and Legal Theory.* Oxford: Clarendon Press, 1978. [5]

———. *H. L. A. Hart.* Stanford University Press, 1981. [5]

Mackie, J. *Ethics: Inventing Right and Wrong.* Harmondsworth, NY: Penguin, 1977. [5]

Martin, M. *The Legal Philosophy of H. L. A. Hart: A Critical Appraisal.* Philadelphia: Temple University Press, 1987. [5]

Miller, S. "On Conventions." *Australasian Journal of Philosophy* (1992). [9]

Millikan, R. "Language Conventions Made Simple." *Journal of Philosophy* (1998). [9]

Morris, H. "Guilt and Suffering." *Philosophy East and West,* 21 (1971), 107–108. [7]

———. "Nonmoral Guilt." In *Responsibility, Character, and the Emotions: New Essays in Moral Psychology,* Ferdinand Schoeman, ed. Cambridge: Cambridge University Press, 1987. [7]

Pettit, P. *The Common Mind: An Essay on Psychology, Society, and Politics.* Oxford: Oxford University Press, 1993. [9]

Piazza, G. "Taylor, Gilbert, e il risveglio (sociale) del sonno dogmatico." *Fenomenologia e Societa* (1996). [3, 9]

———. ed. *Esperienza e Cognoscenza.* Milan: Citta Studi, 1995. [3, 9]

Pink, T. *The Psychology of Freedom.* Cambridge: Cambridge University Press, 1996. [6]

Plato, Crito, *The Collected Dialogues,* E. Hamilton and H. Cairns, eds., Princeton: Princeton University Press, 1978, 51b. [6]

Postema, G. "Coordination and Convention at the Foundations of Law." *Journal of Legal Studies,* 11 (1982) 165–203. [5]

Prichard, H. A. *Moral Obligation and Duty and Interest: Essays and Lectures.* Oxford: Oxford University Press, 1968. [4]

Quinton, A. "Social Objects." *Proceedings of the Aristotelian Society,* 76 (1975), 1–27. [9]

Rawls, J. *A Theory of Justice.* Cambridge, Mass.: Harvard University Press, 1971. [6]

Raz, J. *Practical Reason and Norms.* London: Hutchinson, 1975. [5]

Robins, M. *Promising, Intending, and Moral Autonomy.* Cambridge: Cambridge University Press, 1984. [9]

Rosenberg, J. *One World and Our Knowledge of It.* Dordrecht: Reidel, 1980. [2]

Rousseau, J. J. *On the Social Contract,* Indianapolis: Hackett Publishing Co. (first published in French, 1792.) [6]

Sartorius, R. "The Concept of Law." *Archives for Philosophy of Law and Social Philosophy,* 52 (1966) 161–193. [5]

———. "Positivism and the Foundations of Legal Authority." In *Issues in Contemporary Legal Philosophy: The Influence of H. L. A. Hart,* R. Gavison, ed. Oxford: Clarendon Press, 1987. [5]

Scanlon, T. "Promises and Practices." *Philosophy and Public Affairs,* 19 (1990), 199–226. [9]

Schelling, T. *The Strategy of Conflict.* Oxford: Oxford University Press, 1960. [9]

Schiffer, S. *Meaning.* Oxford: Oxford University Press, 1972. [6, 9]

Schmitt, F., ed. *Socializing Epistemology: The Social Dimensions of Knowledge.* Lanham, Md.: Rowman and Littlefield, 1994. [9]

Searle, J. *Intentionality.* Cambridge: Cambridge University Press, 1983. [9]

———. "Collective Intentions and Actions." In *Intentions in Communication,* P. R. Cohen, J. Morgan, and M. E. Pollack, eds. Cambridge, Mass.: MIT Press, 1990. [2, 9]

———. *The Construction of Social Reality.* New York: Free Press, 1995. [9]

Sellars, W. "Imperatives, Intentions, and the Logic of 'Ought.' " In *Morality and the Language of Conduct,* G. Nakhnikian and H.-N. Castaneda, eds. Detroit: Wayne State University Press, 1963. [2, 9]

Shaffer, J. "An Assessment of Emotion." *American Philosophical Quarterly* 20 (1983), 161–172. [7]

Simmel, G. "How Is Society Possible?" In *Georg Simmel: On Individuality and Social Forms,* D. N. Levine, ed. Chicago: University of Chicago Press, 1971, from the German original, 1908.

Simmons, A. J. *Moral Principles and Political Obligations.* Princeton: Princeton University Press, 1979. [6]

———. "Consent, Free Choice, and Democratic Governments." *Georgia Law Review,* 18 (1984), 791–819. [6]

———. "Associative Political Obligations." *Ethics,* 106 (2), (1996), 47–73. [6, 9]

Sugden, R. "Thinking as a Team: Towards an Explanation of Nonselfish Behavior." In *Altruism.* E. F. Paul, F. D. Miller, and J. Paul, eds. New York: Cambridge University Press, 1993. [9]

Tamir, Y. *Liberal Nationalism.* Princeton: Princeton University Press, 1993. [7]

Thagard, P. "Ulcers and Bacteria I: Discovery and Acceptance." In *Studies in History and Philosophy of Science, Part C, Studies in History and Philosophy of Biological and Biomedical Sciences,* 20 (1998), 107–136. [3]

———. "Ulcers and Bacteria II: Instruments, Experiments, and Social Interaction." In *Studies in History and Philosophy of Science, Part C, Studies in History and Philosophy of Biological and Biomedical Sciences,* 29, 317–342. [3]

Tuomela, R. *A Theory of Social Action.* Dordrecht: Reidel, 1984. [9]

Tuomela, R., and K. Miller. "We-Intentions." *Philosophical Studies,* 53 (1988), 115–137. [2, 9]

———. Review of Margaret Gilbert, *On Social Facts,* 1989. *Philosophia* 20 (1990), 331–338.

———. "Group Beliefs." *Synthese* 91 (3) (1992), 285–318. [9]

———. *The Importance of Us: A Philosophical Study of Basic Social Notions.* Stanford: Stanford University Press, 1995. [2, 9]

Ullman-Margalit, E. *The Emergence of Norms.* Oxford: Oxford University Press, 1977. [5]

Velleman, D. "How to Share an Intention." *Philosophy and Phenomenological Research,* 57 (1997), 29–50. [2, 9]

Weber, M. *Economy and Society,* vol. 1, G. Roth and C. Wittich, eds. Berkeley: University of California Press, 1978, from the posthumous German original, 1922. [1, 7, 8]

Wilkins, B. T. *Terrorism and Collective Responsibility.* London: Routledge, 1992. [8]

Woozley, A. D. "The Existence of Rules." *Nous,* 1 (1967), 63–79. [5]

Index

Note: Bold type indicates that an index entry is a technical term of the author's.

172

About the Author

Margaret Gilbert is professor of philosophy at the University of Connecticut, Storrs. She is the author of *On Social Facts* (1989), *Living Together: Rationality, Sociality, and Obligation* (1996), and numerous articles in professional journals. She has been a member of the School of Historical Studies at the Institute for Advanced Study, Princeton, and a visiting fellow at Wolfson College, Oxford, and has held other distinguished research positions in the United States and Great Britain. She has taught as a visitor at many universities including Princeton University and the University of California at Los Angeles, and she lectures widely to audiences in a range of disciplines including philosophy, economics, sociology, and political theory.